Preliminary Edition Notice

You have been selected to receive a copy of this book in the form of a preliminary edition. A preliminary edition is used in a classroom setting to test the overall value of a book's content and its effectiveness in a practical course prior to its formal publication on the national market.

As you use this text in your course, please share any and all feedback regarding the volume with your professor. Your comments on this text will allow the author to further develop the content of the book, so we can ensure it will be a useful and informative classroom tool for students in universities across the nation and around the globe. If you find the material is challenging to understand, or could be expanded to improve the usefulness of the text, it is important for us to know. If you have any suggestions for improving the material contained in the book or the way it is presented, we encourage you to share your thoughts.

Please note, preliminary editions are similar to review copies, which publishers distribute to select readers prior to publication in order to test a book's audience and elicit early feedback; therefore, you may find inconsistencies in formatting or design, or small textual errors within this volume. Design elements and the written text will likely undergo changes before this book goes to print and is distributed on the national market.

This text is not available in wide release on the market, as it is actively being prepared for formal publication. Accordingly, the book is offered to you at a discounted price to reflect its preliminary status.

If you would like to provide notes directly to the publisher, you may contact us by e-mailing studentreviews@cognella.com. Please include the book's title, author, and 7-digit SKU reference number (found below the barcode on the back cover of the book) in the body of your message.

A Contemporary Student Primer on Race, Gender and Class

Preliminary Edition

Maureen Elgersman Lee

Hampton University

Bassim Hamadeh, CEO and Publisher
Mazin Hassan, Acquisitions Editor
Amy Smith, Project Editor
Alia Bales, Production Editor
Roselia Brooks, Production Assistant
Jackie Bignotti, Production Artist
Alisa Munoz, Licensing Coordinator
Natalie Piccotti, Director of Marketing
Kassie Graves, Vice President of Editorial
Jamie Giganti, Director of Academic Publishing

cognella® | ACADEMIC PUBLISHING

Contents

For Sophia Elizabeth and Gabrielle Grace

INTRODUCTION

To be a student on the cusp of the twenty-first century's third decade is to live in a watershed moment marked by the convergence of a number of increasingly global movements—including #BlackLivesMatter, #BringBackOurGirls, #MeToo, #TimesUp, and #MarchForOurLives—all at different stages in their respective histories.[1] The similarities and differences between these movements bear witness to the ways in which race, gender, and class continue to shape daily life. While any person is larger than the sum of their parts (race, gender, class, religion, age, ability, and others), it is hard to argue against the pervasive racism, sexism, and classism that continues to shape American history and life.

Intersections: A Contemporary Student Primer on Race, Gender, and Class was created to introduce students to fundamental ideas as they pertain to race, gender, and class in American history and contemporary culture. The book's purpose is threefold: to increase students' ability to recognize the intersections of race, gender, and class; to increase students' ability to navigate these intersections in their academic and personal pursuits; and to increase students' capacity to be change agents for justice that comes from recognizing the inherent dignity of their fellow human beings.

This collection of readings comprises nine chapters divided into four units—theoretical foundations, historical perspectives, American culture, and contemporary moments. Unit 1 features "Racial and Ethnic Inequality" by John Iceland and "Distinguishing Features of Black Feminist Thought" by Patricia Hill Collins. The two articles introduce and explore fundamental concepts of race, ethnicity, gender, class, inequality, and power. Unit 2 uses Kevin Gaines' "African-American History" and Elizabeth Abel's "American Graffiti" to examine race and race relations in American history and culture. Unit 3 should be particularly engaging for students. Tamara Winfrey Harris's "Beauty: Pretty for a Black Girl" and R. Fleetwood's "'I am King': Hip Hop Culture, Fashion Advertising, and the Black Male Body" are sure to meet students where they are via discussions of American popular culture and its competing standards of beauty. Unit 4 ends the text with three selections that are rooted in American experiences but also reflect the ever-growing international implications of intersectionality.

Intersections is structured to be a productive learning tool that can be used both inside and outside the classroom. Prior to reading each set of writings, students will be asked a number of questions that relate broadly to the subject matter. These questions encourage students to think critically—and even personally—about how race, gender, and class show up in history and culture. After each set of two or three readings, students will be asked more specific, post-reading questions that encourage them to drill down even deeper and analyze various issues concerning power and empowerment. Both the pre-reading and the post-reading questions are suitable for small-group work, online discussion boards, and individual response papers. Instructors may challenge students to extend the breadth and depth of their knowledge by developing annotated bibliographies on specific subjects. Instructors may

---

[1] For more on the Black Lives Matter, Bring Back Our Girls, Me Too, Times Up, and March for Our Lives movements, see their respective websites: https://blacklivesmatter.com; https://www.bringbackourgirls.ng; https://metoomvmt.org; https://www.timesupnow.com; https://marchforourlives.com.

also encourage students to leverage their own creative abilities by creating original media-based projects around race, gender, class, and their intersections.

A diverse collection of current scholarship, *Intersections* is rich, engaging, challenging, and—still—optimistic. Whether being used as a central text or as a supplemental one, this primer should be pleasing to the student and the instructor, as it explores the intersections and complications of race, gender, and class as found in common discourse of history, politics, economics, sociology, and popular culture.

UNIT 1

THEORETICAL FOUNDATIONS

Any anthology on race, gender, class, and the intersections thereof must provide basic definitions that help the reader understand central topics and increase the reader's capacity to apply these theories to other readings and study questions. In this text, John Iceland's "Race and Ethnic Inequality" and Patricia Hill Collins' "Distinguishing Features of Black Feminist Thought" help create the foundation for examining race, gender, and class in the pages hereafter.

John Iceland's "Racial and Ethnic Inequality" begins the text by defining the concepts of race and ethnicity and exploring how they have been used to construct American power and privilege. Rather than having a central, defining thesis, Iceland's study examines how different racial and ethnic populations in the United States fare economically and to what degree they have been able to transcend America's persistent color line.

Patricia Hill Collins' "Distinguishing Features of Black Feminist Thought" is taken from her book *Black Feminist Thought: Knowledge, Consciousness and the Politics of Empowerment*, which is still considered by many to be the definitive text on Black feminism as both ideology and practice. Collins identifies six distinguishing features that may be used to establish common ground in recognizing how the double binds of race and sex create unique experiences for and distinct oppressions of Black women. Despite her criticisms of race(d) and gender(ed) power systems, Collins is still hopeful. The experiences and oppressions of Black women serve to inform Black feminist activism, which seeks to identify and defeat structures of inequality.

Pre-reading Questions

1. Are race and ethnicity two different things?

2. How do you identify racially and ethnically?

3. What is feminism?

4. Why might there be a need for a Black feminist movement?

5. How do one's racial and gender designations shape their experiences?

Racial and Ethnic Inequality

John Iceland

Racism has a long history in the United States. The country's Founding Fathers were deeply ambivalent about the institution of slavery. On the one hand, slavery stood in opposition to the ideals famously expressed in the Declaration of Independence: "We hold these truths to be self-evident, that all men are created equal, that they are endowed by their Creator with certain unalienable Rights, that among these are Life, Liberty and the pursuit of Happiness." On the other hand, the founders did not advocate for immediate emancipation of slaves for at least three reasons: their need to compromise with pro-slavery advocates to maintain the American republic, their view of slavery as a form of property protected by the Constitution, and their own attitudes about the racial superiority of whites.[1]

The founders themselves had varying views of slavery. George Washington owned hundreds of slaves but generally opposed the institution of slavery and provided for the freeing of his slaves upon the death of his widow. John Adams (the nation's second president) never owned slaves and was against slavery but generally did not take a strong political stand on the divisive issue. Notably, his son, John Quincy Adams, the sixth president, became a strong anti-slavery advocate during his postpresidency congressional career in the 1830s and 1840s. He accused slaveholders of immorality and stridently called for slavery's abolition.

Thomas Jefferson is perhaps the best personification of the nation's ambivalence on the issue. On the one hand, he was the primary author of the lofty language in the Declaration of Independence, and he believed that slavery was an evil stain on the nation's character. As president in 1807, he signed into law a bill that banned the importation of slaves into the United States. In an 1814 letter to Thomas Cooper, he wrote, "There is nothing I would not sacrifice to a practicable plan of abolishing every vestige of this moral and political depravity."[2] On the other hand, he remained a slave owner to his death (at which time his 130 slaves were auctioned off to cover his family's debts), and he believed in the biological inferiority of African Americans. He also believed that freed slaves and their former masters could never live in harmony and that racial mixing would be degrading to whites and to the country. As historian Stephen Ambrose writes, "Jefferson, like all slaveholders and many others, regarded Negroes as inferior, childlike, untrustworthy and, of course, as property."[3] For these reasons, he preferred to gradually free slaves but then deport them to Africa or the West Indies.[4]

Disagreements about slavery festered for decades after the founding of the country, at times threatening to break it apart. The tenuous compromise between slaveholding states of the South and free states of the North finally buckled with the election of Abraham Lincoln, who was feared by many for his anti-slavery convictions. The military victory by the North in the Civil War and the passage of the Thirteenth Amendment to the Constitution that outlawed involuntary servitude settled the issue once and for all. However, despite the abolition of slavery, black subjugation continued for another century in the South in the form of Jim Crow segregation. Northern blacks often fared only a little better, increasingly crowded into ghettos as the twentieth century progressed and facing strong discriminatory barriers in the labor market. Legal barriers to equality final fell during the civil rights movement, which culminated with the passage of a number of laws in the 1950s and 1960s forbidding racial discrimination in many walks of life. Americans attitudes toward race have also continued to liberalize steadily since then.

Many argue that race therefore has a different meaning and significance for the generation coming of age today than for previous ones. For example, National Public Radio (NPR) conducted a series of conversations about race (The Race Card Project), for which thousands of people submitted their thoughts on race and cultural identity today in six words. One respondent that NPR highlighted, George Washington III, an African American married to a white woman in North Carolina, submitted the following entry: "My mixed kids have it differently." By this, he meant that unlike in the past when anyone with any African American ancestry was considered black (the "one drop" rule), his children now have the freedom to identify as mixed race and can celebrate both sides of their family.[5]

With the election of Barack Obama as president in 2008 (and his reelection in 2012), some have argued that the United States is now postracial—that race no longer plays a very meaningful role in people's lives. Others scoff at this notion, arguing that race still plays a central role in determining people's life chances. The goal of this chapter is to examine the role of race in contemporary American society. I describe differences in socioeconomic outcomes across racial and ethnic groups, discuss the factors that contribute to these differences, and reflect on the trajectory of the American color line today.

WHAT IS RACE AND ETHNICITY?

Race commonly has been thought of as a biological concept that distinguishes groups by physical, mental, and genetic traits. While some research activity continues today exploring genetic differences between races, most contemporary social and biological scientists do not believe any evidence exists indicating that racial differences have a deep biological or genetic origin. Instead, most accept the notion that race is a social construction, and as such, meaningful social distinctions between racial groups vary across time and place. During the Enlightenment in the 1700s, many European scholars became interested in understanding racial differences and created all sorts of classification schemes that included anywhere from three to thirty categories of race. Some of these scholars, for example, divided Europeans themselves into four races:

Nordic or northern, Alpine or central, Mediterranean or southern, and Slavic or eastern.[6]

Many southern and eastern European immigrants to the United States in the late nineteenth century and the early twentieth were initially viewed as racially distinct, stoking the fears of nativists and public officials, as previously discussed. Theodore Roosevelt warned of "race suicide" and bemoaned the higher fertility rate among inferior immigrant women compared with that of Anglo-Saxon women. Notions of race were legitimized by scientists who developed theories of eugenics and the role of genes in explaining broad social differences across populations.[7] One of the earliest applications of IQ testing was to show that southern and eastern European immigrants were not as smart as the native stock—a hypothesis that was believed to have been confirmed.[8]

The sociologist Mary Waters notes, "At the peak of immigration from southern and central Europe there was widespread discrimination and hostility against the newcomers by established Americans. Italians, Poles, Greeks, and Jews were called derogatory names, attacked by nativist mobs, and derided in the press. Intermarriage across ethnic lines was very uncommon. . . . The immigrants and their children were residentially segregated, occupationally specialized, and generally poor."[9] Assimilation occurred only gradually through the twentieth century as immigration ebbed, the country's attention turned to two world wars and a depression, and social and economic changes in the post–World War II period further facilitated the upward mobility of the descendants of these immigrants.[10]

Illustrating differences in views about the meaning of race across places, conceptions of race have been more fluid in Latin American societies, where skin color is seen along a continuum, than in the United States, where the division between black and white racial identities has long been sharply defined (perhaps at least until recently). The Brazilian census, for example, has the following categories: white, brown, black, yellow, indigenous, and undeclared. More generally, different societies use different physical attributes to construct racial categories.[11] Skin color seems like an easily observable way to divide people, but is it any more important than eye color, curliness of hair, or any other physical characteristic? Thus, social scientists today see race as representing social relations embedded in a society's specific historical context.[12] Racial distinctions are real and meaningful in a given place to the extent that people are treated differently and have different kinds of life experiences and outcomes.

There is often some confusion about the distinction between "race" and "ethnicity." *Race* typically refers to a group of people who are perceived, by both themselves and others, as possessing distinctive hereditary traits. In the U.S. context, phenotypical difference (skin color) has been the most salient marker of racial difference. In contrast, *ethnicity* refers to a group of people who are differentiated by culture rather than by perceived physical or genetic differences. Nevertheless, the terms *race* and *ethnicity* are often used interchangeably in public conversations today, especially given the growing diversity of the U.S. population, increasing intermarriage, and the changing meaning and importance of group differences. There is also some ambiguity about whether some groups, such as Hispanics or Middle Easterners, are distinct races or ethnicities.[13]

The U.S. Census Bureau has collected data on race/ethnicity in a variety of ways over the years, reflecting changing notions of salient social divisions. It currently collects such information with two questions. The first question asks, "Is this person Spanish/Hispanic/Latino?" There is an answer box for "no" and additional "yes" boxes for people to indicate if they are Mexican, Puerto Rican, or Cuban. There is also a write-in box where respondents can identify other origins. The next question on the form asks, "What is this person's race?" There are answer boxes for White, Black, American Indian, or Alaska Native, and a series of boxes for various Asian groups and Native Hawaiians. People can also mark "some other race," as well as (beginning in the year 2000) two or more races. When disseminating data on race and ethnicity, the Census Bureau essentially uses five race categories (White, Black, American Indian and Alaska Native, Asian, and Native Hawaiian and other Pacific Islander) and one ethnicity (Hispanic origin). A number of respondents are confused by these questions and wonder why Hispanic origin is asked separately.[14] Some advocate using a single combined question that asks more simply about ethnic origins, with the view that "race" has little or no objective basis.[15] Given the fuzziness in the use of these concepts, I often use the terms *race* and *ethnicity* either together (as in the title of this chapter) or interchangeably.

U.S. society has become increasingly racially and ethnically diverse. The proportion of the population that was non-Hispanic white decreased substantially from 83 percent in 1970 to 63 percent in 2011. Meanwhile, the relative size of the black population stayed fairly steady (12 percent in 2011), and the representation of Hispanics (5 to 17 percent) and Asians (1 to 5 percent) increased significantly over the period. In this section we examine changes in the educational attainment, income, poverty, and wealth of different groups to shed light on the extent of racial and ethnic socioeconomic inequality in American society.

Figure 37 shows that college completion has increased markedly for all racial/ethnic groups over time, but significant disparities remain. In 2012, only about 1 in 7 Hispanics who were 25 years old and over had completed college, compared with over a fifth of blacks, over a third of non-Hispanic whites, and over half of Asians. In 1940, only 5 percent of the total population age 25 years and older had a college degree, including 5 percent of whites and just 1 percent of blacks. As one would expect, educational attainment disparities show up in high school graduation rates as well, though the white-black gap is narrower, with 93 percent of non-Hispanic whites and 85 percent of blacks graduating from high school among those age 25 and older in 2012. Hispanics have the lowest levels of high school completion at 65 percent. About 89 percent of Asians had completed high school in 2012.[16]

Racial and ethnic differences persist when looking at median household income (see figure 38). All groups experienced real increases in income over time, with all groups also taking a tumble during the Great Recession. Consistent with the educational differences described above, the median household income was highest among Asians at $65,129, followed by non-Hispanic whites ($55,412). However, even though African Americans had higher levels of education than Hispanics, median household income was higher among Hispanics ($38,624) than blacks ($32,229).

Unsurprisingly, racial and ethnic differences also show up in poverty statistics (figure 39). In 2011, 10 percent of non-Hispanic whites and 12

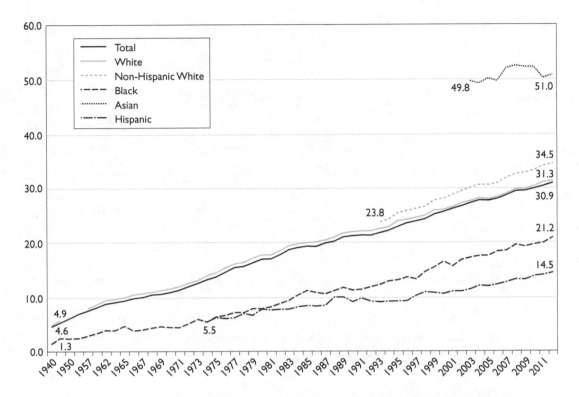

Figure 37. Percentage of people age 25 years and older who have completed college, by race and ethnicity, 1940–2012. Note: Data were collected for different groups at different points in time, which accounts for the various gaps in the graph, including that for whites between ca. 1947 and 1957. Please refer to U.S. Census Bureau 2013d for more information. Source: U.S. Census Bureau 2013d.

percent of Asians were poor, compared with 25 percent Hispanics and 28 percent of African Americans. Notably, the black poverty rate declined significantly over time, from a high of 55 percent in 1959. Nevertheless, the 2000s were a difficult decade for low-income Americans, with blacks experiencing the largest absolute increase in poverty. Finally, racial and ethnic inequality in wealth is even larger than in education, income, or poverty. The mean net worth of white households was $593,000 in 2010, whereas the mean net worth of African American and Hispanic households was only $85,000 and $90,000, respectively. Part of this reflects the fact that non-Hispanic whites are much more likely to be homeowners (75 percent) than African Americans (48 percent) and Hispanics (47 percent), and the value of one's home is most often a household's greatest single asset.[17]

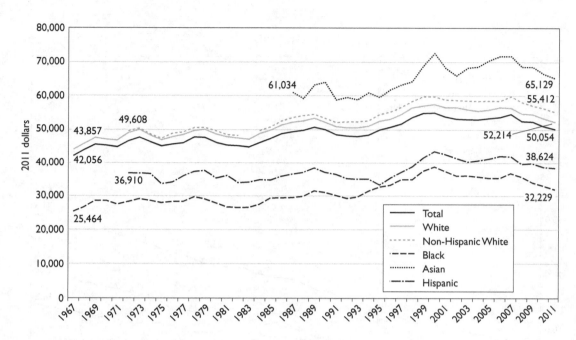

Figure 38. Median household income, by race and ethnicity, 1967–2011 (in constant 2011 dollars). Note: No published data are available for non-Hispanic whites in 1984. Source: U.S. Census Bureau 2012k.

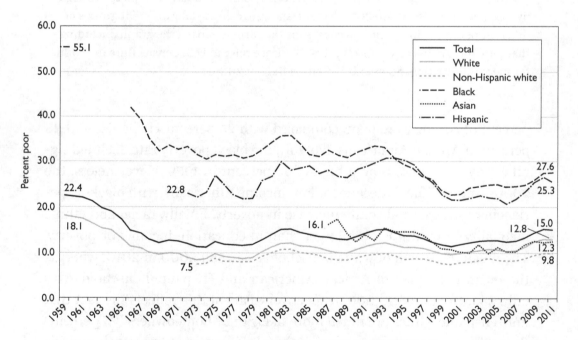

Figure 39. Poverty rates, by race and ethnicity, 1959–2011. Note: No published data are available for blacks between 1959 and 1966. Source: U.S. Census Bureau 2012g.

What factors help explain these disparities? Broad social inequalities in multicultural societies are often a function of what sociologists refer to as "social stratification," which involves members of one group in power seeking to maximize their position by restricting others' access to resources such as jobs, education, health services, and political power. Max Weber noted that usually a social group "takes some externally identifiable characteristic of another group—[such as] race, language, religion, local or social origin, descent, residence, etc.—as a pretext for attempting their exclusion."[18] In this way, broad social boundaries are drawn and maintained.[19] African Americans, Asian Americans, Hispanics, Native Americans, and even many white ethnic and national groups, such as Jews and the Irish, have all at times had to cope with limited opportunities, though their experiences have differed in very important ways. Below I discuss the experiences of contemporary racial and ethnic minority groups in more detail.

African Americans

African Americans have long struggled against racial oppression. They first arrived in the United States in large numbers as involuntary immigrants during the slave trade and were heavily concentrated in southern states. The Civil War and accompanying constitutional amendments ended slavery and conferred citizenship upon African Americans. Nevertheless, after some hope of equality during Reconstruction, from about 1865 to 1877, when blacks gained the right to vote and a number were elected to state legislatures, the U.S. House of Representatives, and even the U.S. Senate, they were relegated to second-class citizenship by the late 1870s, with southern whites reestablishing their own supremacy. Through violence and intimidation, southern whites denied blacks the power to vote. As many as two thousand to three thousand lynchings were perpetrated in the last decade and a half of the nineteenth century.[20] In the economic sphere, blacks in the South often worked as sharecroppers, mainly because they were barred by law or custom from most other full-time jobs outside the black community. Jim Crow laws mandated segregation in all public facilities, ensuring inferior services, including education, for the black community.[21]

Gunnar Myrdal, in his book *An American Dilemma: The Negro Problem and Modern Democracy,* published in 1944, described the nature and extent of black subjugation in the South:

> Violence, terror, and intimidation have been, and still are, effectively used to disfranchise Negroes in the South. Physical coercion is not so often practiced against the Negro, but the mere fact that it can be used with impunity and that it is devastating in its consequences creates a psychic coercion that exists nearly everywhere in the South. A Negro can seldom claim the protection of the police and the courts if a white man knocks him down, or if a mob burns his house or inflicts bodily injuries on him or on members of his family. If he defends himself against a minor violence, he may expect a major violence. If he once "gets in wrong" he may expect the loss of his job or other economic injury, and constant insult and loss of whatever legal rights he may have had.[22]

During the twentieth century many blacks left the oppressive conditions in the South to look for opportunity in the North, especially in booming industries in many northeastern and midwestern cities such as Chicago, Detroit, and New York. This Great Migration resulted in a striking regional redistribution of the black population in the United States. In 1900, about three-quarters of all African Americans lived in rural southern areas; a century later, that figure had declined to about 12 percent. By 1950, more than 2.5 million southern-born African Americans were living outside the region, a number that increased to more than 4 million by 1980.[23] While economic opportunities were better in the North, and the racial climate was not as oppressive (northern blacks, for example, could for the most part vote), blacks still faced a wide range of discriminatory barriers in the labor and housing market and were segregated in congested northern ghettos.

The civil rights movement in the 1950s and 1960s overturned the legal framework that supported the unequal treatment of blacks. In 1954, for example, in the case *Brown v. Board of Education of Topeka,* the Supreme Court ruled that the separate-but-equal doctrine underlying the Jim Crow system was invalid. In the 1960s several laws were passed in Congress (including the far-reaching Civil Rights Act of 1964) that prohibited racial discrimination in employment practices, public accommodations, and housing market transactions. The civil rights movement itself was propelled mainly by nonviolent protest and civil disobedience. The Montgomery Bus Boycott in Alabama in 1955–56, for example, protested racial segregation in the city's public transit system, which relegated blacks to seats in the back of the bus. The campaign began when Rosa Parks, an African American woman active in the movement, refused to give up her seat to a white person. The boycott was a success, and the Supreme Court eventually declared segregation laws to be unconstitutional.

Legal changes have also been accompanied by gradual changes in public opinion. The proportion of whites holding blatantly racist attitudes has dropped considerably over the decades according to national polls. For example, in the 1940s and 1950s, fewer than half of whites surveyed believed that white and black students should attend the same schools or that black and white job applicants should have an equal chance of getting a job. By the 1990s, however, over 90 percent of whites said they believed that schools and employers should treat whites and blacks equally.[24]

The removal of legal barriers and the slowly changing social norms, however, did not translate into immediate social and economic equality. Civil rights legislation was being passed during a time of deindustrialization—when the share of people employed in manufacturing was declining—and when many northeastern and midwestern cities were losing jobs and people through outmigration to the Sun Belt. (Many jobs also went abroad.) For example, in the twenty-year period between 1967 and 1987, Philadelphia lost 64 percent of its manufacturing jobs, Chicago lost 60 percent, New York City lost 58 percent, and Detroit 51 percent. This hurt blacks as well as whites living in those cities and contributed to the increasing poverty of blacks concentrated in inner cities.[25]

Some commentators, such as William Julius Wilson, have argued that race has become less important in determining the labor market success of African Americans and that class position has become more important.[26] From colonial times through the first half of the twentieth century, racial oppression was deliberate and overt. By the latter half of the twentieth century, many traditional barriers were dismantled as a result of political, social, and economic changes of the civil rights era. Wilson emphasizes that although discrimination has become less common though not eliminated, economic conditions have come to play an increasingly important role in shaping opportunities available to African Americans.

He argues that deindustrialization and class segregation in particular have hampered the economic mobility of less-skilled blacks.[27]

Studies show that the economic "penalty" of being African American has declined since the 1960s, in that occupational mobility has increased, as has wage parity.[28] Racial differences in economic outcomes are significantly reduced when one accounts for educational achievement.[29] Measuring the direct effects of discrimination is difficult, because it is not always clear when a discriminatory action has occurred or if general observed differences between whites and blacks are a result of unmeasured differences (e.g., quality of schooling received) or of discrimination itself. Careful examinations of this issue tend to indicate that discrimination still occurs in labor markets and in other areas. For example, "paired-test studies," in which minority job applicants were paired with white applicants with similar backgrounds and trained to be as similar as possible in behavior, have shown that minorities, particularly African Americans and foreign-sounding Latinos, were less likely to be given job interviews and offers, at least in the low-wage labor market.[30] Economists have estimated that perhaps one-quarter of the black-white wage gap is due to prejudice, suggesting that racism continues to contribute to African American economic disadvantage.[31]

Other factors have also contributed to relatively low levels of socioeconomic attainment among African Americans, some related to race and others more nonracial in origin. One race-related factor is residential and social segregation. Because African Americans often live in segregated and disadvantaged communities, they may have fewer economically useful contacts ("social capital") on which to draw to help achieve success. Many people, for example, find a job via word of mouth through friends and neighbors. Those with affluent friends and neighbors typically have access to more and better opportunities.[32] Residential segregation also affects educational disparities because a significant portion of school funding comes from local taxes. Schools in poor neighborhoods often have inferior resources and fewer enrichment programs. High neighborhood poverty rates are strongly correlated with lower student test scores.[33] Declining levels of black segregation in recent decades, along with rapid black suburbanization, has likely reduced the effects of segregation in contributing to racial inequalities over the past couple of decades. However, many cities—particularly some in the Northeast and Midwest such as Chicago, New York, Detroit, and Milwaukee—still have very high levels of black segregation.[34]

Another factor that contributes to higher poverty rates among African Americans is differentials in human-capital skills. Human capital refers to education attainment and subsequent work experience and skills. The gap in average levels of education has declined over the past few decades. Nevertheless, the quality of schooling received by children in the United States still varies widely, and, as mentioned above, African Americans are more likely to attend inferior schools with fewer resources and have lower test scores. Lower employment levels among young African Americans subsequently contribute to earnings differentials. High black incarceration rates (black men are eight times more likely to be incarcerated than white men) translate to a relatively high proportion of young black men entering the labor force with a criminal record, which further dampens their employability. The rapid growth in the prison population from the late 1970s through the mid-2000s exacerbated this problem. Many contend that high black incarceration rates are in part due to racial profiling by law enforcement and racial biases in the sentencing process.[35]

Differences in family structure affect ethnic socioeconomic differentials as well. While 36 percent of white births were to unmarried women, the figure was double (72 percent) among African Americans.[36] This contributes to socioeconomic inequalities because single-parent families are considerably more likely to be poor: about 4 in 10 (41 percent) female-headed families with children were poor in 2011, compared with fewer than 1 in 10 (9 percent) of married-couple families with children.[37] Single parents often struggle to earn sufficient income for their family while also providing an attentive, nurturing environment for their children.

Thus, some have emphasized that an African American disadvantage has persisted across generations because of *cumulative disadvantages*. Racial gaps show up early in childhood and widen through the life course. As author Michael Wenger puts it:

> On average, African Americans begin life's journey several miles behind their white counterparts as a result of the legacy of our history of racial oppression. This disadvantage is compounded by institutional hurdles they encounter at every stage of the journey: the socioeconomic conditions into

which they're born, the system of public education through which they pass, the type of employment they are able to secure, the legacy they are able to leave behind. These hurdles, arduous, relentless, and often withering to the soul, do not confront many white people as they pursue their hopes and dreams.[38]

The importance of cumulative disadvantages suggests that ending inequality has no single easy solution and helps explain why progress has been slow—though some suggest that early childhood interventions revolving around schooling could be the most effective approach to reducing racial disparities.[39] Even as race has become less important in American society, economic inequality and class background have become more important. For example, while the black-white reading gap used to be substantially larger than the rich-poor reading gap in the 1940s, by the 2000s the reverse was true.[40] As a result, while we have seen considerable growth in the black middle class in recent decades, the economic challenges faced by poor African Americans remain daunting.[41]

Hispanics, Asians, and the Role of Immigration

The many racial and ethnic dividing lines in American society have historically reserved privilege for whites. Through much of the twentieth century, some of the factors that impeded African American mobility—discrimination and segregation—also affected Hispanics and Asian Americans. Some of the traditional racial dividing lines have eased, however, mainly since the civil rights era, enabling many members of these groups to achieve socioeconomic mobility and broader incorporation into mainstream society, though people still debate the extent to which racial dividing lines continue to inhibit opportunity.

Hispanics have a long history in the United States, dating at least as far back as the annexation of territory in Florida in the early 1800s. At the request of a growing number of U.S. settlers in what had been Mexican territory, the United States annexed Texas in 1845, precipitating the Mexican-American War. After defeating the Mexican army in 1848, the United States annexed California, New Mexico, Nevada, Arizona, Utah, and Colorado as well. The Mexican-origin population in the American Southwest in 1848 was likely about 80,000 people—roughly one-fifth of the total population of that area.[42] Mexican Americans living in these territories were often treated as second-class citizens. In subsequent decades Mexicans were used as cheap labor in the building of railroads, in mining, and in agriculture. During labor shortages they were often recruited, but at other times they were encouraged to return to Mexico, often with force. Between 1930 and 1960, almost 4 million Mexicans were deported.[43]

The presence of other Hispanic groups is more recent. Puerto Ricans migrated to the U.S. mainland in large numbers in the 1950s and 1960s. Reflecting Puerto Rico's status as a U.S. territory (Spain ceded Puerto Rico to the United States in 1898 as a result of its defeat in the Spanish-American War), Puerto Ricans are U.S. citizens at birth. The Puerto Rican population is generally very mixed, and in the past the darker-skinned Puerto Ricans in particular encountered significant racial barriers.[44] Cubans entered the United States in significant numbers after the Cuban Revolution in 1959. Many of these immigrants were highly educated professionals who had been supporters of the deposed president and dictator, Fulgencio Batista. Another wave entered in 1980 as part of the Mariel Boatlift; this group was decidedly more socioeconomically mixed. Cubans overwhelmingly settled in Miami, and many found success as entrepreneurs and small business owners.[45]

As of 2010, there were 31.8 million Mexican-origin people in the United States (63 percent of the Hispanic population), up from 8.7 million in 1980. The next two traditionally largest groups—Puerto Ricans and Cubans—have been falling as a fraction of the total Hispanic population, from 14 percent and 6 percent, respectively, in 1980 to 9 percent and 4 percent in 2010. In the meantime, the number of Salvadorans, Dominicans, and Guatemalans in the United States has grown rapidly in recent years, though each of these groups still made up no more than about 2 to 3 percent of the Hispanic population nationally in 2010.

Among Asian groups, the Chinese were the first to immigrate in significant numbers around the time of the California gold rush in 1848. In the 1860s, an estimated 12,000 to 16,000 Chinese laborers were employed to build the western leg of the Central Pacific Railroad. Some Chinese also worked in agriculture, and others were entrepreneurs in San Francisco.[46] The Chinese experienced a good deal of discrimination and violence as the community grew; they were viewed as economic competitors who would drive down the wages of native-born Americans. The Naturalization Act of 1870 limited naturalization in the United States to "white persons and persons of African descent"; this meant that the Chinese were aliens ineligible for citizenship and remained so until 1943. The 1882 Chinese Exclusion Act went further, barring the immigration of all Chinese laborers. Because Chinese immigration was so heavily male, the Chinese population in the United States began to gradually decline until about 1920, after which it slowly rebounded as a result of natural increase.[47]

The first group of Japanese arrived in California around 1869 but began to increase more markedly in the 1890s. Initially, most Japanese worked in agriculture, filling a large demand for labor, though many went on to live in larger cities, including San Francisco and Los Angeles, and others became successful farm owners and entrepreneurs. However, white California workingmen and others eventually lobbied for their exclusion. Cognizant of the military might of Japan, which was a considerably more powerful country than China at the time, and not wishing to offend it, the Gentleman's Agreement of 1907 was negotiated between the United States and Japan, ending most kinds of immigration from Japan to the United States, except for family-reunification purposes. In 1913 and 1920 California enacted anti-alien land laws aimed at Japanese farmers, barring "aliens ineligible for citizenship" from purchasing and leasing agricultural land. The resident Japanese population, however, found ways to get around some of these obstacles, and many continued to prosper. Japanese immigration was later completely halted in 1924.[48] Many Japanese on the West Coast were infamously interned in camps during World War II—a fate not suffered by the German American and Italian American communities—indicative of the racism of the time.

Initial migration of Filipinos to the United States came shortly after the American annexation of the Philippines in 1898. In the 1920s and 1930s larger numbers came as farmworkers, filling in the kinds of jobs held by the Chinese and Japanese immigrants in previous years. As Asians, Filipinos were aliens ineligible for citizenship until the 1940s. Filipinos faced a significant amount of prejudice and discrimination. As writer Carlos Bulosan wrote in 1946, "Do you know what a Filipino feels in America? . . . He is the loneliest thing on earth. There is much to be appreciated . . . beauty, wealth, power, grandeur. But is he part of these luxuries? He looks, poor man, through the fingers of his eyes. He's enchained, damnably to his race, his heritage. His is betrayed, my friend."[49] Another time he wrote, "I feel like a criminal running away from a crime that I did not commit. And that crime is that I am a Filipino in America."[50] Filipinos, like other Asians and other minorities, were excluded from a broad array of economic opportunities and were viewed as unwelcome aliens by the native white majority population.

The second wave of immigration after the elimination of discriminatory national-origin quotas in 1965 included Asians from a variety of other countries, including India, Vietnam, and Korea. In 2010, the largest Asian subgroup was Chinese (24 percent of the Asian population), followed by Asian Indians (19 percent) and Filipinos (17 percent). The fraction of the Asian population that is Chinese has stayed roughly the same over the past three decades, with the percentage of Asian Indians growing substantially (they were 10 percent of the Asian population in 1980) and the percentage of Filipinos declining, but slowly (they were 22 percent of the Asian population in 1980). The percentage of Japanese as a share of the Asian population has fallen considerably, from 20 percent in 1980 to 5 percent in 2010, and Korean and Vietnamese each made up 10 percent of Asians in 2010.[51]

In some respects Latinos and Asian Americans share certain experiences, because both groups have been historically discriminated against, both have experienced substantial increases in their population resulting from immigration since the 1960s, and both are heterogeneous in terms of their national origins (though Mexicans are by far the largest group among Latinos and overall). Nevertheless, as figures 37 through 39 indicate, socioeconomic outcomes of Hispanics and Asians differ substantially. For the most part Asians are on equal socioeconomic footing with native-born whites, and in fact their outcomes exceed those of whites in some respects. Because nearly two-thirds of Asians and about 2 in 5 Hispanics are foreign born and many more of both groups are of just the second generation, we need to investigate the characteristics of immigrants from Latin America and Asia to understand their disparate outcomes.[52]

Chapter 5 described patterns of assimilation among Asians and Hispanics and noted important differences in characteristics of the immigrants from different origins, especially in levels of education. Specifically, immigrants from Asia tend to constitute a more "select" group than immigrants from Latin America. Immigrants from Korea, India, and the Philippines achieve higher average levels of education than both Latinos and native-born whites. For example, about 80 percent of immigrants from India have a bachelor's degree or more, compared with 6 percent from Mexico.[53] One factor explaining these differences is that while many immigrants from Asia become eligible to migrate to the United States because of their work-related skills, a larger proportion of immigrants from Latin America immigrate because they have relatives who are U.S. citizens.[54]

It is important to note of course that poverty among immigrants also varies considerably by country of origin; not all subgroups among Asians and Hispanics are similarly advantaged or disadvantaged. Among foreign-born Hispanics, for example, poverty rates in 2007 were high among Dominicans (28 percent) and Mexicans (22 percent) but more moderate among Cubans (16 percent) and Colombians (11 percent).[55] South Americans have nearly reached parity with non-Hispanic whites in terms of both the proportion having a college education and median household income.[56] Among Asian immigrant groups, poverty rates were a little higher for Koreans (17 percent) than for immigrants from Japan (9 percent), India (7 percent), and the Philippines (4 percent).[57] Many of these differences are explained by the average characteristics of the immigrants themselves (especially educational attainment), though as noted above each group has a unique history of immigration to the United States.

Initial disadvantages tend to persist over time and across generations. Native-born Hispanics obtain on average higher levels of education than immigrant Hispanics, but their educational levels still lag behind those of native-born whites, largely because of the lower initial level of family resources of Hispanics.[58] In contrast, native-born Asian Americans tend to achieve high levels of education, which translate into better jobs, higher incomes, and less poverty. Once family characteristics are taken into account, there is little difference in the poverty rates between native-born Asians and native-born non-Hispanic whites.[59] While Latinos are less likely to have a college degree and tend to work in lower-skill, lower-wage jobs, once human capital differences are accounted for (especially education and English-language proficiency), there is not that much difference between whites and Hispanics in terms of occupational status and earnings.[60]

The research literature does not offer a definitive answer as to the extent of racial/ethnic discrimination faced by Asians and Latinos in the labor market. For Asians, it is probably safe to say that discrimination is not widespread enough to significantly affect average levels of socioeconomic achievement. For Latinos, family background characteristics (such as education and income) are likely to play the most prominent role and ethnicity a more minor one. Race appears to continue to play a significant role in explaining lower wages and higher poverty among blacks and darker-skinned Latinos.[61]

Native Americans

The experience of Native Americans, as the original inhabitants of the North American continent, differs from that of all the other groups. At the time when Jamestown was established in 1607, estimates of the number of Native Americans living in what is now the United States is estimated to have varied from about 1 million to 10 million.[62] The population declined substantially over the course of the seventeenth through the nineteenth century, reaching an estimated low of 250,000 in 1890. The most important factor contributing to the decline in population was the diseases brought by American colonists to which Native Americans had little immunity or resistance, including scarlet fever, whooping cough, bubonic plague, cholera, and typhoid. Other causes for population decline include warfare, displacement, the slaughter of buffalo on which some tribes depended, and alcoholism.[63] The Native American population has grown rapidly since the 1970s, not just from natural increase but also in part because a greater number of Americans have asserted some Indian heritage. The civil rights movement and the decline in negative stereotyping of Native Americans—as well as the increase in positive representations of Native Americans in popular culture, such as the movie *Dances with Wolves*—help explain the increase in self-reported Native American identity.[64] As of 2010, 2.9 million Americans identified as solely Native American (0.9 percent of the total U.S. population), and another 2.3 million (0.7 percent) said they were at least part Native American.[65]

Despite this demographic growth, Native Americans tend to have low levels of educational attainment and income and high levels of poverty. In 2010, among the Native American population age 25 years and older, 13 percent had a college degree or more (compared with 30 percent among the population as a whole). Median household income was $35,000 (the national average was $50,000), and their poverty rate was 28 percent (the national average was 15 percent), placing their level of disadvantage near that of African Americans.[66] Native Americans have long had to overcome a dearth of job opportunities in and around reservations and also poor schooling. Although some evidence indicates a decline in the net negative effect of being Native American on wages over the last half of the twentieth century, Native Americans still have lower levels of educational attainment and earnings than otherwise comparable whites.[67] It is not clear whether these differences are explained by discrimination or by other difficult-to-observe factors correlated with being Native American.[68] Research on Native Americans tends to be more limited than that of other groups, in part because of the relatively small Native American population. Additional research on Native Americans, not to mention the other groups, would help shed further light on the complex interrelationship between race and socioeconomic disparities.

MULTIRACIAL AMERICA: ARE WE POSTRACIAL?

The number of mixed-race marriages and multiracial individuals has grown considerably in recent years. The multiracial population grew by 50 percent between 2000 and 2010, from 1.8 million to 4.2 million, making it the fastest growing group of children in the country. Despite this growth, the overall proportion of Americans who report two or more races is still small, at 2.9 percent, according to the 2010 census (the races consist of white, black, American Indian, Asian, and Native Hawaiian). The most common multiracial combination is black and white. Nevertheless, only 2.5 percent of non-Hispanic whites reported more than one race (i.e., among those who reported being white either alone or in combination with another racial group), compared with 6.1 percent of blacks, 13.5 percent of Asians, and 44 percent of Native Americans.[69]

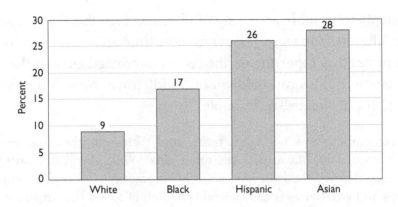

Figure 40. Percentage of newlyweds married to someone of a different race/ethnicity, 2010. Source: Wang 2012, 8.

The number of Americans identifying as multiracial will likely grow rapidly in the coming years because of recent increases in intermarriage. According to one study, about 15 percent of all new marriages in the 2008–10 period involved spouses of different races or ethnicities—more than double the percentage (6.7 percent) in 1980. (In this same study Hispanic origin was considered as a separate race/ethnicity from white.) The percentage of marriages involving a mix of differing races/ethnicities varies across groups, with a low of 9 percent of newlywed whites who married someone of a different race/ethnicity, compared with 17 percent of blacks, 26 percent of Hispanics, and 28 percent of foreign-born and U.S.-born Asians (see figure 40). In fact, nearly half of all U.S.-born Asians marry whites.[70] Overall, about 7 in 10 of mixed-race/ethnicity marriages still involve a white spouse, reflecting the fact that whites constitute the largest racial/ethnic group in the United States. The median household income of mixed-race newlywed couples tends to fall somewhere between the median incomes of couples in the same-race groups.[71]

. Americans have become more accepting of intermarriage. In 2011, nearly two-thirds of Americans (63 percent) said they "would be fine" if a family member married someone of a different race. In contrast, in 1986 (when the question was asked differently), about a third of the public viewed intermarriage as acceptable for everyone, 37 percent said it was acceptable for others but not themselves, and 28 percent said different races marrying one another was not acceptable for anyone. Younger respondents were more accepting of intermarriage than older ones, suggesting differences in views about race over time and across age cohorts.[72]

One news story reporting on the rise in intermarriage told the story of seventeen-year-old Kayci Baldwin of Middletown, New Jersey, who was the daughter of a mixed-race couple:

> She remembers how her black father and white mother often worried whether she would fit in with the other kids. While she at first struggled with her identity, Baldwin now actively embraces it, sponsoring support groups and a nationwide multiracial teen club of 1,000 that includes both Democrats and Republicans.
>
> "I went to my high school prom last week with my date who is Ecuadoran-Nigerian, a friend who is Chinese-white and another friend who is part Dominican," she said. "While we are a group that was previously ignored in many ways, we now have an opportunity to fully identify and express ourselves."[73]

One blogger, Leighton Woodhouse, describes broader social changes and his own experiences in a similar way:

> My girlfriend and I are both of mixed racial heritage. I'm half Japanese and half Anglo. She's half Salvadoran and half Jewish. If and when we have children, they'll be a quarter Asian, a quarter Latino and half white, with the white side split WASP/Jewish. When our kids become 18 and fill out their first voter registration forms, the only ethnic category that will make any sense for them to check off is "Multiracial." Today, checking off that box feels pretty close to checking off "Other" or "None of the above" on a questionnaire on any given topic; it's a throwaway category for misfits that has little if any analytical value to the researchers who review the data, but that has to be in there to get the respondent to the next section. When enough Americans start checking off that box, however, it's going to be impossible to ignore.[74]

So are we postracial? The short answer is no. Changes in American society since the 1950s and 1960s have been momentous. The fall of legal barriers and changes in attitudes have opened up many opportunities that were previously closed, if not unimaginable. African Americans, Hispanics, and Asians hold more high-level jobs in government and in the private sector than they used to, and this pattern is more pronounced among younger cohorts.[75]

However, as long as the socioeconomic disparities highlighted in figures 37 through 39 persist, it will be hard to claim that we are "beyond race." The disparities are caused in part by factors directly related to race (especially in the case of African Americans), such as discrimination. As Woodhouse goes on to say in his blog about the growing multiracial population and its consequences, "That's not to suggest that the age of the generation that follows the Millennials will be some sort of post-racial paradise. Countries like Brazil have had broad racially mixed populations for generations; that hasn't lessened their citizens' propensity for bigotry."[76]

Racial inequality is also exacerbated by factors that are not specifically racial, and they have disparate impacts. Of note, growing economic inequality in American society is serving to hamper the opportunities of low-income Americans and their children. The soaring cost of college has made it more difficult for poor families to utilize a traditionally important avenue to upward mobility. The overrepresentation of blacks and Hispanics among the poor exacerbates racial inequalities and will serve to lengthen the time until racial and ethnic parity is achieved.

INTERNATIONAL COMPARISONS

Examining the experience of minorities around the globe can provide a broader perspective for understanding race relations in the United States. However, rigorous international comparisons of racial and ethnic inequality can be challenging for a number of reasons. For one, ethnic divisions vary widely across countries, making it important to have a deep understanding of local social relations and institutions. In Rwanda, for example, there have been major fault lines between the Tutsi and Hutu people, leading to genocide in 1994. Even though these groups would both be referred to as "black" in the United States, some commentators view them as racially distinct, differing in physical appearance, such as in skin tone and nose width.[77] In some countries, social stratification occurs among religious groups rather than ethnic ones—for example, the Shia-Sunni split in parts of the Middle East and elsewhere in Asia. In other countries, such as many in Europe, ethnic divisions are of relatively recent origin, resulting from the increase in international migration. In these contexts—

as in the United States when discussing outcomes among some groups—separating the effect of nativity from race and ethnicity is difficult.

Chapter 5 discussed the variation in the extent to which immigrants of different origins are integrating in Europe. Immigrants of Muslim and North African origins are often disadvantaged in a number of countries. Various factors contribute to this, including the social background (e.g., level of education and language fluency) of the immigrants and their children and racism and discrimination in the host society.[78] For example, the 1999–2000 European Values Study indicated that between 8 and 33 percent of respondents in various European countries reported to be unwilling to have Muslims as neighbors, with a mean of 15 percent in western European countries and 19 percent in eastern European countries. Although the World Values Survey indicates that racial intolerance extends to all corners of the globe, the degree of intolerance differs from place to place. People in Anglo countries (the United States, Canada, and Australia) and Latin American ones tended to be more tolerant and were less likely to reject a racially different neighbor, while racial intolerance was relatively high in many Middle Eastern and other Asian countries, such as India, Jordan, and Indonesia, where people often reported not wanting to live near a racially distinct neighbor.[79] A caveat of these results is that the question on tolerance might be understood differently in different countries, and in some countries (such as Western democracies) expressing racially intolerant views is more taboo.

More generally, while the groups in conflict vary across countries, a common theme is that ethnic antagonisms are typically based on prejudices and stereotypes that serve to magnify the differences across groups and justify discriminatory behavior. That is not to say that stereotypes have no basis (groups often exhibit different characteristics and practices), but the role of structural factors—such as educational inequalities—in reinforcing disadvantage often goes unacknowledged. One news story on ethnic inequality in Slovakia describes the social and institutional relations between the dominant Slovaks and the disadvantaged Roma (often known as Gypsies), who arrived as migrants in Europe from the Indian subcontinent about fifteen hundred years ago. The Roma have high rates of unemployment, illiteracy, and are often targets of abuse, and many Europeans associate them with criminality. Some activists in Slovakia are pressing for equal rights for the Roma. A lawsuit was brought against one school in which Roma children were segregated into their own playground, did not have access to the school canteen, and were divided into different classes along ethnic lines. The lawsuit was successful, but some are not sure it will solve all problems. The article reports that there is still much wariness of the Roma among the school's faculty: "'These people are interested in only two things: money and sex,' said Vladimir Savov, an English teacher. 'They are lazy and don't want to learn.' Like other teachers, Mr. Savov now accepts that change is necessary, if only to satisfy the court, but he is deeply skeptical about abandoning segregated teaching. 'Mixed classes are a good idea in principle, but the question is how will they work in real life,' he said."[80]

In many immigrant societies the alienation of native-born minority groups is a function of their feeling left out of prosperity. Even Sweden, widely known for its commitment to equality, generous social safety net, and liberal immigration policies, has been the site of ethnic unrest. In May 2013 riots broke out in Stockholm, precipitated by the fatal shooting of a sixty-nine-year-old immigrant wielding a knife. The riots lasted for a few days and mainly involved rock throwing at police and the burning of cars and a school, though with no fatalities. Some attributed the riots to discrimination, high unemployment among the young, and growing income inequality. As one observer, Barbro Sorman, an activist of the opposition Left Party declared, "The rich are getting richer and the poor are getting poorer. Sweden is starting to look like the U.S.A." In contrast, those who viewed the riots with dismay feel the immigrants and their children are ungrateful for the opportunities they have received. One person who was generally sympathetic to immigrants' complaints of discrimination noted, "There are a lot of people aged from 20 to 22 who say, 'I want a job, I want it now, and I want to stay here.' . . . This is their problem, but it becomes a government problem."[81]

In short, many countries around the world are grappling with ethnic diversity. For some, ethnic divisions have long historical roots. For others, diversity is a more recent phenomenon resulting from increases in international migration and the gap between the aspirations of immigrants and their children and the opportunities available. Because racial and ethnic inequalities often have complicated origins, they frequently defy easy solutions.

CONCLUSION

Despite the decline in racial inequality and overt prejudice in the United States in recent decades, we still see significant differences in socioeconomic outcomes across racial and ethnic groups, such as in educational attainment, income, poverty, and wealth. Some of the continuing differences, particularly among blacks and perhaps Native Americans, can be explained by prejudice, stereotypes, and discrimination. However, the importance of race alone in determining life chances has declined substantially in recent decades, and the importance of socioeconomic background has increased. Unfortunately, the increasing importance of socioeconomic background serves to slow progress in reducing racial disparities, as initial disadvantages among groups often persist across generations because of these economic inequities.

1. Diggins 1976, 216.
2. Lipscomb and Bergh 1903–4, 14: 183–84.
3. Ambrose 2003, 4.
4. Peterson 1984, 1343–46.
5. National Public Radio 2013.
6. Arthur 2007, 3731–32.
7. Brodkin 2009, 58.
8. Alba 2009, 30.

9. Waters 2009, 31.

10. Alba 2009, 81–89.

11. Dulitzky 2001, 85; Marger 2011, 282.

12. Omi and Winant 2009, 21.

13. Hirschman, Alba, and Farely 2000, 381–93.

14. Compton et al. 2012.

15. Hirschman, Alba, and Farley 2000, 390–91.

16. U.S. Census Bureau 2013d.

17. Wolff 2013, 15.

18. Weber 1994, 128.

19. See Alba 2009.

20. Gill, Glazer, and Thernstrom 1992, 221.

21. See Foner 1988.

22. Myrdal 1996, 485.

23. Tolnay 2003.

24. Pager 2008, 24–25, from Schuman et al. 2001.

25. W.J. Wilson 1996, 29–30.

26. W.J. Wilson 1978.

27. W.J. Wilson 1987.

28. Hout 1994, 531–42; Sakamoto, Wu, and Tzeng 2000; Farkas and Vicknair 1996.

29. Fryer 2011, 856.

30. See Pager 2009; Cross et al. 1990; Turner, Fix, and Struyk 1991.

31. Charles and Guryan 2008.

32. Loury 2000, 60.

33. Massey and Denton 1993, 141–42.

34. Iceland 2009; Iceland, Sharp, and Timberlake 2013.

35. Western and Wildeman 2009, 221–42; Wakefield and Uggen 2010.

36. Ventura and Bachrach 2000; J.A. Martin et al. 2011; see also Wildsmith, Steward-Streng, and Manlove 2011; and DeParle and Tavernise 2012.

37. U.S. Census Bureau 2012h.

38. Wenger 2013, 1.

39. Lin and Harris 2008, 1–17; Fryer 2011.

40. Reardon 2011.

41. Landry and Marsh 2011.

42. Gill, Glazer, and Thernstrom 1992, 349.

43. Marger 2011, 293.

44. Rodriguez 1989.

45. Portes and Rumbaut 2006.

46. Daniels 2002, 239–43; Gill, Glazer, and Thernstrom 1992, 33.

47. Daniels 2002, 245.

48. Daniels 2002, 250–55; Gill, Glazer, and Thernstrom 1992, 333–34.

49. Bulosan 1946, as quoted in Daniels 2002, 357.

50. San Juan 1995, 9.

51. Iceland, Weinberg, and Hughes 2013 (from decennial censuses).

52. Grieco 2010, 6–8.

53. Camarota 2007, 23.

54. Chiswick and Sullivan 1995, 211–70.

55. Camarota 2007, 18.

56. Logan and Turner 2013, 11.

57. Camarota 2007, 18.

58. White and Glick 2009, 111; see also Bean and Stevens 2003.

59. Takei and Sakamoto 2011.

60. Duncan, Hotz, and Trejo 2006.

61. White and Glick 2009, 148.

62. Healey 2012, 123; Gill, Glazer, and Thernstrom 1992, 30.

63. Gill, Glazer, and Thernstrom 1992, 31.

64. Shoemaker 1999.

65. Norris, Vines, and Hoeffel 2012, 4.

66. U.S. Census Bureau 2010c. Note that the statistics cited here for Native Americans and those cited for other groups come from different surveys (the American Community Survey for Native Americans; and for the other groups see U.S. Census Bureau 2012k). The CPS is too small a survey to provide reliable annual data on Native Americans. Since the data come from different sources, the two sets are not perfectly comparable, but they still provide an accurate general picture of Native American socioeconomic disadvantage in American society.

67. Sakamoto, Wu, and Tzeng 2000; Sandefur and Scott 1983.

68. Huyser, Sakamoto, and Takei 2010.

69. Saulny 2011; see also Humes, Jones, and Ramirez 2011.

70. Qian and Licther 2007.

71. Wang 2012, 8 and 19.

72. Wang 2012, 7.

73. Yen 2009.

74. Woodhouse 2012.

75. Alba 2009, 90–135.

76. Woodhouse 2012.

77. Mamdani 2001, 45.

78. Heath, Rothon, and Kilpi 2008, 218.

79. Fisher 2013.

80. Higgins 2013a.

81. Higgins 2013b.

DISTINGUISHING FEATURES OF BLACK FEMINIST THOUGHT

Patricia Hill Collins

I am a product of an intellectual tradition which until twenty-five years ago did not exist within the academy. Like patchwork in a quilt, it is a tradition gathered from meaningful bits and pieces. My tradition has no name, because it embraces more than womanism, Blackness, or African studies, although those terms will do for now.

BARBARA OMOLADE 1994, ix

It seems I am running out of words these days. I feel as if I am on a linguistic treadmill that has gradually but unmistakably increased its speed, so that no word I use to positively describe myself or my scholarly projects lasts for more than five seconds. I can no longer justify my presence in academia, for example, with words that exist in the English language. The moment I find some symbol of my presence in the rarefied halls of elite institutions, it gets stolen, co-opted, filled with negative meaning.

PATRICIA WILLIAMS 1995, 27

U.S. Black women's struggles on this "linguistic treadmill" to name this tradition with "no name" reveal the difficulties of making do with "terms [that] will do for now." Widely used yet increasingly difficult to define, U.S. Black feminist thought encompasses diverse and often contradictory meanings. Despite the fact that U.S. Black women, in particular, have expended considerable energy on naming Black women's knowledge, definitional tensions not only persist but encounter changing political climates riddled with new obstacles. When the very vocabulary used to describe Black feminist thought comes under attack, Black women's self-definitions become even more difficult to achieve. For example, despite continued acceptance among many African-Americans of Afrocentrism as a term referencing traditions of Black consciousness and racial solidarity, academics and media pundits maligned the term in the 1980s and 1990s. Similarly, the pejorative meanings increasingly attached to the term feminist seem designed to discredit a movement dedicated to women's empowerment. Even the term *Black* fell victim to the deconstructive moment, with a growing number of "Black" intellectuals who do "race" scholarship questioning the very terms used to describe both themselves and their political struggles (see, e.g., Gilroy 1993). Collectively, these developments produced a greatly changed political and intellectual context for defining Black feminist thought.

Despite these difficulties, finding some sort of common ground for thinking through the boundaries of Black feminist thought remains important because, as U.S. Black feminist activist Pearl Cleage reminds us, "we have to see clearly that we are a unique group, set undeniably apart because of race and sex with a unique set of challenges" (Cleage 1993, 55). Rather than developing definitions and arguing over naming practices—for example, whether this thought should be called Black feminism, womanism, Afrocentric feminism, Africana womanism, and the like—a more useful approach lies in revisiting the reasons why Black feminist thought exists at all. Exploring six distinguishing features that characterize Black feminist thought may provide the common ground that is so sorely needed both among African-American women, and between African-American women and all others whose collective knowledge or thought has a similar purpose. Black feminist thought's distinguishing features need not be unique and may share much with other bodies of knowledge. Rather, it is the *convergence* of these distinguishing features that gives U.S. Black feminist thought its distinctive contours.

WHY U.S. BLACK FEMINIST THOUGHT?

Black feminism remains important because U.S. Black women constitute an oppressed group. As a collectivity, U.S. Black women participate in a *dialectical* relationship linking African-American women's oppression and activism. Dialectical relationships of this sort mean that two parties are opposed and opposite. As long as Black women's subordination within intersecting oppressions of race, class, gender, sexuality, and nation persists, Black feminism as an activist response to that oppression will remain needed.

In a similar fashion, the overarching purpose of U.S. Black feminist thought is also to resist oppression, both its practices and the ideas that justify it. If intersecting oppressions did not exist, Black feminist thought and similar oppositional knowledges would be unnecessary. As a critical social theory, Black feminist thought aims to empower African-American women within the context of social injustice sustained by intersecting oppressions. Since Black women cannot be fully empowered unless intersecting oppressions themselves are eliminated, Black feminist thought supports broad principles of social justice that transcend U.S. Black women's particular needs.

Because so much of U.S. Black feminism has been filtered through the prism of the U.S. context, its contours have been greatly affected by the specificity of American multiculturalism (Takaki 1993). In particular, U.S. Black feminist thought and practice respond to a fundamental contradiction of U.S. society. On the one hand, democratic promises of individual freedom, equality under the law, and social justice are made to all American citizens. Yet on the other hand, the reality of differential group treatment based on race, class, gender, sexuality, and citizenship status persists. Groups organized around race, class, and gender in and of themselves are not inherently a problem. However, when African-Americans, poor people, women, and other groups discriminated against see little hope for group-based advancement, this situation constitutes social injustice.

Within this overarching contradiction, U.S. Black women encounter a distinctive set of social practices that accompany our particular history within a unique matrix of domination characterized by intersecting oppressions. Race is far from being the only significant marker of group difference—class, gender, sexuality, religion, and citizenship status all matter greatly in the United States (Andersen and Collins 1998). Yet for African-American women, the effects of institutionalized racism remain visible and palpable. Moreover, the institutionalized racism that African-American women encounter relies heavily on racial segregation and accompanying discriminatory practices designed to deny U.S. Blacks equitable treatment. Despite important strides to desegregate U.S. society since 1970, racial segregation remains deeply entrenched in housing, schooling, and employment (Massey and Denton 1993). For many African-American women, racism is not something that exists in the distance. We encounter racism in everyday situations in workplaces, stores, schools, housing, and daily social interaction (St. Jean and Feagin 1998). Most Black women do not have the opportunity to befriend White women and men as neighbors, nor do their children attend school with White children. Racial segregation remains a fundamental feature of the U.S. social landscape, leaving many African-Americans with the belief that "the more things change, the more they stay the same" (Collins 1998a, 11–43). Overlaying these persisting inequalities is a rhetoric of color blindness designed to render these social inequalities invisible. In a context where many believe that to talk of race fosters racism, equality allegedly lies in treating everyone the same. Yet as Kimberle Crenshaw (1997) points out, "it is fairly obvious that treating different things the same can generate as much inequality as treating the same things differently" (p. 285).

Although racial segregation is now organized differently than in prior eras (Collins 1998a, 11–43), being Black and female in the United States continues to expose African-American women to certain common experiences. U.S. Black women's similar work and family experiences as well as our participation in diverse expressions of African-American culture mean that, overall, U.S. Black women as a group live in a different world from that of people who are not Black and female. For individual women, the particular experiences that accrue to living as a Black woman in the United States can stimulate a distinctive consciousness concerning our own experiences and society overall. Many African-American women grasp this connection between what one does and how one thinks. Hannah Nelson, an elderly Black domestic worker, discusses how work shapes the perspectives of African-American and White women: "Since I have to work, I don't really have to worry about most of the things that most of the white women I have worked for are worrying about. And if these women did their own work, they would think just like I do—about this, anyway" (Gwaltney 1980, 4). Ruth Shays, a Black inner-city resident, points out how variations in men's and women's experiences lead to differences in perspective. "The mind of the man and the mind of the woman is the same" she notes, "but this business of living makes women use their minds in ways that men don't even have to think about" (Gwaltney 1980, 33).

A recognition of this connection between experience and consciousness that shapes the everyday lives of individual African-American women often pervades the works of Black women activists and scholars. In her autobiography, Ida B. Wells-Barnett describes how the lynching of her friends had such an impact on her worldview that she subsequently devoted much of her life to the anti-lynching cause (Duster 1970). Sociologist Joyce Ladner's discomfort with the disparity between the teachings of mainstream scholarship and her experiences as a young Black woman in the South led her to write *Tomorrow's Tomorrow* (1972), a groundbreaking study of Black female adolescence. Similarly, the transformed consciousness experienced by Janie, the light-skinned heroine of Zora Neale Hurston's (1937) classic *Their Eyes Were Watching God*, from obedient granddaughter and wife to a self-defined African-American woman, can be directly traced to her experiences with each of her three husbands. In one scene Janie's second husband, angry because she served him a dinner of scorched rice, underdone fish, and soggy bread, hits her. That incident stimulates Janie to stand "where he left her for unmeasured time" and think. And in her thinking "her image of Jody tumbled down and shattered . . . [S]he had an inside and an outside now and suddenly she knew how not to mix them" (p. 63).

Overall, these ties between what one does and what one thinks illustrated by *individual* Black women can also characterize Black women's experiences and ideas as a *group*. Historically, racial segregation in housing, education, and employment fostered group commonalities that encouraged the formation of a group-based, collective standpoint.[1] For example, the heavy concentration of U.S. Black women in domestic work coupled with racial segregation in housing and schools meant that U.S. Black women had common organizational networks that enabled them to share experiences and construct a collective body of wisdom. This collective wisdom on how to survive as U.S. Black women constituted a distinctive Black women's standpoint on gender-specific patterns of racial segregation and its accompanying economic penalties.

The presence of Black women's collective wisdom challenges two prevailing interpretations of the consciousness of oppressed groups. One approach claims that subordinate groups identify with the powerful and have no valid independent interpretation of their own oppression. The second assumes the oppressed are less human than their rulers, and are therefore less capable of interpreting their own experiences (Rollins 1985; Scott 1985). Both approaches see any independent consciousness expressed by African-American women and other oppressed groups as being either not of our own making or inferior to that of dominant groups. More importantly, both explanations suggest that the alleged lack of political activism on the part of oppressed groups stems from our flawed consciousness of our own subordination.[2]

Historically, Black women's group location in intersecting oppressions produced commonalities among individual African-American women. At the same time, while common experiences may predispose Black women to develop a distinctive group consciousness, they guarantee neither that such a consciousness will develop among all women nor that it will be articulated as such by the group. As historical conditions change, so do the links among the types of experiences Black women will have and any ensuing group consciousness concerning those experiences. Because group standpoints are situated in, reflect, and help shape unjust power relations, standpoints are not static (Collins 1998a, 201–28). Thus, common challenges may foster similar angles of vision leading to a group knowledge or standpoint among African-American women. Or they may not.

DIVERSE RESPONSES TO COMMON CHALLENGES WITHIN BLACK FEMINISM

A second distinguishing feature of U.S. Black feminist thought emerges from a tension linking experiences and ideas. On the one hand, all African-American women face similar challenges that result from living in a society that historically and routinely derogates women of African descent. Despite the fact that U.S. Black women face common challenges, this neither means that individual African-American women have all had the same experiences nor that we agree on the significance of our varying experiences. Thus, on the other hand, despite the common challenges confronting U.S. Black women as a group, diverse responses to these core themes characterize U.S. Black women's group knowledge or standpoint.

Despite differences of age, sexual orientation, social class, region, and religion, U.S. Black women encounter societal practices that restrict us to inferior housing, neighborhoods, schools, jobs, and public treatment and hide this differential consideration behind an array of common beliefs about Black women's intelligence, work habits, and sexuality. These common challenges in turn result in recurring patterns of experiences for individual group members. For example, African-American women from quite diverse backgrounds report similar treatment in stores. Not every *individual* Black woman consumer need experience being followed in a store as a potential shoplifter, ignored while others are waited on first, or seated near restaurant kitchens and rest rooms, for African-American women as a collectivity to recognize that differential *group* treatment is operating.

Since standpoints refer to group knowledge, recurring patterns of differential treatment such as these suggest that certain themes will characterize U.S. Black women's group knowledge or standpoint. For example, one core theme concerns multifaceted legacies of struggle, especially in response to forms of violence that accompany intersecting oppressions (Collins 1998d). Katie Cannon observes, "[T]hroughout the history of the United States, the interrelationship of white supremacy and male superiority has characterized the Black woman's reality as a situation of struggle—a struggle to survive in two contradictory worlds simultaneously, one white, privileged, and oppressive, the other black, exploited, and oppressed" (1985, 30). Black women's vulnerability to assaults in the workplace, on the street, at home, and in media representations has been one factor fostering this legacy of struggle.

Despite differences created by historical era, age, social class, sexual orientation, skin color, or ethnicity, the legacy of struggle against the violence that permeates U.S. social structures is a common thread binding African-American women. Anna Julia Cooper, an educated, nineteenth-century Black woman intellectual, describes Black women's vulnerability to sexual violence:

> I would beg . . . to add my plea for the *Colored Girls* of the South:—that large, bright, promising fatally beautiful class . . . so full of promise and possibilities, yet so sure of destruction; often without a father to whom they dare apply the loving term, often without a stronger brother to espouse their cause and defend their honor with his life's blood; in the midst of pitfalls and

snares, waylaid by the lower classes of white men, with no shelter, no protection.

(Cooper 1892, 240)

Yet during this period Cooper and other middle-class U.S. Black women built a powerful club movement and numerous community organizations (Giddings 1984, 1988; Gilkes 1985).

Stating that a legacy of struggle exists does not mean that all U.S. Black women share its benefits or even recognize it. For example, for African-American girls, age often offers little protection from assaults. Far too many young Black girls inhabit hazardous and hostile environments (Carroll 1997). In 1975 I received an essay titled "My World" from Sandra, a sixth-grade student who was a resident of one of the most dangerous public housing projects in Boston. Sandra wrote, "My world is full of people getting rape. People shooting on another. Kids and grownups fighting over girls-friends. And people without jobs who can't afford to get a education so they can get a job . . . winos on the streets raping and killing little girls." Her words poignantly express a growing Black feminist sensibility that she may be victimized by racism, misogyny, and poverty. They reveal her awareness that she is vulnerable to rape as a form of sexual violence. Despite her feelings about her neighborhood, Sandra not only walked the streets daily but managed safely to deliver three siblings to school. In doing so she participated in a Black women's legacy of struggle. Sandra prevailed, but at a cost. Unlike Sandra, others simply quit.

This legacy of struggle constitutes one of several core themes of a Black women's standpoint. Efforts to reclaim U.S. Black women's intellectual traditions have revealed Black women's long-standing attention to additional core themes first recorded by Maria W. Stewart (Richardson 1987). Stewart's perspective on intersecting oppressions, her call for replacing derogated images of Black womanhood with self-defined images, her belief in Black women's activism as mothers, teachers, and Black community leaders, and her sensitivity to sexual politics are all core themes advanced by a variety of Black feminist intellectuals.

Despite the common challenges confronting African-American women as a group, individual Black women neither have identical experiences nor interpret experiences in a similar fashion. The existence of core themes does not mean that African-American women respond to these themes in the same way. Differences among individual Black women produce different patterns of experiential knowledge that in turn shape individual reactions to the core themes. For example, when faced with controlling images of Black women as being ugly and unfeminine, some women—such as Sojourner Truth—demand, "Ain't I a woman?" By deconstructing the conceptual apparatus of the dominant group, they challenge notions of Barbie-doll femininity premised on middle-class White women's experiences (duCille 1996, 8–59). In contrast, other women internalize the controlling images and come to believe that they are the stereotypes (Brown-Collins and Sussewell 1986). Still others aim to transgress the boundaries that frame the images themselves. Jaminica, a 14-year-old Black girl, describes her strategies: "Unless you want to get into a big activist battle, you accept the stereotypes given to you and just try and reshape them along the way. So in a way, this gives me a lot of freedom. I can't be looked at any worse in society than I already am—black and female is pretty high on the list of things not to be" (Carroll 1997, 94–95).

Many factors explain these diverse responses. For example, although all African-American women encounter institutionalized racism, social class differences among African-American women influence patterns of racism in housing, education, and employment. Middle-class Blacks are more likely to encounter a pernicious form of racism that has left many angry and disappointed (Cose 1993; Feagin and Sikes 1994). A young manager who graduated with honors from the University of Maryland describes the specific form racism can take for middle-class Blacks. Before she flew to Cleveland to explain a marketing plan for her company, her manager made her go over it three or four times in front of him so that she would not forget her marketing plan. Then he explained how to check luggage at an airport and how to reclaim it. "I just sat at lunch listening to this man talking to me like I was a monkey who could remember but couldn't think," she recalled. When she had had enough, "I asked him if he wanted to tie my money up in a handkerchief and put a note on me saying that I was an employee of this company. In case I got lost I would be picked up by Traveler's Aid, and Traveler's Aid would send me back" (Davis and Watson 1985, 86). Most middle-class Black women do not encounter such blatant incidents, but many working-class Blacks do. Historically, working-class Blacks have struggled with forms of institutionalized racism directly organized by White institutions and by forms mediated by some segments of the Black middle class. Thus, while it shares much with middle-class Black women, the legacy of struggle by working-class Blacks (Kelley 1994) and by working-class Black women in particular will express a distinctive character (Fordham 1993).

Sexuality signals another important factor that influences African-American women's varying responses to common challenges. Black lesbians have identified heterosexism as a form of oppression and the issues they face living in homophobic communities as shaping their interpretations of everyday events (Shockley 1974; Lorde 1982, 1984; Clarke et al. 1983; Barbara Smith 1983, 1998; Williams 1997). Beverly Smith describes how being a lesbian affected her perceptions of the wedding of one of her closest friends: "God, I wish I had one friend here. Someone who knew me and would understand how I feel. I am masquerading as a nice, straight, middle-class Black 'girl' " (1983, 172). While the majority of those attending the wedding saw only a festive event, Beverly Smith felt that her friend was being sent into a form of bondage. In a similar fashion, varying ethnic and citizenship statuses within the U.S. nation-state as well also shape differences among Black women in the United States. For example, Black Puerto Ricans constitute a group that combines categories of race, nationality, and ethnicity in distinctive ways. Black Puerto Rican women thus must negotiate a distinctive set of experiences that accrue to being racially Black, holding a special form of American citizenship, and being ethnically Latino.

Given how these factors influence diverse response to common challenges, it is important to stress that no homogeneous Black *woman's* standpoint exists. There is no essential or archetypal Black woman whose experiences stand as normal, normative, and thereby authentic. An essentialist understanding of a Black woman's standpoint suppresses differences among Black women in search of an elusive group unity. Instead, it may be more accurate to say that a Black *women's* collective standpoint does exist, one characterized by the tensions that accrue to different responses to common challenges. Because it both recognizes and aims to incorporate heterogeneity in crafting Black women's oppositional knowledge, this Black *women's* standpoint eschews essentialism in favor of democracy. Since Black feminist thought both arises within and aims to articulate a Black *women's* group standpoint regarding experiences associated with intersecting oppressions, stressing this group standpoint's heterogeneous composition is significant.

Moreover, in thinking through the contours of a Black women's standpoint, it is equally important to recognize that U.S. Black women also encounter the same challenges (and correspondingly different expressions) as women of African descent within a Black diasporic context. This context in turn is situated within a transnational, global context. The term *diaspora* describes the experiences of people who, through slavery, colonialism, imperialism, and migration, have been forced to leave their native lands (Funani 1998, 417). For U.S. Black women and other people of African descent, a diasporic framework suggests a dispersal from Africa to societies in the Caribbean, South America, North America, and Europe. Understandings of African-American womanhood thus reflect a distinctive pattern of dispersal associated with forced immigration to the United States and subsequent enslavement (Pala 1995). Since a diasporic framework is not normative, it should not be used to assess the authenticity of people of African descent in reference to an assumed African norm. Rather, Black diasporic frameworks center analyses of Black women within the context of common challenges experienced transnationally.

The version of Black feminism that U.S. Black women have developed certainly must be understood in the context of U.S. nation-state politics. At the same time, U.S. Black feminism as a social justice project shares much with comparable social justice projects advanced not only by other U.S. racial/ethnic groups (see, e.g., Takaki 1993), but by women of African descent across quite diverse societies. In the context of an "intercontinental Black women's consciousness movement" (McLaughlin 1995, 73), women of African descent are dispersed globally, yet the issues we face may be similar. Transnationally, women encounter recurring social issues such as poverty, violence, reproductive concerns, lack of education, sex work, and susceptibility to disease (*Rights of Women* 1998). Placing African-American women's experiences, thought, and practice in a transnational, Black diasporic context reveals these and other commonalities of women of African descent while specifying what is particular to African-American women.

BLACK FEMINIST PRACTICE AND BLACK FEMINIST THOUGHT

A third distinguishing feature of Black feminist thought concerns the connections between U.S. Black women's experiences as a heterogeneous collectivity and any ensuing group knowledge or standpoint. One key reason that standpoints of oppressed groups are suppressed is that self-defined standpoints can stimulate resistance. Annie Adams, a Southern Black woman, describes how she became involved in civil rights activities:

> When I first went into the mill we had segregated water fountains. . . . Same thing about the toilets. I had to clean the toilets for the inspection room and then, when I got ready to go to the bathroom, I had to go all the way to the bottom of the stairs to the cellar. So I asked my boss man, "what's the difference? If I can go in there and clean them toilets, why can't I use them?" Finally, I started to use that toilet. I decided I wasn't going to walk a mile to go to the bathroom.
>
> (Byerly 1986, 134)

In this case Ms. Adams found the "boss man's" point of view inadequate, developed one of her own, and acted on it. On the individual level, her actions illustrate the connections among lived experiences with oppression, developing one's own point of view concerning those experiences, and the acts of resistance that can follow. A similar relationship characterizes African-American women's group knowledge. U.S. Black women's collective historical experiences with oppression may stimulate a self-defined Black women's standpoint that in turn can foster Black women's activism.

As members of an oppressed group, U.S. Black women have generated alternative practices and knowledges that have been designed to foster U.S.

Black women's group empowerment. In contrast to the dialectical relationship linking oppression and activism, a *dialogical* relationship characterizes Black women's collective experiences and group knowledge. On both the individual and the group level, a dialogical relationship suggests that changes in thinking may be accompanied by changed actions and that altered experiences may in turn stimulate a changed consciousness. For U.S. Black women as a collectivity, the struggle for a self-defined Black feminism occurs through an ongoing dialogue whereby action and thought inform one another.

U.S. Black feminism itself illustrates this dialogical relationship. On the one hand, there is U.S. Black feminist practice that emerges in the context of lived experience. When organized and visible, such practice had taken the form of overtly Black feminist social movements dedicated to the empowerment of U.S. Black women. Two especially prominent moments characterize Black feminism's visibility. Providing many of the guiding ideas for today, the first occurred at the turn of the century via the Black women's club movement. The second or modern Black feminist movement was stimulated by the antiracist and women's social justice movements of the 1960s and 1970s and continues to the present. However, these periods of overt political activism where African-American women lobbied in our own behalf remain unusual. They appear to be unusual when juxtaposed to more typical patterns of quiescence regarding Black women's advocacy.

Given the history of U.S. racial segregation, Black feminist activism demonstrates distinctive patterns. Because African-Americans have long been relegated to racially segregated environments, U.S. Black feminist practice has often occurred within a context of Black community development efforts and other Black nationalist-inspired projects. Black nationalism emerges in conjunction with racial segregation—U.S. Blacks living in a racially integrated society would most likely see less need for Black nationalism. As a political philosophy, Black nationalism is based on the belief that Black people constitute a people or "nation" with a common history and destiny. Black solidarity, the belief that Blacks have common interests and should support one another, has long permeated Black women's political philosophy. Thus, Black women's path to a "feminist" consciousness often occurs within the context of antiracist social justice projects, many of them influenced by Black nationalist ideologies. In describing how this phenomenon affects Black women in global context, Andree Nicola McLaughlin contends, "[A]mong activist Black women, it is generally recognized that nationalist struggle provides a rich arena for developing a woman's consciousness" (McLaughlin 1995, 80). To look for Black feminism by searching for U.S. Black women who self-identify as "Black feminists" misses the complexity of how Black feminist practice actually operates (Collins 1993a).

Similar views have been expressed about the feminism of women in Africa. When a colleague asked Obioma Nnaemeka to describe African feminists' definition of African feminism, her off-the-cuff response was telling: "[T]he majority of African women are not hung up on 'articulating their feminism'; they just do it." In Nnaemeka's view, "It is *what* they do and *how* they do it that provide the 'framework'; the 'framework' is not carried to the theater of action as a definitional tool. . . . Attempts to mold 'African feminism' into an easily digestible ball of pointed yam not only raise definitional questions but create difficulties for drawing organizational parameters and unpacking complex modes of engagement" (Nnaemeka 1998a, 5). Here Nnaemeka provides a compelling argument concerning the interconnectedness of experiences and ideas, one that differs markedly from accepted models of how one defines social justice movements. Her model references the dialogical relationship, and points to a different way of thinking about Black feminist thought as knowledge. Specifically, Black feminist practice requires Black feminist thought, and vice versa.

When it comes to the dialogical relationship within U.S. Black feminism, on the other hand, there is U.S. Black feminist thought as a critical social theory. Critical social theory constitutes theorizing about the social in defense of economic and social justice. As critical social theory, Black feminist thought encompasses bodies of knowledge and sets of institutional practices that actively grapple with the central questions facing U.S. Black women as a group. Such theory recognizes that U.S. Black women constitute one group among many that are differently placed within situations of injustice. What makes critical social theory "critical" is its commitment to justice, for one's own group and for other groups.

Within these parameters, knowledge for knowledge's sake is not enough—Black feminist thought must both be tied to Black women's lived experiences and aim to better those experiences in some fashion. When such thought is sufficiently grounded in Black feminist practice, it reflects this dialogical relationship. Black feminist thought encompasses general knowledge that helps U.S. Black women survive in, cope with, and resist our differential treatment. It also includes more specialized knowledge that investigates the specific themes and challenges of any given period of time. Conversely, when U.S. Black women cannot see the connections among themes that permeate Black feminist thought and those that influence Black women's everyday lives, it is appropriate to question the strength of this dialogical relationship. Moreover, it is also reasonable to question the validity of that particular expression of Black feminist thought. For example, during slavery, a special theme within Black feminist thought was how the institutionalized rape of enslaved Black women operated as a mechanism of social control. During the period when Black women worked primarily in agriculture and service, countering the sexual harassment of live-in domestic workers gained special importance. Clear connections could be drawn between the content and purpose of Black feminist thought and important issues in Black women's lives.

The potential significance of Black feminist thought goes far beyond demonstrating that African-American women can be theorists. Like Black feminist practice, which it reflects and which it seeks to foster, Black feminist thought can create a collective identity among African-American women about the dimensions of a Black women's standpoint. Through the process of *rearticulation*, Black feminist thought can offer African-American women a different view of ourselves and our worlds (Omi and Winant 1994, 99). By taking the core themes of a Black women's standpoint and infusing them with new meaning, Black feminist thought can stimulate a new consciousness that utilizes Black women's everyday, taken-for-granted knowledge. Rather than raising consciousness, Black feminist thought affirms, rearticulates, and provides a vehicle for expressing in public a consciousness that quite often already exists. More important, this rearticulated consciousness aims to empower African-American women and stimulate resistance.

Sheila Radford-Hill stresses the importance of rearticulation as an essential ingredient of an empowering Black feminist theory in her essay "Considering Feminism as a Model for Social Change." In evaluating whether Black women should espouse feminist programs, Radford-Hill suggests, "[T]he essential issue that black women must confront when assessing a feminist position is as follows: If I, as a black woman, 'become a feminist,' what basic tools will I gain to resist my individual and group oppression?" (1986, 160). For Radford-Hill, the relevance of feminism as a vehicle for social change must be assessed in terms of its "ability to factor black women and other women of color into alternative conceptions of power and the consequences of its use" (p. 160). Thus Black feminist thought as critical social theory aims to aid African-American women's struggles against intersecting oppressions.

At first glance, these connections between Black feminist practice and Black feminist thought might suggest that only African-American women can participate in the production of Black feminist thought and that only Black women's experiences can form the content of that thought. But this model of Black feminism is undermined as a critical perspective by being dependent on those who are biologically Black and female. Exclusionary definitions of Black feminism which confine "black feminist criticism to black women critics of black women artists depicting black women" (Carby 1987, 9) are inadequate because they are inherently separatist. Instead, the connections here aim for autonomy. Given this need for self-definition and autonomy— an important objective of "an intellectual tradition which until twenty-five years ago did not exist within the academy" (Omolade 1994, ix)—what is the significance of Black women intellectuals within Black feminist thought?

DIALOGICAL PRACTICES AND BLACK
WOMEN INTELLECTUALS

A fourth distinguishing feature of Black feminist thought concerns the essential contributions of African-American women intellectuals. The existence of a Black women's standpoint does not mean that African-American women, academic or otherwise, appreciate its content, see its significance, or recognize its potential as a catalyst for social change. One key task for Black women intellectuals of diverse ages, social classes, educational backgrounds, and occupations consists of asking the right questions and investigating all dimensions of a Black women's standpoint with and for African-American women. Historically, Black women intellectuals stood in a special relationship to the larger community of African-American women, a relationship that framed Black feminist thought's contours as critical social theory. Whether this relationship will persist depends, ironically, on Black women intellectuals' ability to analyze their own social locations.

Very different kinds of "thought" and "theories" emerge when abstract thought is joined with pragmatic action. Denied positions as scholars and writers which allow us to emphasize purely theoretical concerns, the work of most Black women intellectuals has been influenced by the merger of action and theory. The activities of nineteenth-century educated Black women intellectuals such as Anna J. Cooper, Frances Ellen Watkins Harper, Ida B. Wells-Barnett, and Mary Church Terrell exemplify this tradition of merging intellectual work and activism. These women both analyzed the intersecting oppressions that circumscribed Black women's lives and worked for social justice. The Black women's club movement they created was both an activist and an intellectual endeavor. Working-class Black women also engaged in a parallel joining of ideas and activism. But because they were denied formal educations, the form of their activism as well as the content of the ideas they developed differed from those of middle-class Black women. The live performances of classic Black women blues singers in the 1920s can be seen as one important arena where working-class women gathered and shared ideas especially germane to them (Davis 1998).

Many contemporary Black women intellectuals continue to draw on this tradition of using everyday actions and experiences in our theoretical work. Black feminist historian Elsa Barkley Brown describes the importance her mother's ideas played in the scholarship she eventually produced on African-American washerwomen. Initially Brown used the lens provided by her training as a historian and saw her sample group as devalued service workers. But over time she came to understand washerwomen as entrepreneurs. By taking the laundry to whoever had the largest kitchen, they created a community and a culture among themselves. In explaining the shift of vision that enabled her to reassess this portion of Black women's history, Brown notes, "It was my mother who taught me how to ask the right questions—and all of us who try to do this thing called scholarship on a regular basis are fully aware that asking the right questions is the most important part of the process" (1986, 14).

This special relationship of Black women intellectuals to the community of African-American women parallels the existence of two interrelated levels of knowledge (Berger and Luckmann 1966). The commonplace, taken-for-granted knowledge shared by African-American women growing from our everyday thoughts and actions constitutes a first and most fundamental level of knowledge. The ideas that Black women share with one another on an informal, daily basis about topics such as how to style our hair, characteristics of "good" Black men, strategies for dealing with White folks, and skills of how to "get over" provide the foundations for this taken-for-granted knowledge.

Experts or specialists who participate in and emerge from a group produce a second, more specialized type of knowledge. Whether working-class or middle-class, educated or not, famous or everyday, the range of Black women intellectuals discussed in Chapter 1 are examples of these specialists. Their theories that facilitate the expression of a Black women's standpoint form the specialized knowledge of Black feminist thought. The two types of knowledge are interdependent. While Black feminist thought articulates the often taken-for-granted knowledge shared by African-American women as a group, the consciousness of Black women may be transformed by such thought. Many Black women blues singers have long sung about taken-for-granted situations that affect U.S. Black women. Through their music, they not only depict Black women's realities, they aim to shape them.

Because they have had greater opportunities to achieve literacy, middle-class Black women have also had greater access to the resources to engage in Black feminist scholarship. Education need not mean alienation from this dialogical relationship. The actions of educated Black women within the Black women's club movement typify this special relationship between one segment of Black women intellectuals and the wider community of African-American women:

> It is important to recognize that black women like Frances Harper, Anna Julia Cooper, and Ida B. Wells were not isolated figures of intellectual genius; they were shaped by and helped to shape a wider movement of Afro-American women. This is not to claim that they were representative of all black women; they and their counterparts formed an educated, intellectual elite, but an elite that tried to develop a cultural and historical perspective that was organic to the wider condition of black womanhood.
>
> (Carby 1987, 115)

The work of these women is important because it illustrates a tradition of joining scholarship and activism. Because they often lived in the same neighborhoods as working-class Blacks, turn-of-the-century club women lived in a Black civil society where this dialogical relationship was easier to establish. They saw the problems. They participated in social institutions that encouraged solutions. They fostered the development of a "cultural and historical perspective that was organic to the wider condition of black womanhood." Contemporary Black women intellectuals face similar challenges of fostering dialogues, but do so under greatly changed social conditions. Whereas racial segregation was designed to keep U.S. Blacks oppressed, it fostered a form of racial solidarity that flourished in all-Black neighborhoods. In contrast, now that Blacks live in economically heterogeneous neighborhoods, achieving the same racial solidarity raises new challenges.

Black women intellectuals are central to Black feminist thought for several reasons. First, our experiences as African-American women provide us with a unique angle of vision concerning Black womanhood unavailable to other groups, should we choose to embrace it. It is more likely for Black women, as members of an oppressed group, to have critical insights into the condition of our oppression than it is for those who live outside those structures. One of the characters in Frances Ellen Watkins Harper's 1892 novel, *Iola Leroy*, expresses this belief in the special vision of those who have experienced oppression:

> Miss Leroy, out of the race must come its own thinkers and writers. Authors belonging to the white race have written good books, for which I am deeply grateful, but it seems to be almost impossible for a white man to put himself completely in our place. No man can feel the iron which enters another man's soul.
>
> (Carby 1987, 62)

Only African-American women occupy this center and can "feel the iron" that enters Black women's souls, because while U.S. Black women's experiences resemble others, such experiences remain unique. The importance of Black women's leadership in producing Black feminist thought does not mean that others cannot participate. It does mean that the primary responsibility for defining one's own reality lies with the people who live that reality, who actually have those experiences.

Second, Black women intellectuals both inside and outside the academy are less likely to walk away from Black women's struggles when the obstacles seem overwhelming or when the rewards for staying diminish. In discussing Black women's involvement in the feminist movement, Sheila Radford-Hill stresses the significance of taking actions in one's own behalf:

Black women now realize that part of the problem within the movement was our insistence that white women do for/with us what we must do for/with ourselves: namely, frame our own social action around our own agenda for change. . . . Critical to this discussion is the right to organize on one's own behalf. . . . Criticism by black feminists must reaffirm this principle.

(1986, 162)

For most U.S. Black women, engaging in Black feminist research and scholarship is not a passing fad—these issues affect both contemporary daily life and intergenerational realities.

Third, Black women intellectuals from all walks of life must aggressively push the theme of self-definition because speaking for oneself and crafting one's own agenda is essential to empowerment. As Black feminist sociologist Deborah K. King succinctly states, "Black feminism asserts self-determination as essential" (1988, 72). Black feminist thought cannot challenge intersecting oppressions without empowering African-American women. Because self-definition is key to individual and group empowerment, ceding the power of self-definition to other groups, no matter how well-meaning or supportive of Black women they may be, in essence replicates existing power hierarchies. As Patrice L. Dickerson contends, "A person comes into being and knows herself by her achievements, and through her efforts to become and know herself, she achieves" (personal correspondence 1988). Like Dickerson, individual African-American women have long displayed varying types of consciousness regarding our shared angle of vision. When these individual expressions of consciousness are articulated, argued through, contested, and aggregated in ways that reflect the heterogeneity of Black womanhood, a collective group consciousness dedicated to resisting oppression becomes possible. Black women's ability to forge these individual, often unarticulated, yet potentially powerful expressions of everyday consciousness into an articulated, self-defined, collective standpoint is key to Black women's survival. As Audre Lorde points out, "It is axiomatic that if we do not define ourselves for ourselves, we will be defined by others—for their use and to our detriment" (1984, 45).

Fourth, Black women intellectuals are central in the production of Black feminist thought because we alone can foster the group autonomy that fosters effective coalitions with other groups. Recall that Black women intellectuals need not be middle-class, educated, middle-aged, or recognized as such by academia or other establishments. Black women intellectuals constitute a highly diverse group. Rather than assuming that Black women intellectuals constitute a Black female version of William E. B. DuBois's Talented Tenth—a common misperception advanced by some elitist academics who apparently have difficulty imagining everyday Black women as bona fide intellectuals (see, e.g., Gilroy 1993, 53)—the type of intellectual leadership envisioned here requires collaboration among diverse Black women to think through what would constitute Black women's autonomy. Moreover, although Black feminist thought originates within Black women's communities, it cannot flourish isolated from the experiences and ideas of other groups. Black women intellectuals must find ways to place our own heterogeneous experiences and consciousness at the center of any serious efforts to develop Black feminist thought without having our thought become separatist and exclusionary.

This autonomy is quite distinct from separatist positions whereby Black women withdraw from other groups and engage in exclusionary politics. In her introduction to *Home Girls, A Black Feminist Anthology*, Barbara Smith describes this difference: "Autonomy and separatism are fundamentally different. Whereas autonomy comes from a position of strength, separatism comes from a position of fear. When we're truly autonomous we can deal with other kinds of people, a multiplicity of issues, and with difference, because we have formed a solid base of strength" (1983, xl). As mothers, college presidents, grassroots activists, teachers, musicians, and corporate executives, Black women intellectuals who contribute to articulating an autonomous, self-defined standpoint are in a position to examine the usefulness of coalitions with other groups, both scholarly and activist, in order to develop new models for social change. Autonomy to develop a self-defined, independent analysis means neither that Black feminist thought has relevance only for African-American women nor that we must confine ourselves to analyzing our own experiences. As Sonia Sanchez points out, "I've always known that if you write from a black experience, you're writing from a universal experience as well. . . . I know you don't have to whitewash yourself to be universal" (Tate 1983, 142).

By advocating, refining, and disseminating Black feminist thought, individuals from other groups who are engaged in similar social justice projects—Black men, African women, White men, Latinas, White women, and members of other U.S. racial/ethnic groups, for example—can identify points of connection that further social justice projects. Very often, however, engaging in the type of coalition envisioned here requires that individuals become "traitors" to the privileges that their race, class, gender, sexuality, or citizenship status provide them. For example, in *Memoir of a Race Traitor*, Mab Segrest (1994) writes of how coming to terms with her lesbian identity spurred her recognition of how her Whiteness gave her unearned privileges. Unlike most U.S. White women, Segrest turned her back on this privilege, embraced her new identity as a "race traitor," and came to see her role as confronting social injustice.[3] Similarly, sociologist Joe Feagin's antiracist scholarship exemplifies a similar rejection of the unearned privileges of Whiteness. Feagin chooses to use benefits that may accrue to him as a White male to engage in collaborative scholarship with Black men (Feagin and Sikes 1994) and with Black women (St. Jean and Feagin 1998). While many might see Segrest and Feagin as "race traitors," their intellectual work illustrates how coalition building that advances Black feminist thought might operate.

Just as African-American women who aim to advance Black feminism as a social justice project can support other social justice projects—U.S. Black women who are respectful of the importance of Latina autonomy to Latina social justice projects can study, learn from, research, and teach about Latinas if they do so in non-exploitative ways—so can others approach Black feminist thought in a similar fashion. Thus, U.S. Black feminist thought fully actualized is a collaborative enterprise. It must be open to coalition building with individuals engaged in similar social justice projects.

Coalition building such as this requires simultaneous if not prior dialogues among Black women intellectuals and within the larger African-American women's community. Exploring the common themes of a Black women's standpoint is an important first step. Moreover, finding ways of handling internal dissent is especially important for building Black women's intellectual communities. Evelynn Hammonds describes how maintaining a united front for Whites stifles her thinking: "What I need to do is challenge my thinking, to grow. On white publications sometimes I feel like I'm holding up the banner of black womanhood. And that doesn't allow me to be as critical as I would like to be" (in Clarke et al. 1983, 104). Cheryl Clarke observes that she has two dialogues: one with the public and the private ones in which she feels free to criticize the work of other Black women. Clarke states that the private dialogues "have changed my life, have shaped the way I feel . . . have mattered to me" (p. 103).

Coalition building also requires dialogues with groups engaged in similar social justice projects. Black women intellectuals can use our outsider-within location in building effective coalitions and stimulating dialogue with others who are similarly located. Barbara Smith suggests that Black women develop dialogues from a "commitment to principled coalitions, based not upon expediency, but upon our actual need for each other" (1983, xxxiii). Dialogues among and coalitions with a range of groups, each with its own distinctive set of experiences and specialized thought embedded in those experiences, form the larger, more general terrain of intellectual and political discourse necessary for furthering Black feminism. Through dialogues exploring how domination is maintained and changed, parallels between Black women's experiences and those of other groups become the focus of investigation.

Dialogues associated with ethical, principled coalition building create possibilities for new versions of truth. Alice Walker's answer to the question of what she felt were the major differences between the literature of African-Americans and Whites offers a provocative glimpse of the types of truths that might emerge through epistemologies that embrace dialogues and coalition building. Walker did not spend much time considering this question, since it was not the difference between them that interested her, but, rather, the way Black writers and White writers seemed to be writing one immense story, with different parts of the story coming from a multitude of different perspectives. In a conversation with her mother, Walker refines this epistemological vision: "I believe that the truth about any subject only comes when all sides of the story are put together, and all their different meanings make one new one. Each writer writes the missing parts to the other writer's story. And the whole story is what I'm after" (1983, 49). Her mother's response to Walker's vision of the possibilities of dialogues and coalitions hints at the difficulty of sustaining such dialogues across differences in power: " 'Well, I doubt if you can ever get the *true* missing parts of anything away from the white folks,' my mother says softly, so as not to offend the waitress who is mopping up a nearby table; 'they've sat on the truth so long by now they've mashed the life out of it' " (1983, 49).

BLACK FEMINISM AS DYNAMIC AND CHANGING

A fifth distinguishing feature of U.S. Black feminist thought concerns the significance of change. In order for Black feminist thought to operate effectively within Black feminism as a social justice project, both must remain dynamic. Neither Black feminist thought as a critical social theory nor Black feminist practice can be static; as social conditions change, so must the knowledge and practices designed to resist them. For example, stressing the importance of Black women's centrality to Black feminist thought does not mean that all African-American women desire, are positioned, or are qualified to exert this type of intellectual leadership. Under current conditions, some Black women thinkers have lost contact with Black feminist practice. Conversely, the changed social conditions under which U.S. Black women now come to womanhood—class-segregated neighborhoods, some integrated, far more not—place Black women of different social classes in entirely new relationships with one another.

African-American women as a group may have experiences that provide us with a unique angle of vision. But expressing a collective, self-defined Black feminist consciousness is problematic precisely because dominant groups have a vested interest in suppressing such thought. As Hannah Nelson notes, "I have grown to womanhood in a world where the saner you are, the madder you are made to appear" (Gwaltney 1980, 7). Ms. Nelson realizes that those who control school curricula, television programs, government statistics, and the press typically prevail in establishing their viewpoint as superior to others.

An oppressed group's experiences may put its members in a position to see things differently, but their lack of control over the ideological apparatuses of society makes expressing a self-defined standpoint more difficult. Elderly domestic worker Rosa Wakefield assesses how the standpoints of the powerful and those who serve them diverge:

> If you eats these dinners and don't cook 'em, if you wears these clothes and don't buy or iron them, then you might start thinking that the good fairy or some spirit did all that. . . . Black folks don't have no time to be thinking like that. . . . But when you don't have anything else to do, you can think like that. It's bad for your mind, though.
>
> (Gwaltney 1980, 88)

Ms. Wakefield has a self-defined perspective growing from her experiences that enables her to reject standpoints advanced by more powerful groups. And yet ideas like hers are typically suppressed by dominant groups. Groups unequal in power are correspondingly unequal in their ability to make their standpoint known to themselves and others.

The changing social conditions that confront African-American women stimulate the need for new Black feminist analyses of the common differences that characterize U.S. Black womanhood. Some Black women thinkers are already engaged in this process. Take, for example, Barbara Omolade's (1994) insightful analysis of Black women's historical and contemporary participation in mammy work. Most can understand mammy work's historical context, one where Black women were confined to domestic service, with Aunt Jemima created as a controlling image designed to hide Black women's exploitation. Understanding the limitations of domestic service, much of Black women's progress in the labor market has been measured by the move out of domestic service. Currently, few U.S. Black women work in domestic service in private homes. Instead, a good deal of this work in private homes is now done by undocumented immigrant women of color who lack U.S. citizenship; their exploitation resembles that long visited upon African-American women (Chang 1994). But, as Omolade points out, these changes do not mean that U.S. Black women have escaped mammy work. Even though few Aunt Jemimas exist today, and those that do have been cosmetically altered, leading to the impression that mammy work has disappeared, Omolade reminds us that mammy work has assumed new forms. Within each segment of the labor market—the low-paid jobs at fast-food establishments, nursing homes, day-care centers, and dry cleaners that characterize the secondary sector, the secretaries and clerical workers of the primary lower tier sector, or the teachers, social workers, nurses, and administrators of the primary upper tier sector—U.S. Black women still do a remarkable share of the emotional nurturing and cleaning up after other people, often for lower pay. In this context, the task for contemporary Black feminist thought lies in explicating these changing relationships and developing analyses of how these commonalities are experienced differently.

The changing conditions of Black women's work overall have important implications for Black women's intellectual work. Historically, the suppression of Black feminist thought has meant that Black women intellectuals have traditionally relied on alternative institutional locations to produce specialized knowledge about a Black women's standpoint. Many Black women scholars, writers, and artists have worked either alone, as was the case with Maria W. Stewart, or within African-American community organizations, the case for Black women in the club movement and in Black churches. The grudging incorporation of work on Black women into curricular offerings of historically White colleges and universities, coupled with the creation of a critical mass of African-American women writers such as Toni Morrison, Alice Walker, and Gloria Naylor within these institutional locations, means that Black women intellectuals can now find employment within academia. Black women's history and Black feminist literary criticism constitute two focal points of this renaissance in Black women's intellectual work (Carby 1987). Moreover, U.S. Black women's access to the media remains unprecedented, as talk show hostess Oprah Winfrey's long-running television show and forays into film production suggest.

The visibility provided U.S. Black women and our ideas via these new institutional locations has been immense. However, one danger facing African-American women intellectuals working in these new locations concerns the potential isolation of individual thinkers from Black women's collective experiences—lack of access to other U.S. Black women and to Black women's communities. Another is the pressure to separate thought from action—particularly political activism—that typically accompanies training in standard academic disciplines or participating in allegedly neutral spheres like the "free" press. Yet another involves the inability of some Black women "superstars" to critique the terms of their own participation in these new relations. Blinded by their self-proclaimed Black feminist diva aspirations, they feel that they owe no one, especially other Black women. Instead, they become trapped within their own impoverished Black feminist universes. Despite these dangers, these new institutional locations provide a multitude of opportunities for enhancing Black feminist thought's visibility. In this new context, the challenge lies in remaining dynamic, all the while keeping in mind that a moving target is more difficult to hit.

U.S. BLACK FEMINISM AND OTHER SOCIAL JUSTICE PROJECTS

A final distinguishing feature of Black feminist thought concerns its relationship to other projects for social justice. A broad range of African-American women intellectuals have advanced the view that Black women's struggles are part of a wider struggle for human dignity, empowerment, and social justice. In an 1893 speech to women, Anna Julia Cooper cogently expressed this worldview:

> We take our stand on the solidarity of humanity, the oneness of life, and the unnaturalness and injustice of all special favoritisms, whether of sex, race, country, or condition. . . . The colored woman feels that woman's cause is one and universal; and that . . . not till race, color, sex, and condition are seen as accidents, and not the substance of life; not till the universal title of humanity to life, liberty, and the pursuit of happiness is conceded to be inalienable to all; not till then is woman's lesson taught and woman's cause won—not the white woman's nor the black woman's, not the red woman's but the cause of every man and of every woman who has writhed silently under a mighty wrong.
>
> (Loewenberg and Bogin 1976, 330–31)

Like Cooper, many African-American women intellectuals embrace this perspective regardless of particular political solutions we propose, our educational backgrounds, our fields of study, or our historical periods. Whether we advocate working through autonomous Black women's organizations, becoming part of women's organizations, running for political office, or supporting Black community institutions, African-American women intellectuals repeatedly identify political actions such as these as a *means* for human empowerment rather than ends in and of themselves. Thus one important guiding principle of Black feminism is a recurring humanist vision (Steady 1981, 1987).[4]

Alice Walker's preference for the term *womanist* addresses this notion of the solidarity of humanity. "Womanist is to feminist as purple is to lavender," she writes. To Walker, one is "womanist" when one is "committed to the survival and wholeness of entire people, male and female." A womanist is "not a separatist, except periodically for health" and is "traditionally universalist, as is 'Mama, why are we brown, pink, and yellow, and our cousins are white, beige, and black?' Ans.: 'Well, you know the colored race is just like a flower garden, with every color flower represented' " (1983, xi). By redefining all people as "people of color," Walker universalizes what are typically seen as individual struggles while simultaneously allowing space for autonomous movements of self-determination.[5]

In assessing the sexism of the Black nationalist movement of the 1960s, lawyer Pauli Murray identifies the dangers inherent in separatism as opposed to autonomy, and also echoes Cooper's concern with the solidarity of humanity:

> The lesson of history that all human rights are indivisible and that the failure to adhere to this principle jeopardizes the rights of all is particularly applicable here. A built-in hazard of an aggressive ethnocentric movement which disregards the interests of other disadvantaged groups is that it will become parochial and ultimately self-defeating in the face of hostile reactions, dwindling allies, and mounting frustrations. . . . Only a broad movement for human rights can prevent the Black Revolution from becoming isolated and can insure ultimate success.
>
> (Murray 1970, 102)

Without a commitment to human solidarity and social justice, suggests Murray, any political movement—whether Black nationalist, feminist, or anti-elitist—may be doomed to ultimate failure.

Former congresswoman Shirley Chisholm also points to the need for self-conscious struggle against the stereotypes that support social injustice. In "working toward our own freedom, we can help others work free from the traps of their stereotypes," she notes. "In the end, antiblack, antifemale, and all forms of discrimination are equivalent to the same thing—antihumanism. . . . We must reject not only the stereotypes that others have of us but also those we have of ourselves and others" (1970, 181).

This humanist orientation within U.S. Black feminism also resembles similar stances taken with Black diasporic feminisms. Ama Ata Aidoo, a former minister of education in Ghana and author of novels, poetry, and short stories, describes the inclusive nature of her political philosophy:

> When people ask me rather bluntly every now and then whether I am a feminist, I not only answer yes, but I go on to insist that every woman and every man should be a feminist—especially if they believe that Africans should take charge of African land, African wealth, African lives, and the burden of African development. It is not possible to advocate independence for the African continent without also believing that African women must have the best that the environment can offer. For some of us, this is the crucial element in our feminism.
>
> (Aidoo 1998, 39)

Aidoo recognizes that neither African nor U.S. Black women nor any other group will ever be empowered in situations of social injustice. Social justice projects are not either/or endeavors where one can say, "We have our movement and you have yours—our movements have nothing to do with one another." Instead, such projects counsel, "We have our movement, and we support yours." In a context of intersecting oppressions, Black feminism requires searching for justice not only for U.S. Black women, but for everyone.

The words and actions of these diverse Black women intellectuals may address markedly different audiences. Yet in their commitment to Black women's empowerment within a context of social justice, they advance the strikingly similar theme of the oneness of all human life. Perhaps the most succinct version of the humanist vision in U.S. Black feminist thought is offered by Fannie Lou Hamer, the daughter of sharecroppers and a Mississippi civil rights activist. While sitting on her porch, Ms. Hamer observed, "Ain' no such thing as I can hate anybody and hope to see God's face" (Jordan 1981, xi).

Post-reading Questions

1. Does race have the same meaning in the absence of whiteness as it does in the presence of whiteness?

2. What does race mean between different populations of color, such as Native Americans and African Americans?

3. What are some important terms that Collins introduces as essential in Black feminist thought?

4. What remains unfinished in the work of Black feminist practice? What is the biggest challenge faced by Black feminists today?

5. What is the value of Black feminist thought to those who are not Black or female?

UNIT 2

HISTORICAL CONSIDERATIONS

Although brief, this unit provides a sound overview of the history of African-descended people in the United States and their relationship with Americans of other races. It also provides a solid overview of African American historiography—that is, the history of *how* Black people's history in the United States has been written over time.

Kevin Gaines' "African-American History" is an engaging survey of African American history and historiography. The historical narrative that is African American history is written by various individuals with different disciplinary backgrounds including history, politics, journalism, economics, and religion. Gaines admits that this creates an imperfect, overlapping historical narrative that reflects the oversights and biases of its narrators. However, Gaines' work provides a sound timeline of African American history that provides important historical context needed to understand other chapters found in this collection.

In "American Graffiti: Social Life of Jim Crow Signs," Elizabeth Abel reminds the reader that the history of race relations in the United States is not only about law and custom. Segregation was present in the very fabric of American visual and material culture for decades. While the Supreme Court decision in *Plessy v. Ferguson* (1896) did not create "separate but equal," it did sanction it by declaring it constitutional and within the police power of the state. "Whites Only" and "Colored Only" signs bore physical, spatial witness to segregation's grip on American society. These signs, as Abel explores, were the products of conscious decisions about physical context, messaging, and even aesthetics. This legal graffiti blended into the landscape of American social life as much as its messages of rigidity and intolerance stood out.

Pre-reading Questions

1. What is a central theme that runs through both American history and African American history?

2. If you were writing a history of African Americans, what would your top three topics be? Why?

3. How were slavery and segregation similar? How were they different?

4. How did racial segregation shape the lives of White Americans as well as Black Americans?

5. Why might a study of "Whites Only" and "Colored Only" signs be informative?

African-American History

KEVIN GAINES

Academic historians have no monopoly on the production of historical narratives. Historians engage in lively public debates about the meaning of the past with many actors, including journalists, politicians, political and religious leaders, and members of civic associations. History is, thus, produced in a set of overlapping sites, including those outside of academia. History is also, as Michel-Rolph Trouillot observed, laden with silences. Academic historians and others with a stake in the matter are often selective in their interests, and not immune to blind spots.

Such overlapping sites of production and silences have shaped the field of African-American history. In its formative period, the history of African Americans was written against the silences, evasions and propaganda of a U.S. historical profession that, until the mid-twentieth century, was dominated by those who had little regard for the humanity of blacks. Early historians of the African-American experience, including W.E.B. Du Bois, Carter G. Woodson, and Benjamin Quarles, confronted either negative depictions of black people or their outright erasure from narratives about the American past. Excluded from the white-dominated academy, these historians recorded the integral contributions of African Americans to the development of constitutional freedom and democracy in the United States. Gaining a doctorate in history at Harvard in 1912, Woodson, the son of former slaves, assumed the vital task of building an infrastructure and audience for African-American history, founding the Association for the Study of Negro Life and History in 1915 and the *Journal of Negro History* the following year, as well as a publishing company. In 1926, Woodson founded Negro History Week, initially celebrated during February, now expanded to the entire month. "Negro history," as promoted by Woodson and others, and taught almost exclusively in black schools and colleges, had a dual character as both a public and academic endeavor, taking aim at racial prejudice in American society and the historical profession. The efforts of Woodson and countless others have paid off today, in the transformative impact of African-American history on the writing of U.S. history and through the field's strong global presence within college and university curricula.

The past is always with us, though we often fail to notice. Occasionally it resurfaces, tangibly. In 1991, construction work uncovered the graves of 427 enslaved Africans at the site of a planned 34-story federal office building in Lower Manhattan. The graves were just a portion of what has become known as the African burial ground, a graveyard of approximately 10,000 to 20,000 people paved over as the city expanded northward.

Forensic archaeologists' examination of the skeletal remains suggests the physical suffering of the slaves. In many of the adult skeletons, hollow lesions in the legs, arms, and shoulders offer mute testimony that in life the strain of hard labor severed ligaments and muscle from bone. As Brent Staples wrote in the *New York Times*, "The brutality etched on these skeletons easily matches the worst of what we know of slavery in the South."

Another recent encounter with the past involves the amateur Historian in Chief, Barack Obama, who in July 2009, during a state visit to Ghana, visited the Cape Coast Castle, a massive seaside fortress that served as the seat of Britain's Gold Coast colony and a major transit point for the Atlantic slave trade. Extensive media coverage of the visit of the first African-American president to a major slave-trading fort brought worldwide attention to a place and a history invisible to many Americans. Obama acknowledged the "evil" of the trade, and the tragically double-edged meaning of the place for African Americans, who, like many Caribbean and Latin American people of African descent (but not Obama himself), can trace their origins to places like Cape Coast Castle.

These two events were emblematic of the development of the field of African-American history since the 1990s. Studies of the slave trade and of slavery in the Northern colonies and states have addressed silences in the historical record and in public awareness. These works present U.S. slavery, North and South, as a global system of market relations integral to the development of the American nation-state. Recent scholarship on slavery is noteworthy for its shift away from a prior emphasis on the autonomy of slave culture and on slave "agency" in favor of an emphasis on exploitation and its consequences, including psychological ones, analyzing the impact of slavery's market-driven commodification on the lives of its victims and enslavers alike.

Amid growing public awareness of the foundational significance of Africa and the slave trade, historians have extended their gaze beyond U.S. boundaries, making the African diaspora the key unit of analysis. Moreover, just as the history of slavery in colonial New York disrupts the idea of slavery as a uniquely southern institution, historians of the civil rights movement have expanded their attention to black struggles for equality in the North, as well as those in the South. In this chapter, I will offer an overview of three main periods that reflect significant developments in the writing of African-American history over roughly the last twenty years: slavery and the slave trade; the era of segregation, in both the North and South; and "the long civil rights movement."

SLAVERY

Slavery was the source of unrivaled political and economic power in the antebellum United States. On the eve of the Civil War, the economic value of slaves in the United States was $3 billion in 1860 currency, a sum that exceeded the combined value of all the factories, railroads, and banks in the country. Members of the merchant and political class in New York City were actively involved in the domestic slave trade, and gleaned profits from the cotton trade as well. Not surprisingly, staunch defenders of the institution could be found among their ranks. According to an 1852 report to Congress, the maritime shipment of the cotton crop was a vast enterprise, with 1.1 million tons of American-bound shipping to eastern and southern gulf ports, employing upward of 55,000 American maritime workers.

An appreciation of the vast profitability of the domestic slave trade and slave-produced cotton is essential for students of U.S. history. But there is another dimension of this history. Inspired by the historian Nell Painter's call for a "fully loaded cost accounting" of slavery, scholars have assessed the psychological toll of slavery's physical and sexual abuse on its victims. Painter challenged historians to ponder slavery's impact as a defining feature of American society, politics, and nation building, past and present. Recent scholars have answered the call by foregrounding the subjectivity and actions of the enslaved, and the impact of slavery's routine violence on its victims, on slave owners, and on American society. They have interrogated the conditions of life within a system of domination that Orlando Patterson has termed "social death."

This scholarship shows how far the field has come since the late 1960s. Then, almost without exception, male historians studied male slaves. And the question of that generic male slave's personality loomed large, as historians shied away from issues of political economy raised by Eric Williams in *Capitalism and Slavery* (1944). Stanley Elkins set the terms of debate in 1959, when, in describing the crippling impact of slavery, he portrayed slaves as too traumatized to resist their lot. Elkins's view of the slaves' childlike, compliant personality was based on studies of the inmates of Nazi concentration camps. To be sure, Elkins's account of the brutality of slavery and its traumatized victims countered enduring myths of the plantation legend that portrayed slavery as a benevolent institution. At that time, by a similar logic of paternalism, segregationists parried rising demands for equality by asserting that Jim Crow society bestowed upon African Americans a higher standard of living than most of the world's peoples. The damage-victimization thesis invoked by Elkins and others was subjected to critical analysis by Daryl Michael Scott's study *Contempt and Pity* (1997), but in Elkins's time the idea of blacks damaged by racial segregation was a staple of liberal demands for civil rights and was endorsed by black and white scholars alike. No less than E. Franklin Frazier and Howard Zinn lauded Elkins's account of the crippling impact of the "closed system" of plantation slavery on the personality of the slaves.

The most influential challenge to Elkins came from Sterling Stuckey's 1968 essay "Through the Prism of Folklore: The Black Ethos in Slavery." Stuckey's essay called for more rigorous investigation of African-American culture as a site of resistance. Stuckey's subsequent work on the salience of the African past for the study of African-American history and culture helped inspire among scholars of slavery an increased emphasis on the African diaspora as the central unit of analysis. Over the past twenty years, Michael A. Gomez, Dylan Penningroth, Sharla Fett, Stephanie Smallwood, and others explored the West African social and cultural roots of the Afro-American experience of slavery.

Rejecting Elkins's thesis of slave docility, such scholars as John Blassingame, Herbert Gutman, Stuckey and others emphasized the survival of family, community and autonomous cultural identities, and practices of resistance. But claims of community strength and resistance, and an emphasis on Africanity, while important in their time, deferred consideration of slavery as a sociopolitical and legal system with gender as a defining feature of its power relationships. The pioneering work of Deborah Gray White and subsequent studies of slavery informed by women's and gender history, including the work of Stephanie Camp, Thavolia Glymph, and Stephanie McCurry, have deepened our understanding of resistance, moving away from the limited, all-or-nothing, male-centered image of slave revolts at the heart of the dispute between Elkins, on one side, and his critics, on the other.

Jennifer Morgan has been especially influential in employing gender analysis to complicate issues of resistance. In *Laboring Women*, Morgan writes of the intolerable burden of enslaved women forced to bear children in addition to the agricultural labor they performed. Slave owners in the colonial Bahamas referred to their female slaves as "increasors." Besides physical and sexual abuse, these women endured the constant threat of separation from their offspring through sale. Morgan warns us of the difficulty of defining resistance in this degrading situation rife with contradictions. Enslaved women enriched their captors while at the same time playing a vital role in creating the communities that would foster a complex dynamic of opposition to and compliance with racial slavery. Under such abject conditions, the meanings enslaved women might ascribe to their fertility or infertility defy generalization. Morgan cautions historians against imposing modern assumptions about resistance or motherhood in assessing the behavior of enslaved women.

While historians have written extensively about the slaves' culture and resistance, some have focused their attention on the slave trade. Since the publication of Philip Curtin's classic study *The Atlantic Slave Trade*, historians have debated estimates of the number of Africans caught up in this forced mass migration. In *Saltwater Slavery*, Stephanie Smallwood goes beyond this quantitative approach by focusing on the experience of the captives. Inventively mining the records of the Royal African Company, Smallwood follows the captives from enslavement on the Gold Coast in Africa and detention in the dungeons of Cape Coast and Elmina to the crossing of the ocean in the so-called Middle Passage and, finally, to sale in the British colonies of the Americas. Smallwood describes how the Atlantic slave trade and forced migration across the water transformed people into commodities. Smallwood not only attends to the subjectivity and actions of enslaved Africans, but also seeks to understand the traders themselves, along with the world that produced them. Smallwood demonstrates how African captives made meaning of the terror, death, and suffering that underwrote the destruction of the bonds of community and kinship, in sum, their social annihilation. In so doing, she succeeds in bringing the captives aboard slave ships to life as subjects of American social history.

Focusing on a different site of commodification, the antebellum slave market, Walter Johnson examines the internal slave trade in his influential work *Soul by Soul*. Johnson lays bare the dehumanizing market logic of slavery and the racial and ideological assumptions, transmogrified into notions of value and worthlessness, that underlay its mundane transactions. He writes vividly of the moral, spiritual, and physical annihilation of the bodies and souls of the enslaved that took place in the slave pen. The negotiations between traders and buyers and the inspections of the bodies of the enslaved enacted racial theories positing the disobedience of slaves as evidence of biological depravity and reinforcing invidious distinctions between blackness and whiteness. Johnson, like Morgan, writes of the limits of notions of agency and resistance for those subject to the violent logic of the slave market. Johnson nevertheless shows the slaves as thinking, even calculating, beings, who sought to gain whatever leverage they could, attempting to manipulate the decisions of buyers and sellers to their potential advantage.

In addition to work that reads the records of slave traders and planters against the grain to recover the experience of those reduced to property by the market relations of slavery, recent studies have expanded our understanding of the scope of the institution. Tiya Miles's groundbreaking *Ties That Bind*, a study of an Afro-Cherokee family shaped by antebellum slaveholding among Native Americans, challenges popular assumptions about race, exploitation, and community. Writing the largely untold history of black slaves in Cherokee country, Miles pieces together the story of Doll, the African-American concubine of the Cherokee war hero Shoe Boots. Mobilizing secondary literature on the sexual oppression of enslaved women, Miles writes with sensitivity about Doll's likely feelings regarding the narrow range of choices she faced as Shoe Boots's slave and mother of his children.

Miles's study locates the genesis of present-day conflict between the Cherokee nation and Afro-Cherokees in the nineteenth-century trauma of removal from Georgia. The forced separation from Cherokee ancestral lands destroyed a shared past of personal and communal ties between native and black Cherokees. Miles foregrounds the "psychological and spiritual reverberations" of Indian removal. She contends that it "was more than the relocation of bodies and possessions. It was the tearing of the flesh of the people from the same flesh of the land, a rupture of soul and spirit. . . . [R]emoval created a legacy of detachment between Cherokees and blacks that would lessen potential for cross-racial alliances and narrow the possibility of subverting racial hierarchies."

Annette Gordon-Reed provides still another rich portrait of enslaved women's experience in her magisterial work the *Hemingses of Monticello: An American Family*, the definitive history of the Hemings family *and* the family of Thomas Jefferson, whose blood ties to the Hemingses belie the racial fiction of separateness. Making a powerful case for Hemings's historical importance, Gordon-Reed ultimately provides an account of American slavery worthy of Painter's injunction to study the inner lives of the enslaved, in Gordon-Reed's words, "to see slavery through the eyes of the enslaved." At the same time, Gordon-Reed's study of the Hemings family breaks with Patterson's view of slavery as social death, a view which, while theoretically compelling, is also challenged by Penningroth's study of property ownership among slaves and Fett's book on slave healing practices, both of which suggest that the lives of slaves were defined by creativity and resiliency as much as social and spiritual annihilation. It does not mitigate the horror of slavery to write, as Gordon-Reed does, "That the Hemingses were enslaved did not render them incapable of knowing who they were, of knowing their mothers, fathers, sisters and brothers. Slavery did not destroy their ability to observe, remember and reason."

Gordon-Reed's chapters on the genesis of the relationship between Sally Hemings, a girl of sixteen, and the widowed Jefferson, thirty years her senior, while the latter was on a diplomatic mission in France, are a tour de force. Seeking to unlock the "mystery" of what transpired between them from the record of Jefferson and Hemings's five years in Paris, Gordon-Reed mines numerous sources, including the vast biographical record of Jefferson's actions and temperament, the historiography of courtship and marriage in early America (whose legal status and protections were unavailable to Hemings), and the reminiscences of Madison Hemings, the son of Jefferson and Hemings.

The work of Leslie Harris, Joanne Melish, and others reminds us that slavery, though largely domestic in the North, was hereditary and permanent. As Melish shows for New England and Harris for New York City, the racial and gendered hierarchies at the core of the system survived its abolition in northern states, constraining the lives of emancipated and free blacks. As a buffer against this stark prejudice and discrimination, free blacks in the antebellum North and many areas of the South developed vibrant communities of their own, replete with churches, schools, and mutual aid institutions. By 1830, America's free black population had grown to almost a quarter of a million. Roy E. Finkenbine and Richard S. Newman have written of the outspoken leadership of "black founders" of the early republic, who condemned slavery and the exclusion of blacks from northern white churches, schools, and civic organizations, laying a solid foundation for the abolitionist and civil rights movements of the nineteenth and twentieth centuries. As the work of Julius Scott and Maurice Jackson has shown, the Haitian Revolution loomed large in the political imagination of these "black founders," enslaved and free persons throughout the Atlantic world, and less renowned African-American seamen.

AFTER SLAVERY: AFRICAN-AMERICAN POLITICAL BEHAVIOR IN THE ERA OF SEGREGATION

As W.E.B. Du Bois wrote of emancipation and Reconstruction in 1935, "The slave went free, stood a brief moment in the sun, then moved back again towards slavery. The whole weight of America was thrown to color caste." Reconstruction revolutionized the South's and the nation's politics, outlawing slavery and enfranchising black male citizens. Black men were elected to office in substantial numbers, serving in Congress, state legislatures, and municipal governments throughout the South. African-American elected officials, in tandem with white Republicans, redefined the scope of government for the South and the entire nation, enacting a broader vision of freedom. Reconstruction state governments throughout the South supported free public education and universal male suffrage, outlawed racial discrimination, and expanded the public infrastructure.

But the defeated slave owners and their political representatives waged incessant war against Reconstruction governments and the voting rights of blacks. With the withdrawal of federal troops from the South in 1877, antiblack violence escalated in the region. Blacks were deprived of the suffrage and barred from juries, police forces, and electoral offices. Silences and willful acts of forgetting continue to define the violent legacy of post-Reconstruction. In recent years, some states have conducted official investigations into atrocities of the era of segregation and disfranchisement, seeking some measure of civic healing. In 2006, the 1898 Wilmington Riot Commission appointed by the state of North Carolina concluded that the overthrow of Wilmington's Republican interracial "fusion" government was an insurrection planned for months by white supremacists. Following a spate of inflammatory newspaper articles demonizing black political power as a threat to white womanhood, an unknown number of blacks were killed in broad daylight, in the words of the report, as "part of a statewide effort to put white supremacist Democrat[ic Party members] in office and stem the political advances of black citizens." After the violence, white Democrats enacted laws that disfranchised blacks until the Voting Rights Act of 1965. Noting the continuing debate over voting rights in Congress and the courts, the state archivist who helped research the report noted, "More than a hundred years later, we're still trying to resolve the issues."

Investigative commissions on events like the Wilmington massacre are much-needed attempts to educate the public. It is also true that African Americans were not simply the passive victims of the post-Reconstruction onslaught against their political and civil rights, a period termed "the Nadir" by historian Rayford Logan. Following Logan, scholars often centered their accounts on the rise of segregation, the coerced labor of the sharecropping system, disfranchisement, and lynching. Sexual violence against women, neglected until recently, has been studied by Darlene Clark Hine, Hannah Rosen, and Crystal Feimster. If works on slavery have moved from highlighting agency to a recent concern with exploitation, since the late 1990s the trend seems to have gone in the opposite direction for historians of the era of segregation. Their earlier narratives of antiblack oppression have given way to accounts of agency, resistance, grassroots organization, and mass activism.

Over the last three decades, historians have grappled with the problem of defining the political behavior of African Americans reduced to statelessness by the systematic repeal of their civil and political rights. Shane and Graham White have explored the bodily displays and comportment of African Americans in urban public spaces as acts of individual and collective transgression of white expectations of deference under slavery and Jim Crow. "From Reconstruction through the early decades of the twentieth century," they write, "African-American parades became an established feature of the southern urban landscape," with a plethora of black civic associations staging processions on Emancipation Day and the Fourth of July, using these occasions to express a sense of unity and pride. But such manifestations were impossible for African Americans in besieged rural areas. Under such dire conditions, migration to southern cities, and later, to the relative freedom of the urban North during World War I, constituted the most viable means of escape from poverty and the constant threat of violence through lynching and rape.

Nell Painter's *Exodusters*, a study of the mass migration of some five to seven thousand blacks from the Louisiana and Mississippi Delta to Kansas in 1879, enriched our understanding of the political behavior of poor and working African-American people. The immediate causes of the Kansas Exodus were chronic poverty and a surge of political violence against rural blacks in Louisiana. But the Exodus also reflected the freedpeople's enduring aspirations for economic independence and freedom from white dominance. Painter's study highlighted the importance of emigration and an African diaspora perspective, along with the black folk religion derived from the Old Testament Exodus story, for blacks in the rural South. The initial destination of the migrants had been Liberia, which soon proved beyond their resources.

For impoverished African Americans, migration—voting with one's feet—was their strongest collective protest against exploitation and terror. The journalist and antilynching activist Ida B. Wells understood this fact when she convinced many blacks in Memphis to punish white civic and business leaders who condoned lynching by leaving the city, taking with them their labor and purchasing power. Equally aware of the stakes for employers, Booker T. Washington rejected migration, famously urging the southern black masses in 1895 to "cast down your bucket where you are." Painter contrasts grassroots black leaders such as Henry Adams and Joseph "Pap" Singleton, both of whom supported the Exodus, with Frederick Douglass and less renowned "representative colored men" who implored would-be migrants to stand their ground against rampant political terror, lest the depletion of their numbers erode the strength of the Republican Party.

Painter's study, along with subsequent scholarship on the era of Jim Crow segregation, brought into focus an indigenous black politics as a defining feature of African-American life. In much of this work, the class dynamics of African-American leadership and politics are a central concern. All told, recent scholarship on the Nadir points to a varied repertoire of African-American political activism, both within and outside the formal domains of party, electoral, and trade union politics, and reflecting assertions of economic and cultural citizenship that were often inseparable from the quest for political and civil rights.

A Nation under Our Feet, Steven Hahn's study of the grassroots thought and politics of southern African Americans from Emancipation to the Great Migration to the North during World War I, builds on Painter's work and Robin D. G. Kelley's study of African-American Communists in Alabama during the 1930s. For Hahn, emancipation and aspirations for economic independence and the redistributive justice of "forty acres and a mule" were integral to African-American politics over generations. Labor concerns were at the core of black aspirations, nurtured despite the constant threat of white violence within a vibrant black civil society. During the late 1880s and 1890s, after the violent ouster of Reconstruction and fusion interracial coalitions, populist and labor challenges to white landowners reached a crescendo throughout the region. Excluded from white agrarian organizations, African Americans organized Colored Farmer's Alliance locals all over the Deep South. The Knights of Labor, which recruited blacks, spread from such cities as Richmond, Raleigh, Birmingham, and Little Rock to nearly two thousand local assemblies in small towns, more than two-thirds in rural counties in the former Confederacy. These organizations "appear to have tapped and fed on an institutional infrastructure of benevolent, church, and political associations commonly known to African Americans as 'secret societies,' which had been developing in the countryside for years." Secrecy was essential, as landowners and authorities organized white militias and "regulators" with the aim of intimidating black labor insurgencies and their leaders into submission.

Undaunted, African Americans demanded justice at public assemblies, with black women often playing prominent roles. The assault on black electoral politics and labor insurgency led to the rise of separate black neighborhoods and enclaves and the rise of an extensive black civil society, with scores of benevolent societies, schools, churches, and associations, and an explosion of black newspapers in cities and towns across the South. "It may well have been," writes Hahn, "that the exclusion of black men from the official arenas of politics in the 1890s and early 1900s" helped give "new voice and authority . . . to black women who, for years had been actively involved in community mobilizations through churches, schools, charitable organizations, and auxillaries, not to mention Union Leagues, Republican Parties, and benevolent societies."

The prominence of African-American women within the intraracial politics of class, gender, and sexuality is an even more central theme in Michele Mitchell's analysis of the discourse of racial destiny of African Americans, from the post-Reconstruction South to the Garvey movement of the 1920s. Racial destiny was the preoccupation of black reformers and spokespersons of middle- and striving-class status. In a bid for cultural citizenship, these reformers voiced an intense concern with the race's biological reproduction, viewed as synonymous with its social well-being. Mitchell analyzes a neglected archive of frank public discussions of sexuality and hygiene. Breaking with late Victorian norms of reticence about sexuality, these "race activists" opposed the ubiquitous racial and sexual stereotypes that justified the oppression of black men and women, while openly confronting threats to the community's well-being posed by a lack of instruction in sexual matters and by self-destructive sexual behaviors. Mitchell surveys their efforts in a number of gendered sites: late-nineteenth-century emigrationist movements, scientific and popular discourses on eugenics, anthologies of race progress, "better baby" contests, conduct manuals, tracts asserting the importance of homes for black progress, and black nationalist discourses of motherhood and child rearing. For Mitchell, the activities of domestic reformers, particularly women, constituted an ephemeral grassroots politics. Mitchell's study illuminates how perennial concerns about sexuality, well-being, and the role of patriarchy mitigated an effective response to public health problems in African-American communities.

Taken together, these studies expand the purview of black politics during the ordeal of racial segregation, North and South, indicating a departure from narratives about the integration of black people into the U.S. nation. Instead of a focus on black participation in the mainstream areas of electoral politics, civil rights activism, the labor movement, and military service in domestic and foreign wars, with pride of place given to the thought and actions of educated elites, the work of Painter, Hahn, and Mitchell, among others, offers examples of indigenous and grassroots politics emerging from a black civil society suffused with the long memory of postemancipation struggles for economic independence and full citizenship. In these accounts, African Americans confront the barriers of segregation by seeking inclusion into the American nation on their own terms.

Just as one almost suspects that all the stories have been researched and told, one is startled by the seeming infinity of the past and its enduring silences. Mary Frances Berry tells the remarkable story of an indigenous black mass movement led by an unlettered black woman who petitioned the U.S. government for ex-slave pensions and was undone by federal agencies in her quest for justice. In recounting the activism of the former slave and Nashville washerwoman Callie House, Berry recovers a neglected strain of grassroots politics that illustrates the simultaneous production of scholarship and silences. Inspired by the payment of pensions to Civil War veterans and a pamphlet and proposed legislation for a pension for ex-slaves during the 1890s, House and others organized the Ex-Slave Mutual Relief, Bounty, and Pension Association, backing legislation proposed in Congress that would provide pensions for former slaves. As one of the officers of the organization, House traveled throughout the South, gaining the support and dues of thousands of former slaves and their relatives. As House and others gathered names on petitions in support of the ex-slave pension bill, the association provided mutual aid for its impoverished members and held national conventions. But House ran afoul of the Justice Department, which enlisted the Post Office to seek the destruction of the organization through accusations of mail fraud. Despite the lack of support, if not outright contempt, of middle-class black leaders and journalists, House and her organization withstood the hostility of the federal government for years, a testament to the popularity of the cause with southern blacks. House was released from federal prison in 1918, and the association was largely forgotten at the time of her death in 1928. But elderly ex-slaves had not forgotten, writing letters to Presidents Herbert Hoover and Franklin D. Roosevelt inquiring about pensions for ex-slaves. Berry views Callie House and her movement as a precursor for the contemporary reparations movement.

Berry's study, along with other studies of the era of segregation, suggests the varied nature of black struggles, often against difficult odds. Diverse expressions of indigenous politics, including migration and emigration, civil society reform efforts, parades and public commemorations, and claims for reparations, defy normative generalizations or teleological assumptions about integration into the U.S. nation. Of course, state-centered approaches have generated much important work on the legal, constitutional, and legislative dimensions of the struggle for equality, and much more work remains to be done in these areas. But what seems to have emerged is a composite view of black struggles that foregrounds the economic and cultural dimensions of the struggle for full citizenship and views internationalism and "overlapping black diasporas," in Earl Lewis's phrase, as resources for African Americans against the constraints imposed by the U. S. government and civil society.

For example, Beth Bates's study of A. Philip Randolph and the Brotherhood of Sleeping Car Porters reminds us that the brotherhood's conception of "manhood rights" was more than a struggle for the suffrage, but held at its core a vision of economic justice dating back to Reconstruction. Winston James's *Holding Aloft the Banner of Ethiopia*, a study of Caribbean radicalism in the early twentieth century, highlights the diasporic cosmopolitanism of black public culture, particularly in a Harlem shaped by immigration from the West Indies as well as urban migration from the South. Brenda Gayle Plummer produced the first comprehensive study of African Americans' engagement with foreign affairs over the course of the twentieth century. African Americans across the political spectrum, from civil rights leaders and organizations to left-wing activists and grassroots nationalist groups, were intensely engaged in foreign affairs, seeking to influence U.S. policy toward Africa and Haiti, forging alliances between anticolonial movements and U.S. black struggles for equality, and using the United Nations as a forum for crafting a vision of global order that would encompass the democratic aspirations of blacks and colonized peoples. More recently, Clare Corbould has argued that a central theme in black public life in Harlem during the interwar years was a formative engagement with African art, history, and expressive cultures. The search for a usable African past and present was manifested in the New Negro Renaissance, the Garvey movement, protests against the U.S. occupation of Haiti, and Italy's invasion of Ethiopia in 1935.

The Long Civil Rights Movement

The outpouring of work over the past three decades on the history of the black freedom struggle defies easy summation. Scholars in the last decade have adopted the term "the long civil rights movement," to describe this proliferation of scholarship, but also to register qualms about mass-media representations of the movement. Nikhil Singh and Jacquelyn Hall use the phrase to refer to the blossoming of studies whose overall impact challenges a narrow master narrative of the movement. That narrative chronicles a "short" civil rights movement beginning with the 1954 *Brown v. Board of Education* decision and concluding with the passage of the Civil Rights Act of 1964 and the Voting Rights Act of 1965. Subsequent events—urban riots, the Vietnam war, black militancy, feminism, student revolts, busing, and affirmative action—signal the unraveling of America and the decline of the movement. Martin Luther King, Jr., remains fixed at the Lincoln Memorial in 1963, his dream of a color-blind America endlessly replayed while his opposition to the Vietnam War and support of campaigns for economic justice are expunged from popular memory.

This triumphant but diminished image of the movement prevents it, Hall writes, "from speaking effectively to the challenges of our time." Against this distortion of the movement, Hall emphasizes "a more robust, more progressive and truer story" of a "long civil rights movement" that took root during the New Deal and the Popular Front, accelerated during World War II, extended far beyond the South, was hotly contested, and persisted with considerable force into the 1970s. By situating the post-*Brown* struggle for civil rights legislation within that longer story, Hall not only reinforces the moral authority of those who fought for change, but also seeks to "make civil rights harder. . . . [H]arder to simplify, appropriate and contain."

But the "long civil rights movement" thesis has not gone unchallenged. Sundiata K. Cha-Jua and Clarence Lang argue that the thesis expands the time period and regional scope of the movement beyond all recognition. These critics seem most concerned with the potential marginalization of the southern struggle for civil and voting rights during the 1960s, which for many Americans retains an unquestioned moral authority. As the work of John Dittmer, Tim Tyson, and others has shown, however, the southern freedom movement encompassed the local and the global, and rested on the shoulders of traditions of black resistance that predate the modern civil rights movement. It did not burst onto the scene, sui generis, in splendid historical or regional isolation. Rather, its possibilities were forged in the immediate aftermath of the eclipse of a wartime liberal-left alliance between labor, civil rights, and anticolonial activists.

Several influential studies viewing the southern movement from the vantage point of indigenous and grassroots politics have challenged accounts centered on high-level administration officials and such national civil rights leaders as King. Taking issue with the view of the 1954 *Brown* decision as the catalyst for the movement, Aldon Morris emphasized the indigenous resources that gave rise to the modern struggle for equality, with the black church supplying crucial leadership, organization, and fundraising. Breaking from top-down approaches to the movement, Clayborne Carson's book on the Student Nonviolent Coordinating Committee (SNCC) foregrounded the southern movement's radical wing, with SNCC organizers Robert Moses, John Lewis, and Fannie Lou Hamer, under the inspiration of veteran civil rights organizer Ella Baker, adopting the strategy of grassroots organizing for voting rights in Mississippi. Laboring in rural communities far from the media spotlight and facing the constant threat of violence, SNCC sought to empower the most downtrodden blacks in the Deep South. In a somewhat different vein, Charles Payne's magisterial study of the "organizing tradition" in Mississippi recounts the deep egalitarian and democratic structures of black southern life that informed SNCC's ethos and efforts, rooted in generations of struggle. Through their voter education efforts, the young activists in SNCC "were bringing back to the rural Black South a refined, codified version of something that had begun there, an expression of the historical vision of ex-slaves, men and women who understood that, for them, maintaining a deep sense of community was itself an act of resistance." Eschewing triumphalism, Payne explores the limits of liberal consensus. He notes SNCC's fraught relationship with liberalism and the Democratic Party. The activists' faith in government as an ally and their own ideals of interracial cooperation were tested by their mounting frustration at the nation's apparent indifference to the loss of black life. Particularly telling is Payne's discussion of the impact of the news media, which, by focusing on Dr. King's nonviolent direct action campaigns and largely ignoring SNCC's undramatic grassroots organizing, set the tone for histories of the movement that rendered indigenous mass activism invisible.

A similar interest in recovering traditions of resistance and struggle obscured by "mainstream" perspectives has guided the efforts of scholars working at the juncture of African-American, southern, and labor history, focusing on what Robert Korstad has called civil rights unionism. As Patricia Sullivan has shown, the New Deal's federal relief programs and pro-labor policy opened the solid South to labor organizing and voting rights campaigns mounted by black labor and civil rights activists and southern liberals and progressives. This revival of mass activism shocked those convinced of black acquiescence to Jim Crow. In Theodore Rosengarten's *All God's Dangers*, Ned Cobb, an Alabama sharecropper and organizer with the Southern Tenant Farmer's Union, recalled a white employer's alarmed response to the union's popularity among blacks: "The Lord is bringing down the world." Whether or not African-American workers believed their fight against workplace discrimination enjoyed a divine sanction, the wartime mood of antiracism and rights consciousness fueled the alliance between civil rights organizations and the Congress of Industrial Organizations (CIO). The vibrant labor–civil rights pact recounted by Sullivan, Korstad, Michael Honey, and others became a casualty of the red scare's campaign against liberal-left unionism in northern bastions such as Detroit and southern cities including Memphis and Winston-Salem. While the Supreme Court's majority opinion in *Brown v. Board of Education* (1954) cited the importance of desegregation as an asset in the cold war struggle against the Soviet Union, cold war anticommunism also provided segregationists with a formidable weapon in their opposition to Court-ordered desegregation. The cold war consensus in national politics pressured civil rights leaders to jettison demands for economic justice for the pursuit of formal equality through legal and legislative remedies.

Martha Biondi's *To Stand and Fight* brings together several aspects of the approach to the long civil rights movement, writing the history of the movement from the standpoint of postwar northern liberalism. Moving beyond an exclusive emphasis on the Jim Crow South, Biondi shows that discrimination in public accommodations, housing, and the workplace, as well as police brutality, were deeply entrenched in New York City. Biondi's account of racial apartheid in the North leads her to debunk the notion of "de facto segregation," an argument reinforced by the work of Matthew Countryman on Philadelphia and Thomas Sugrue on Detroit. Public policies of real estate, banking, and insurance companies; federal, state, and local governments; and members of the judiciary promoted and upheld segregation in New York and other northern cities. Black mobilizations against discriminatory practices and policies gained momentum from the antiracist thrust of wartime popular sentiment and from a vibrant liberal-left political culture that Biondi terms a "Black popular front." These mobilizations, in which trade unions played a crucial role, influenced the national Democratic Party and served as incubators for political leadership and legal support for the southern civil rights movement. Although the movement in New York and many of its left-wing and labor activists were casualties of the cold war, Biondi concludes that their campaigns against discrimination in housing and employment were influential in providing the basis for such national reforms as affirmative action and the Great Society. Biondi highlights the global consciousness of local black activists, some of them products of multiple histories of racism and colonialism, migrating from the Caribbean and the Panama Canal Zone to societies differently structured in racial dominance in Harlem and New York City.

Indeed, African Americans' interactions with the broader colonial world has been an important dimension of African-American historiography as well as politics, stretching back to the early work of W.E.B. Du Bois, Carter Woodson, and C.L.R. James, to name just a few. As Nikhil Singh has shown, black radical and liberal intellectuals responded to the crises of segregation, depression, and war with a critical discourse of "Black worldliness" that framed U.S. black demands for equality within the democratic aspirations of colonized and oppressed peoples on a global scale. As Rayford Logan phrased the issue in *What the Negro Wants* (1944), a collection of essays by fourteen black intellectuals, "We want the Four Freedoms to apply to black Americans as well as to the brutalized peoples of Europe and to other underprivileged peoples of the world."

Since the mid-1990s, such scholars as Brenda Gayle Plummer, Penny Von Eschen, and James Meriwether have explored the fluid wartime order defined by the collapse of Europe's colonial empires, decolonization, and African and Asian nonaligned movements. What Von Eschen has termed "the politics of the African Diaspora," took shape in the form of African-American activists' linkage of their struggle against U.S. racism with accelerating anticolonial movements in Africa and Asia. Led by stalwarts of the black left—W.E.B. Du Bois, Paul Robeson, and Alphaeus Hunton— the broad-based advocacy of African anticolonial struggles and international labor was grounded in such institutions as the nationally circulated black press, labor unions, and churches, and attracted broad support from African Americans of all political persuasions. As civil rights organizations and black civil society institutions sought representation at the United Nations to lobby on behalf of anticolonial causes, and amid the global war against fascism, internationalism seemed to be a viable strategy for opposing Jim Crow and campaigning for political and economic rights. However, with the advent of the cold war, such figures as Rayford Logan, Walter White, and A. Philip Randolph opposed discrimination within the framework of anticommunism, rather than anticolonialism. Cold war ideology demanded that African Americans limit their political and civic affiliations to the American nation, discrediting wartime expressions of solidarity with African and Asian anticolonial struggles.

Although the cold war's rollback of progressive labor–civil rights–anti-colonial projects blocked hopes for a more democratic global order, a dissident black worldliness persisted among a younger generation of black radicals critical of cold war liberalism and U.S. foreign policy toward Africa. Such diverse figures as Du Bois, James Baldwin, Lorraine Hansberry, Malcolm X, and others wondered how African Americans on the threshold of full citizenship would define themselves in relation to political change in Africa and the colonized world. In 1959, while visiting India, Martin Luther King himself declared that "the strongest bond of fraternity was the common cause of minority and colonial peoples in America, Africa, and Asia struggling to throw off racism and imperialism." Whether as expatriates in Ghana or as part of the Harlem-based activist community, some African Americans reserved the right to define their U.S. citizenship in affiliation with Africa and its diaspora, breaking from the ideological tenets of U.S. cold war liberalism. As hopes for nonviolent change in the United States and Africa yielded to the bloodshed that in the minds of many would join Mississippi and Birmingham with South Africa and the Congo, black Americans critical of cold war liberalism declared themselves Afro-American nationalists, fending off reflexive accusations of communism. The former Nation of Islam minister Malcolm X's meeting with voting rights activists in Selma, Alabama, signaled, according to Clayborne Carson, a transformation of his politics from racial-religious separatism to militant political engagement. Malcolm's interactions with young SNCC activists and the high esteem in which they held him indicate the growing influence of his radical pan-African internationalism.

To date, the scholarship produced under the banner of the long civil rights movement tends to cluster around locating the movement's origins in the decades spanning the New Deal and World War II. But the long civil rights movement also includes a growing number of studies of the black power movement. Some of this scholarship challenges the master narrative's declension story by blurring the line between civil rights and black power. Such a view can be seen in Tim Tyson's study of Robert F. Williams, the militant North Carolina NAACP official whose advocacy of armed self-defense during the late 1950s led to his ouster from that organization and his increasingly radical critique of cold war liberalism. Recent scholarship on northern struggles for equality, such as Matthew Countryman's work on Philadelphia, views black power activism in that city not as a rupture, but as an outgrowth of the limited gains of civil rights organizations in the face of persistent discrimination in the workplace and public schools. Historian Peniel Joseph has been a leading contributor to the emerging field of "Black Power studies." The work of Joseph, William Van Deburg, and Jeffrey Ogbar has emphasized the transformative cultural significance of black power. Though not focused on black power per se, Rhonda Williams, Premilla Nadasen, and Annelise Orleck have studied black women's involvement in public housing and welfare rights activism, both key expressions of black power's shift to struggles for economic and social justice after the passage of civil rights reforms. Komozi Woodard's groundbreaking study of Amiri Baraka and black power politics in Newark suggests the need for more local studies of black power.

Scholarship on black power faces its sternest challenge not from the "normative" studies of liberal consensus historians of the "short civil rights movement," but from such scholars of the southern movement as Clayborne Carson and Charles Payne. Carson notes a deep disconnect between black power leaders and mass mobilizations. In his view, black power spokespersons gained national status through media coverage, but they could only react to spontaneous urban rebellions and were unable to deliver any tangible results to the masses they purported to lead. For his part, Payne views the "radical-nationalist thrusts" after the mid-1960s as diametrically opposed to the nonhierarchical assumptions of the organizing tradition. "While their analysis was in fact growing sharper in many ways," according to Payne, "movement activists lost the ability to relate to one another in human terms." The growing number of studies of local black struggles during the 1960s and 1970s that might perhaps be grouped under the heading of Black Power studies seems analogous to the aforementioned trend of scholarship on grassroots black struggles during the era of segregation, more legible as an efflorescence of local struggles rather than as a full-fledged national movement with dedicated leadership.

As with studies of slavery, a focus on women, gender, and sexuality has transformed the study of the civil rights movement. Barbara Ransby's *Ella Baker and the Black Freedom Movement: A Radical Democratic Vision*, along with other studies of women in the movement, greatly enhances our understanding of the movement's gendered dimension. Ransby grounds Baker's long career as an activist for civil and women's rights, from the Popular Front era to the 1970s, in her rural North Carolina origins and the traditions of black southern resistance that were bequeathed to her and many others. Baker, who had contended with the sexism of male-dominated leadership during her brief tenure as executive director of the Southern Christian Leadership Conference, inspired SNCC workers with her democratic vision of grassroots organizing and an ideal of social change that transcended struggles for civil and political rights. Biography appears to be a fruitful means of exploring issues of gender and sexuality. Like Ransby's book on Ella Baker, John D'Emilio's biography of Bayard Rustin complicates triumphalist narratives of the movement, illuminating the dilemma of Rustin, the African-American pacifist and gifted organizer of the 1963 March on Washington, whose homosexuality made him a convenient target of segregationists and often estranged him from his ostensible allies in the movement.

African-American history continues to thrive as a vital subfield of U.S. history. Its subject matter continues to provide occasions for scholarly and public debate, some measured, others strident, on the nation's tortured history of racial and social conflict. In a nation that continues to be afflicted by racial segregation, scholarship outstrips understanding. Many continue to deny the wide gulf separating America's promises and its practices, resulting, for example, in cumulative wealth disparities between blacks and whites. African-American history offers all Americans a unique opportunity for understanding past and present inequalities and ultimately, reconciling differences. Indeed, reconciliation and humanism are central themes of the African-American story. That much is illustrated by those who have experienced the worst treatment at the hands of whites in Jim Crow Mississippi and yet concluded, as did Lou Emma Allen, "Of course there is no way I can hate anybody and hope to see God's face." In addition, one cannot fail to notice African Americans' unmatched fidelity to ideals of freedom and citizenship, grounded in a long memory of generations of struggle and the sacrifices of millions. Darrell Kenyatta Evers once argued with his mother, claiming that he did not see the point of voting. Myrlie Evers ended the discussion by showing her son the bloodied poll-tax receipt his father, Medgar Evers, had been carrying when he was gunned down in his driveway in 1963. At a moment when the progress and legacy of the civil rights movement remain hotly contested, a final lesson that we can derive from African-American history is the extent to which past social and political advances of African Americans have been subject to backlash and reversal by the forces of reaction. That final lesson raises the stakes for the production of future scholarship that advances the field and meaningfully engages public audiences.

BIBLIOGRAPHY

Bates, Beth. *Pullman Porters and the Rise of Protest Politics in Black America, 1925–1945*. Chapel Hill: University of North Carolina Press, 2001.

Berry, Mary Frances. *My Face Is Black Is True: Callie House and the Struggle for Ex-Slave Reparations*. New York: Knopf, 2005.

Biondi, Martha. *To Stand and Fight: The Struggle for Civil Rights in Postwar New York City*. Cambridge, MA: Harvard University Press, 2003.

Blassingame, John. *The Slave Community: Plantation Life in the Antebellum South*. New York: Oxford University Press, 1972.

Camp, Stephanie. *Closer to Freedom: Enslaved Women and Everyday Resistance in the Plantation South*. Chapel Hill: University of North Carolina Press, 2004.

Carson, Clayborne. "African American Leadership and Mass Mobilization." *The Black Scholar* 24 (Fall 1994): 2–7.

———. *In Struggle: SNCC and the Black Awakening of the 1960s*. Cambridge, MA: Harvard University Press, 1981.

Cha-Jua, Sundiata Keita, and Clarence Lang. "The 'Long Movement' as Vampire: Temporal and Spatial Fallacies in Recent Black Freedom Studies." *Journal of African American History* 92 (Spring 2007): 265–288.

Corbould, Clare. *Becoming African Americans: Black Public Life in Harlem, 1919–1939*. Cambridge, MA: Harvard University Press, 2009.

Countryman, Matthew. *Up South: Civil Rights and Black Power in Philadelphia*. Philadelphia: University of Pennsylvania Press, 2006.

Curtin, Philip. *The Atlantic Slave Trade: A Census*. Madison: University of Wisconsin Press, 1969.

D'Emilio, John. *Lost Prophet: The Life and Times of Bayard Rustin*. New York: Free Press, 2003.

Dittmer, John. *Local People: The Struggle for Civil Rights in Mississippi*. Urbana: University of Illinois Press, 1995.

Du Bois, W.E.B. *Black Reconstruction*. New York: Oxford University Press, 2007 [1935].

Elkins, Stanley M. *Slavery: A Problem in American Institutional and Intellectual Life*. Chicago: University of Chicago Press, 1959.

Feimster, Crystal. *Southern Horrors: Women and the Politics of Rape and Lynching*. Cambridge, MA: Harvard University Press, 2009.

Fett, Sharla. *Working Cures: Healing, Health, and Power on Southern Slave Plantations*. Chapel Hill: University of North Carolina Press, 2002.

Finkenbine, Roy E., and Richard S. Newman, "Black Founders in the New Republic: Introduction." *William and Mary Quarterly* 64 (January 2007): 83–94.

Frazier, E. Franklin. *Black Bourgeoisie*. New York: Collier, 1962.

Glymph, Thavolia. *Out of the House of Bondage: The Transformation of the Plantation Household*. New York: Cambridge University Press, 2008.

Gomez, Michael A. *Exchanging Our Country Marks: The Transformation of African Identities in the Colonial and Antebellum South*. Chapel Hill: University of North Carolina Press, 1998.

Gordon-Reed, Annette. *The Hemingses of Monticello: An American Family*. New York: W. W. Norton, 2008.

Gutman, Herbert. *The Black Family in Slavery and Freedom*. New York: Pantheon, 1976.

Hahn, Steven. *A Nation under Our Feet: Black Political Struggles in the Rural South, from Slavery to the Great Migration*. Cambridge, MA: Belknap/Harvard University Press, 2003.

Hall, Jacquelyn. "The Long Civil Rights Movement and the Political Uses of the Past." *Journal of American History* 91 (March 2005): 1233–1263.

Harris, Leslie. *In the Shadow of Slavery: African Americans in New York City, 1626–1863*. Chicago: University of Chicago Press, 2003.

Hine, Darlene Clark. "Rape and the Inner Lives of Black Women in the Middle West: Preliminary Thoughts on the Culture of Dissemblance." In Beverly Guy-Sheftall, ed., *Words of Fire: An Anthology of African-American Feminist Thought*, 380–388. New York: New Press, 1995.

Honey, Michael. *Southern Labor and Black Civil Rights: Organizing Memphis Workers*. Urbana: University of Illinois Press, 1993.

Jackson, Maurice. "'Friends of the Negro! Fly with Me, the Path Is Open to the Sea': Remembering the Haitian Revolution in the History, Music, and Culture of the African American People." *Early American Studies* 6 (Spring 2008): 59–103.

James, Winston. *Holding Aloft the Banner of Ethiopia: Caribbean Radicalism in Early Twentieth-Century America*. London: Verso, 1998.

Johnson, Walter. *Soul by Soul: Life inside the Antebellum Slave Market*. Cambridge, MA: Harvard University Press, 1999.

Joseph, Peniel. *Waiting 'til the Midnight Hour: A Narrative History of Black Power in America*. New York: Henry Holt, 2006.

Kelley, Robin D. G. *Hammer and Hoe: Alabama Communists during the Great Depression*. Chapel Hill: University of North Carolina Press, 1990.

Korstad, Robert. *Civil Rights Unionism: Tobacco Workers and the Struggle for Democracy in the Mid-Twentieth-Century South.* Chapel Hill: University of North Carolina Press, 2003.

Lewis, Earl. "'To Turn as on a Pivot': Writing African Americans into a History of Overlapping Diasporas." *American Historical Review* 100 (June 1995): 765–787.

Logan, Rayford. *The Betrayal of the Negro, from Rutherford B. Hayes to Woodrow Wilson.* New York: Da Capo Press, 1997.

———. *What the Negro Wants.* Notre Dame, IN: University of Notre Dame Press, 1944.

McCurry, Stephanie. *Masters of Small Worlds: Yeoman Households, Gender Relations, and the Political Culture of the Antebellum South Carolina Low Country.* New York: Oxford University Press, 1995.

Melish, Joanne Pope. *Disowning Slavery: Gradual Emancipation and "Race" in New England, 1780–1860.* Ithaca, NY: Cornell University Press, 1998.

Meriwether, James. *Proudly We Can Be Africans: Black Americans and Africa, 1935–1961.* Chapel Hill: University of North Carolina Press, 2002.

Miles, Tiya. *Ties That Bind: The Story of an Afro-Cherokee Family in Slavery and Freedom.* Berkeley: University of California Press, 2005.

Mitchell, Michele. *Righteous Propagation: African Americans and the Politics of Racial Destiny after Reconstruction.* Chapel Hill: University of North Carolina Press, 2004.

Morgan, Jennifer. *Laboring Women: Reproduction and Gender in New World Slavery.* Philadelphia: University of Pennsylvania Press, 2004.

Morris, Aldon. *The Origins of the Civil Rights Movement: Black Communities Organizing for Change.* New York: Free Press, 1984.

Nadasen, Premilla. *Welfare Warriors: The Welfare Rights Movement in the United States.* New York: Routledge, 2005.

Ogbar, Jeffrey. *Black Power: Radical Politics and African American Identity.* Baltimore: Johns Hopkins University Press, 2005.

Orleck, Annelise. *Storming Caesar's Palace: How Black Mothers Fought Their Own War on Poverty.* Boston: Beacon Press, 2005.

Painter, Nell Irvin. *Exodusters: Black Migration to Kansas after Reconstruction.* New York: W. W. Norton, 1977.

———. "Soul Murder and Slavery: Toward a Fully Loaded Cost Accounting." In *Southern History across the Color Line,* 15–39. Chapel Hill: University of North Carolina Press, 2002.

Patterson, Orlando. *Slavery and Social Death: A Comparative Study.* Cambridge, MA: Harvard University Press, 1982.

Payne, Charles. *I've Got the Light of Freedom: The Organizing Tradition and the Mississippi Freedom Struggle.* Berkeley: University of California Press, 1995.

Penningroth, Dylan. *The Claims of Kinfolk: African American Property and Community in the Nineteenth Century South.* Chapel Hill: University of North Carolina Press, 2003.

Plummer, Brenda Gayle. *Rising Wind: Black Americans and U.S. Foreign Affairs, 1935–1960.* Chapel Hill: University of North Carolina Press, 1996.

Quarles, Benjamin. *Black Mosaic: Essays in Afro-American History and Historiography.* Amherst: University of Massachusetts Press, 1988.

Ransby, Barbara. *Ella Baker and the Black Freedom Movement: A Radical Democratic Vision.* Chapel Hill: University of North Carolina Press, 2003.

Rosen, Hannah. *Terror in the Heart of Freedom: Citizenship, Sexual Violence, and the Meaning of Race in the Postemancipation South.* Chapel Hill: University of North Carolina Press, 2009.

Rosengarten, Theodore. *All God's Dangers: The Life of Nate Shaw.* New York: Knopf, 1974.

Scott, Daryl Michael. *Contempt and Pity: Social Policy and the Image of the Damaged Black Psyche.* Chapel Hill: University of North Carolina Press, 1997.

Scott, Julius. "'Negroes in Foreign Bottoms': Sailors, Slaves, and Communication." In Laurent Dubois and Julius Scott, eds., *Origins of the Black Atlantic: Rewriting Histories,* 69–98. New York: Routledge, 2010.

Singh, Nikhil Pal. *Black Is a Country: Race and the Unfinished Struggle for Democracy.* Cambridge, MA: Harvard University Press, 2004.

Sitkoff, Harvard. *A New Deal for Blacks: The Emergence of Civil Rights as a National Issue.* New York: Oxford University Press, 1978.

Smallwood, Stephanie. *Saltwater Slavery: A Middle Passage from Africa to American Diaspora.* Cambridge, MA: Harvard University Press, 2007.

Staples, Brent. "History Lessons Learned from the Slaves of New York." *New York Times,* January 9, 2000.

Stuckey, Sterling. *Slave Culture: Nationalist Theory and the Foundations of Black America.* New York: Oxford University Press, 1987.

———. "Through the Prism of Folklore: The Black Ethos in Slavery." *Massachusetts Review* 9 (Summer 1968): 417–437.

Sugrue, Thomas. *Sweet Land of Liberty: The Forgotten Struggle for Civil Rights in the North.* New York: Random House, 2008.

Sullivan, Patricia. *Days of Hope: Race and Democracy in the New Deal Era.* Chapel Hill: University of North Carolina Press, 1996.

Trouillot, Michel-Rolph. *Silencing the Past: Power and the Production of History.* Boston: Beacon Press, 1995.

Tyson, Timothy B. *Radio Free Dixie: Robert F. Williams and the Roots of Black Power.* Chapel Hill: University of North Carolina Press, 1999.

Van Deburg, William. *New Day in Babylon: The Black Power Movement and American Culture, 1965–1975.* Chicago: University of Chicago Press, 1992.

Von Eschen, Penny. *Race against Empire: Black Americans and Anticolonialism, 1937–1957.* Ithaca, NY: Cornell University Press, 1997.

White, Deborah Gray. *Ar'n't I a Woman: Female Slaves in the Plantation South.* New York: W. W. Norton, 1985.

White, Shane, and Graham White. *Stylin': African American Expressive Culture from Its Beginnings to the Zoot Suit.* Ithaca, NY: Cornell University Press, 1998.

Williams, Eric E. *Capitalism and Slavery.* New York: Capricorn Books, 1966 [1944].

Williams, Rhonda. *The Politics of Public Housing: Black Women's Struggles against Urban Inequality.* New York: Oxford University Press, 2004.

Wilmington Race Riot Commission. Final Report. May 31, 2006. www.history.ncdcr.gov/1898-wrrc/report/report.htm.

Woodard, Komozi. *A Nation within a Nation: Amiri Baraka (LeRoi Jones) and Black Power Politics.* Chapel Hill: University of North Carolina Press, 1999.

Zinn, Howard. *The Southern Mystique.* New York: Knopf, 1964.

American Graffiti

The Social Life of Jim Crow Signs
Elizabeth Abel

*Every little southern town is a fine stage-set for Southern Tradition to use
as it teaches its children the twisting turning dance of segregation. Few words
are needed for there are signs everywhere. White . . . colored . . . white . . .
colored . . . over doors of railroad and bus stations, over doors of public toi-
lets, over doors of theaters, over drinking fountains.*

LILLIAN SMITH, *KILLERS OF THE DREAM,* 1949

*We have to follow the things themselves, for their meanings are inscribed in
their forms, their uses, their trajectories. It is only through the analysis of these
trajectories that we can interpret the human transactions and calculations that
enliven things. . . . it is the things-in-motion that illuminate their human and
social context.*

ARJUN APPADURAI, "INTRODUCTION,"
THE SOCIAL LIVES OF THINGS, 1988

White . . . colored . . . white . . . colored: the shorthand for segregation. In Lillian
Smith's Southern Everytown, all Jim Crow signs are one master sign, a superscript
over all social spaces and relations. Circumventing the channels of cognition, the
signs write race directly on the body, which is programmed to dance to segregation's piper. Th e choreography is various, the words invariant. Scarcely material-
ized in written form, their incantation appears to be intoned instead by a disembodied voice that speaks from beyond the historical scene, as if the language of Jim
Crow bypassed graphic mediation to be written directly in human nerves and flesh.

Collapsing the space between Jim Crow signs and the bodies they imprint is a
common trope of narratives of race. For African American writers in particular,
the first encounter with a segregation sign is a defining moment of social inscription, a painful rite of passage that spells the fall into race. To learn to read the "Colored" sign is to learn that one has already been read by a law that writes its terms
on a body forever af t er "branded and tagged and set apart from the rest of mankind

83

upon the public highways, like an unclean thing."[1] Typically recounted through the optic of the child, the law's cutting force is registered not in the adult language of status and rights, but in the experience of bodily pain—the jerk on the arm or the shout in the ear—and the foreclosure of specific bodily pleasures: the fresh breeze on the face at the front of the trolley, the iced Coke at the drugstore counter. The body is affronted time and again, and each impact and withholding aches distinctively; yet within the coming-of-age narratives they serve, these incidents are condensed into a single originary scene that (like the scene of castration in the narrative of gender) performs the work of allegory. After recounting his traumatic childhood experience of being refused a Coke at a Mississippi drugstore counter, the civil rights activist James Forman recasts this moment as "a cliché of the black experience, so often has it happened to our children in one form or another."[2]

Clichés tell important truths, but only by obscuring others. By redirecting our attention from the bodies that are racially inscribed to the bodies of the signs (also described in considerable detail by African American writers) that are the objects as well as agents of inscription, this chapter seeks to uncover the stories relayed by things instead of by authors. Jim Crow signs conduct their own social lives independent of the racial choreography Lillian Smith describes.

As Arjun Appadurai argues in his introduction to *The Social Lives of Things*, which offers a counterpoint to the epigraph from Lillian Smith, the pathways of things-in-motion provide windows into the social transactions that enliven things. It may be strange to think of Jim Crow signs as things in motion, securely tacked to structures as they were; but as things that were subject to the concessions and contingencies of material existence, rather than as transcendent and transparent vehicles of power, they were expressive and eventually portable objects that could be adapted to a range of cultural purposes. They have a history of production and a lively posthistorical existence after they were detached from walls and thrust into circulation. The messier and longer stories they convey route power through economic and cultural transactions that redistribute it less unilaterally and reconfigure race in a broader matrix of social relations.

The strange career of Jim Crow signs extends across a century, significantly outliving the statutes that gave rise to it. Its trajectory follows the general course that anthropologists attribute to the "cultural biography of things."[3] The contours of this biography enlarge the context for local arguments about the politics of collecting black memorabilia and the relative claims of preserving and undoing an oppressive history at the same time that the specificity of these things recruits the generic biography of things to the charged and contested practices of race making.[4] The cultural biography of Jim Crow signs can be divided into several interdependent chapters.

The biography begins with the production of the signs over the first half of the twentieth century, a chapter that reveals surprising variations in the ways that social authority was both articulated and complicated. Formal features allowed the signs to pivot between intentional command and inadvertent signature. Making signs entailed negotiating between public and private, class and race, and self-authorization and self-exposure on both sides of the color line. This extended period of production finally slowed with the early stirrings of the civil rights movement and the growing recognition that the signs would offer evidence of a regime that would appear increasingly incredible to successive generations. A new chapter of the biography begins with the efforts of African American activists to pry the signs loose from the structures that supported them. Diverted from their historical function, repossessed as trophies, segregation signs were transported from a disciplinary regime to an economy of consumption.

This chapter unfolds in accordance with Michel de Certeau's effort (in contradistinction to Foucault's) "not to make clearer how the violence of order is transmuted into a disciplinary technology, but rather to bring to light the clandestine forms taken by the dispersed, tactical, and makeshift creativity of groups or individuals already caught in the nets of 'discipline.' Pushed to their ideal limits, these procedures and ruses of consumers compose the network of an antidiscipline." Certeau's account of consumption as "*another* production"—devious, dispersed, and often invisible "because it does not manifest itself through its own products, but rather through its *ways of using* the products" imposed by a dominant order—gives us a good handle on the tactics of the signs' earliest, most determined and defiant consumers.[5]

This first generation could salvage only a small percentage of the signs, however, and as this limited supply failed to satisfy a growing demand for a material record of a vanishing history, a new market and new chapter emerged, whose trademark was reproductions. Signs initially, intentionally, and often illicitly taken to be preserved as historical evidence crossed paths with commodities manufactured for general circulation. After constituting "another production," consumption generated a more conventional mode of mass production as commercial producers, no less resourceful than Certeau's devious consumers and inspired perhaps by some of their tricks, devised new and profitable uses of the signs in this most controversial chapter of their biography.

As an engine of reproductions and reinventions whose diversions can be read as either resisting or repressing the burden of segregation's history, the marketplace inevitably generates debates about the proper place of things in a historically grounded cultural identity. For David Pilgrim, the founder and curator of the Jim Crow Museum of Racist Memorabilia at Ferris State University, the commodification of segregation artifacts is more perversion than diversion, an "ugly intersection of money and race."[6] Pilgrim's museum, whose name sends an unambiguous message about the nature of its holdings, takes historical artifacts and meanings out of circulation to preserve them from contamination on the marketplace. But neither the museum nor the marketplace is a singular entity, especially in relation to the traffic in signs, typically transacted at sites outside the repository of history.

The long career of Jim Crow signs reveals the ways they served to unravel their original intent by complicating not only the racial division they enforced, but also other oppositions that share its binary structure and territorial design: past and present, production and consumption, original and copy, museum and marketplace, history and memory. This is a strange career indeed, not only because of its surprising twists and turns, but also because its overall direction can be read both as an emancipatory evolution away from the dominant culture's stranglehold over racial definitions toward a more democratic proliferation, and as a trivializing devolution from the understanding of the signs' historical consequences to an empty, dehistoricizing, commodified form of play. The entanglements that come to the fore of the most recent chapter of the signs' biography provide a lens for reexamining the origins of the signs, which were created, discarded, and preserved through relations of complicity and agency across and within divergent groups that, neither passively inscribing nor inscribed, took the words of segregation into their own hands.

. . .

Jim Crow signs occupy a unique place in the history of public signage in the United States. Despite their narrow content, their heterogeneous sources and forms embraced a spectrum of expression that escaped regulation from the state or marketplace. Drawing their authority from their status as regulatory signage, a mode of public address that emerged in the middle of the nineteenth century, racial restrictions could claim kinship with safety or traffic regulations that instructed citizens where to stand or walk.[7] From this stemmed the perception of a far-reaching mandate to post private prejudice in public view. Subject to only minimal regulation in even its civic varieties—a Maryland ordinance specifying that railroads must have segregation signs in each coach with "appropriate words, in plain letters, in some conspicuous place" is a characteristically vague formulation, as is a Mississippi ordinance declaring that signs had to be visible from all quarters of intercity streetcars and buses—the enticement to post racial signage was both empowering and treacherous to some of the voices it teased out of hiding, as the lack of explicit guidelines also kept out of view the implicit norms of speaking for the public.[8] A surprisingly broad cross-section of the American public consequently left its racial signature in this perversely democratic mode of expression that, encompassing public officials and private individuals, professional signmakers and amateur scribblers, could be characterized as an American graffiti.

At one pole were the signs commercially manufactured for transportation and entertainment companies, business and merchant organizations, and government agencies. These are relatively standardized. At the center in block capitals is a generic formula: either the minimal announcement "White" or "Colored" or more specific

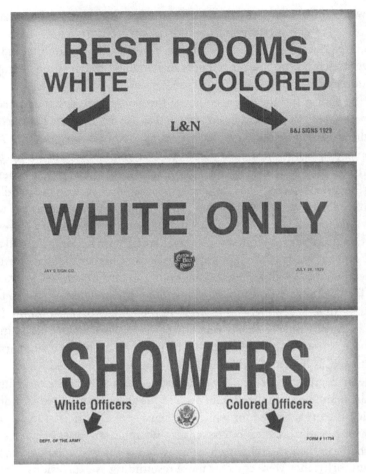

FIGURE 4. Assorted Jim Crow signs (reproductions).

yet still multipurpose messages, such as "Colored Seated in Rear," which could apply not only on public transportation but also in courtrooms, waiting rooms, and county or state offices. This instructional message stands on a tripod of authority. In smaller print below are the name or logo of the commissioning organization—the Cotton Belt Route, the Louisville and Nashville Railroad Company (L&N), or the United States Army (which had the distinction of segregating its members simultaneously along the axes of race and rank, dividing "white" from "colored" soldiers and enlisted men from officers), for example—along with by the name of the company that manufactured the sign and the date or number of the segregation ordinance (figure 4).

Presenting themselves as the announcement of a policy determined previously and elsewhere, these signs provide at least some fictive origins for their statements. The rhetoric of direct and disinterested address, divorced from personal attitude or gain, encourages the perception of a neutral general will. Unmodified nouns and passive verbs give arbitrary arrangements an axiomatic cast; restrained graphic design reinforces the impression of impersonal necessity.

Both the choice and the arrangement of the words were designed as codes for public speech, but the public they constructed as the origin as well as the object of their address took more than one shape, as suggested by two signs from Alabama that reference the same ordinance (figure 5). The Montgomery drinking-fountain sign illustrates the classic strategy for legitimating a segregated public sphere. With its precise symmetry, it rests its miniature cartography of race on the parallel foundations of space (on the left) and time (on the right): the sign arranges words to create an imaginary space that supplants the material conditions they represent (almost certainly a large refrigerated cooler and a small basin nearby). Behind the state ordinance it cites by date, the sign implicitly draws a higher mandate for this idealized racial map through a silent quotation of the formula of *Plessy*. By contrast, the sign for the Selma swimming pool abandons any pretense of an equitably divided public sphere. Through either a slip of the tongue or a slap in the face, the sign makes explicit what is usually kept quiet by bringing the word *public* into view. Public space is not partitioned here: it is blatantly restricted to a single race, and gratuitously so, as the word *public* could easily have been avoided.

The Selma sign suggests that any sign that served the interests of whites could assume the mantle of a public dictum even in the absence of a cited authority. The less explicit the organization for which the signs spoke or the statutory nature of their provenance, the broader the consensus they appeared to articulate. Less stringent, perhaps, in their disciplinary overtones than signs that stipulated the source of their authority, they were equal or more resounding as expressions of a general will. Even the most minimal form—a single racial word—functioned as a citation of the larger social framework that backed that word's authority.

More than any other formal feature of the Jim Crow signs, consequently, the physical frame conferred legitimacy, not only by virtue of the economy of expression it inevitably imposed, but also by the participation it signaled in a distinctive discursive order. That the symbolic value of the frame was widely recognized is suggested by the frequency with which private citizens painted one around the racial restrictions they stenciled or scribbled on family businesses: the frame not only called attention to the words but also situated them in a larger social context (see figures 55 and 56). Whether hand-painted or professionally manufactured, Jim Crow signage provided a conduit through which the private voice could be invested with the authority of the collective. This was a heady incentive, especially for those whose economic status afforded little access to a public voice, but effecting this translation demanded adherence to the conventions of public speech.

FIGURE 5. Two Jim Crow signs citing an Alabama ordinance from July 14, 1931 (reproductions).

The most obvious taboo was the personal signature. Because the sign must appear to emanate from some impersonal source, even the name of a public official could compromise the fiction of the collective, as a signed variant of a standard formula makes clear (figure 6). This handwritten sign, posted on a tree standing sentry over a park, is given some weight by the substantial signboard, framed at the top, but the highly unprofessional, almost childish inscription—the uncertain penmanship, uneven lines, smudged paint, misspelling, and lack of foresight in spacing—seriously compromises its authority, posing the question of who—child or semiliterate or even prankster—could have written it. Perhaps to circumvent that question and to recover some lost authority, the sign is uncharacteristically dignified with a signature of sorts. But the name that is signed has the opposite effect: intentionally or not, it tilts the sign from amateurism to absurdity, and possibly to parody. Whether E. W. Grove is the name of a park commissioner or an area of the park (the east and west groves?), its inclusion creates the comical impression that the tree is speaking on its own behalf.

The crudely made sign also reveals that the signature is inscribed in more than one way. The rare (because counterproductive) inclusion of a name is only the most obvious version of a self-identification that could also take the form of handwriting, diction, spelling, or choice of color. The anonymity of the discursive form was countered by the individuality of the graphic form, which provided a handprint in

FIGURE 6. Hand-lettered park sign. From *The Negro Almanac*. Dorothy Sterling Collection, Amistad Research Center, Tulane University.

the absence of a name. Even less idiosyncratic sign makers had recourse to graphic options that exposed the messenger as they honed the message. Tonal differences could be rendered through variations in lettering: the typical reliance on block capitals yielded to the courtesies of cursive to insinuate class or racial distinctions. Size could serve as a register of sound: the larger the letters, the louder the voice, the more inflated the authority. Pauli Murray recalls that the signs she saw as a child in Durham, North Carolina, "literally screamed" at her from streetcars and drinking fountains, and she reproduces their loud voice on the printed page through over-size block capitals that show up Lillian Smith's quieter italics: "FOR WHITE ONLY, FOR COLORED ONLY, WHITE LADIES, COLORED WOMEN, WHITE, COLORED."[9] Choices of color, sometimes deployed mimetically for a partially literate public (white signs for white people, black signs for black people), had their expressive qualities as well: as his train crosses the Virginia border a few months after that state had enacted its separate-car law, Charles A. Chesnutt's fictional protagonist Dr. Miller notes a large framed card "containing the legend 'White,' in letters about a foot long, painted in white upon a dark background, typical, one might suppose, of the distinction thereby indicated."[10] Painting the word *colored* in black, conversely, effects a silent translation from the polite social term to its aggressive underside, blurring the distinction between those African Americans who had garnered a modicum of status and the underclass usually designated by the blunt color label *black*.

The range of expressive options distinguished Jim Crow signs not only from the more uniform regulatory signage but also from commercial signage, for Jim Crow signs were not subject to marketplace pressures to develop a consistent style. According to David M. Henkin, the increasing standardization of commercial signage over the nineteenth century derived from a common stake in professionalization. Because, as a visiting Argentinian statesman observed about commercial signs in New York in 1847, "a crooked or fat letter or a mistake in spelling would be enough to ensure a deserted counter for the shopkeeper," commercial signs developed a uniform typography and style. This consistency subsumed their competitive interests into the semblance of a "single, official voice" that contributed to the evolving perception of a coherent public space.[11] Because segregation signs were not promoting goods for sale, they risked no penalties for casual or sloppy expression, and there was no need to gain credibility among competing signs. Jim Crow signs thus share with their commercial counterparts the interrelation Henkin proposes between private interests and public language, but they work it in reverse. Like commercial signs, segregation signs fostered and gained power from the impression of impersonal authority, but this putatively public discourse, whose function was to articulate a general policy rather than to advertise the names and trades of individuals, was both deliberately and inadvertently a vehicle of self-disclosure. Paradoxically, whereas the commercial signage that had no intrinsic claim to public status played a cru-

FIGURE 7. Inscription on outhouse, North Carolina. Harry Golden Papers, University of North Carolina, Charlotte.

cial role in developing the concept of the public sign, the racial signage that was defined as the voice of the public became a mode of private expression.

In addition, there were no constraints on who could produce these signs, or how. It did not require status, money, education, or expertise to enter one's production into the public colloquy. It was not even necessary to know how to spell. Consequently, Jim Crow signage elicited a spectrum of expressions from commercial organizations, rednecks, and kooks who, for reasons of class or psychological disenfranchisement, perceived racial language as a medium for asserting what they took to be their underrecognized rights. Before the spray-paint can gave anyone the means and the incentive to impress a private signature on a public place, Jim Crow signage offered a frame for social writing that encouraged self-expression from the fringes as well as the center. Individuals drawn to this mode of self-aggrandizement revealed more than they knew, for they were also framed by the legitimating frame by which they were seduced.

The writing furthest from the center is at once the most revealing and the hardest to read. Consider, for example, the side wall of an outhouse in a field in North Carolina (figure 7). The racial restriction appears to be an exercise in absurdity: who would want to use this collapsing "tolit," whose tilt seems to suggest the precarious structure of white supremacy itself? More an act of self-definition than of practical instruction, the broadcasting of racial exclusivity seems almost pathetically compensatory. Racial entitlement attempts to remedy a class disadvantage that is visible in the diction as well as in the spelling. Yet whereas an officially printed version of the same message would pose few interpretive conundrums, these tell-tale markers are tantalizing but opaque. We can attribute the misspellings to inferior education—and perhaps to youth as well—but what kind of intentionality or meaning should we ascribe to the backwards *F* in "For"? Is it the signature of a dyslexic or child writer, as is famously intimated by the backwards *R* in the corporate logo of Toys "Я" Us? A clever attempt to superimpose the number 4 on its homonym? A sinister allusion to the swastika the reversed letter also resembles? The signifier that captures our attention does not answer our inquiries.

It is not only through the insistence of the letter that the material foundation of the sign is brought to our attention, however. Background as well as foreground plays a role in its formation. For it is as much the invitation tendered by the outermost board, I would argue, as the urgency of an internal state that elicits this inscription. By demarcating public space for racial writing, Jim Crow reconfigured the built environment as a series of blank pages that invited public expression of private sentiments. This had bitter and long-term consequences, but it also exposed the spectrum of racial discourse for future scrutiny.

. . .

Racial inscription included ingenious African American variations. The most inspired occurred in cartoons designed by and for readers who had thoroughly mastered Jim Crow's visual codes. The *Chicago Defender* fostered this visual play during and after World War II in the form of a comic strip about Mr. Jim Crow, a clueless white man with a crow mask who is continually forced to eat the crow produced by the rebound of the "No Collud" and "For White" signs he has tacked up everywhere. In 1950, the comic strip was opened to a competition among readers, with a prize of five dollars offered for the "most amusing 'Jim Crow' experience." This would be translated into comic form by the *Defender* cartoonist (whose name—or pseudonym—was Whyte). Even before that extended exercise, however, the *Defender* published individual cartoons that capitalized on the sign system's graphic (rather than semantic) codes, sometimes by playing with capitalization. One favorite trick was to call attention to the fact that *Negro* was typically written in lowercase by capitalizing all but the first letter of the word. Thus, for example, on a page supporting the reelection of Franklin Delano Roosevelt a few days before the 1944 election, a cartoon of Roosevelt welcoming a Negro delegation at the front door of the White House was juxtaposed with a sign for Thomas Dewey's home town that included a standard formula, with a single letter altered: "nEGRO, DON'T LET THE SUN SET ON YOU HERE!" A few months later, that strategy was deftly redeployed with another standard formula in a cartoon by Jay Jackson in which a streetcar conductor points to a sign declaring "FROM HERE BACK FOR nEGROES" (figure 8). Beneath the sign, a Caucasian-featured woman protests: "But I'm not! I got this tan out at the beach." By playing with the conventions of case and color in the graphic sign, the cartoon suggests that race's somatic signs are equally unstable.

Although the actual signs afforded less room for play, African American versions reveal a distinctive cultural signature directed at viewers within the community. Sometimes the same word simply registered differently. Whereas a white-made "Colored" sign signified a humiliating back-door entry, for example, the same word on a black-owned store signaled a refuge from humiliating (or no) service in the larger culture. An insult in one context became an offering in the other: the accent fell implicitly on the preposition *for*. A gesture of outreach, the "Colored" sign could also alert an agitated community that black-owned businesses were on their side: during the 1943 Harlem riots, African American proprietors hung hastily handmade "Colored Store" signs in their windows as a notice to looters to spare their stores.

This engagement with the community meant that commercial and racial signage were often interwoven. Rather than a separate "Colored" sign, race could be written into an establishment's name explicitly or implicitly—"The Pit Colored Café," "Al's Café for Colored," and "The Black Cat," for example. Color coding could also be more subtle, as in the use of *silver* as a substitute for black, a code derived from the practice of American engineers during the construction of the Panama Canal of paying Negro workers in silver, white workers in gold. This usage was appropriated as a form of self-designation by African Americans in the South in names like "The Silver Moon Café" and "The Silver Dollar Finest Colored Club." Color could also be expressed in adjectival form—the Silver Moon Café advertises itself as a "colorful restaurant"—or through a proper name—the Booker Tea Washington Café. Signifying on race was a way to convert a stigma into a component of communal conversation and play. In these contexts, the mass-produced "Colored" signs rarely were displayed, and segregation statutes were certainly not cited.

Such practices had real liabilities, however, for they meant that African American attempts to defend the boundaries of their segregated world, to consolidate its potential as a safe and nurturing space, had little state sanction or support. As a result, the adverb *only* was frequently invoked: "For Colored Only" signs were as common on African American hamburger joints, taxi cab companies, movie theaters, or rooming houses as they were uncommon on "Colored" entries to white-owned facilities. Putting teeth into that *only* required stronger measures, however. A hand-painted "Colored Only" sign posted, ostensibly for the benefit of both races, on a juke joint for migratory workers in the Belle Glades region of Florida was reinforced with the words "Police Order." "Colored" space, then, was at once all too public—its boundaries were permeable, undefended, so vulnerable to trespass that they

SO WHAT? — — — — By Jay Jackson

"... But I'm not! I got this tan out at the beach."

FIGURE 8. Cartoon, *Chicago Defender,* July 7, 1945. Courtesy of the *Chicago Defender.*

needed police protection—and external to the public, beyond the statutory safe-guards of the public will.

Institutions with greater economic clout could assert their boundaries more confidently. The boldest strategy was to turn the tables by deploying the signs' structuring conventions and formulas in reverse. In the sign commissioned from the Ace Sign Company by the black-owned Lenox Theater in Augusta, Georgia, the color terms are switched in two standard (and redundant) formulas uttered in the traditional passive voice that indicates authority is speaking from elsewhere (figure 9). The theater seized the structure of the sign in a strongly worded double address to imaginary white readers behind the primary audience; a more common alternative was to deploy visual cues directed at insiders. Although white sign producers made

FIGURE 9. Lenox Theater sign, Augusta, Georgia.

deliberate choices of materials to match specific settings (wood for railroad stations, Tiffany glass for high-class restaurants), the goal was less to communicate information visually than to create an aesthetically harmonious environment, especially under the pressure of a modernist aesthetic that encouraged harmonizing all signage with other design features.[12] African American sign makers, however, devised ingenious strategies for implying visually what could not be verbalized overtly.

These strategies become apparent in the contrast between two signs, one produced by the county, the other by the black community, for Florida beaches at which African Americans gained the right to swim in the 1930s and '40s. The sign for Virginia Beach, marking a victory gained in 1945 after six African Americans staged a swim-in to establish access to a beach in Dade County, is a minimalist concession of territory that specifies simply the name of the county, the beach, and the message "Colored Only." The sign for American Beach, established in the 1930s by the Afro-American Life Insurance Company in Jacksonville, which created a recreation area for its members by buying property on an isolated stretch of beach on an island north of Jacksonville, is a suggestive emblem produced by a financially secure, proud, and resourceful community (figure 10).[13]

The sign both embraces and teases the color line. That autonomy could cohabit with a claim to nationality is asserted in the community's self-presentation as first and foremost an American beach that is secondarily a "playground" for African Americans. Here, the iconography suggests, signifying is one form of play. The swordfish on the left, its elongated body and jaw reclining on and extending almost the length of the word *American,* appears more the subject than the object of aggressive sport. On this American beach, the fished (the hunted, the hounded, the pursued, and the persecuted) are transformed into the fisher, whose sword is aimed directly at a light-skinned bathing beauty in a two-piece bathing suit. This reclamation of phallic potency, this fishing license that resists the relentless desexualization of African Americans in commercially produced iconography of perpetual childhood and happy servitude, points along the reclaimed stretch of beach to the

FIGURE 10. Sign from American Beach, Florida. Photograph courtesy Stetson Kennedy and Southern Labor Archives, Special Collections Department, Georgia State University.

racially ambiguous American girl whose turned back defines her more as prey than as playmate—prey that, stepping off the sign, gestures outward like the figurehead she resembles toward a less circumscribed field of play.

. . .

Opportunities for invention expanded dramatically after the signs were carried quite literally into the next chapter of their biography through the determination and fore-sight of the people they were designed to control. It is a chapter characterized by two interrelated developments: as the signs migrated from the field of production to that of consumption, there was a corollary shift from white to black predomi-nance in the collection of black memorabilia. The heroic mode of covert con-sumption yielded quickly to more conventional and therefore controversial con-sumer practices fostered by a marketplace willing to supply copies of signs whose shrinking supply of originals could not keep pace with a growing demand.

Jim Crow signs did not disappear overnight: indeed, signs of those signs con-tinue to linger as evidence of a system that was haphazardly repurposed rather than radically purged. Succumbing to the pressures of the civil rights movement, the sig-nage gradually disappeared through the 1960s and 1970s (occasionally lingering into the 1980s). It was sometimes sandblasted or painted over lightly in ways in-tended to keep the message legible, sometimes reinstated in less explicit forms, such as doors color-coded black or white, and sometimes partially dismantled but al-lowed to remain as broken but decipherable fragments (see figure 11). Some traces are still visible in the built environment, as symmetrical holes drilled into the mar-ble surface above drinking fountains; as decentered or redundant restrooms that betray their prior duplication by race; as ceilings lowered in theaters to conceal a segregated bank of upper seats; and as insipid messages on adjacent waiting rooms, such as "Safety First," whose primary function appears to be filling in the blank space left by painted-over segregation signs. As these traces became increasingly obscure, the signs themselves became increasingly difficult to find. Typically produced on perishable materials (paper and cardboard more often than metal, glass, or wood), most of them rapidly deteriorated after they were taken down, as the progressive Southern writer Stetson Kennedy poignantly describes: "I raced around to dumpsters collecting discarded 'White' and 'Colored' signs, thinking they would be of some interest to posterity in a Museum of Horrors. Alas, I stored them under my house, where termites got them, which may be just as well."[14]

As a Southern white, Kennedy was unusual, and perhaps unusually careless in his habits. Although his experience is undoubtedly representative of that of countless other ambivalent sign retrievers—in conjunction with that of the intentional sign destroyers who, whether out of anger, bitterness, triumph, or shame, worked to make these hateful reminders disappear—there were also some determined and deliberate collectors and preservers. We owe the preservation of the few remaining original signs almost entirely to the courage of a generation of African Americans who came of age during the civil rights movement and who collected the signs as a form of activism. Acquiring the signs in the final years of their regime literally required activism. The collectors risked jail to lift them surreptitiously from buses under cover of darkness; pilfered them from hotels or restaurants in which African Americans were employed; snatched them from trash cans after they were taken down by law; or returned to abandoned buildings, gutted by natural disasters, to detach them from walls still reeking of smoke. Those with less audacity but equal foresight scoured flea markets and yard sales for the signs that others had collected, stored in attics, and eventually discarded. For some, the encounter with a sign triggered the passion for collecting; for others, especially for college students raised in the North, the sign became a prize possession to bring back home.[15] By retrieving these tools of subjugation, these activist collectors—Certeau-style consumers—turned segregation signs around to testify against their makers.

This generation changed the character and cast of collecting black memorabilia. Since the late eighteenth century there has been an industry in black-themed mass-produced souvenirs, novelties, toys, kitchen items, dolls, and ceramic figurines, all characterized by the literal and figurative diminishment of African Americans. This market, however, was driven by a white middle class eager to fill its homes with iconographic evidence of its own superiority. Only as that desire came under fire did African Americans begin to seek to "keep the memory alive" before it was too attenuated, to preserve a record of what was "all true . . . to understand why it was done."[16] As this era receded further into a tenuous memory, the drive to collect its material remains became increasingly urgent. By the close of the twentieth century,

FIGURE 11. Painted-over "White Men" sign. Southern Conference Educational Fund (SCEF) Collection, Special Collections and Archives, Georgia State University Library.

the number of African American collectors had tripled to approximately fifty thousand; the number of museums of African American history had increased from approximately a dozen in the 1960s to approximately a hundred by the late 1990s; a rash of websites dedicated to assessing the value and sources of black memorabilia had been newly constructed; and the field had shifted definitively from white to African American leadership. Jeanette Carson founded the Black Memorabilia Collectors Association in 1984 to educate and encourage African Americans to collect their own history, to recognize the value of what they already owned, and to retain their collections in the face of increasingly seductive financial incentives. She notes that African Americans made up 50 to 70 percent of collectors by the end of the century, as opposed to 30 percent when the association was formed.[17] Although the economic downturn of the early twenty-first century has slowed this activity, it has not altered the racial balance of the collectors.

During this transitional chapter of their biography, Jim Crow signs continued to function as racial markers. Whether accomplished by theft, purchase, or inheritance, African American possession of these signs implies some narrative of agency, which may be one reason why some white antique dealers in the South who are happy to sell African Americans a variety of "cute little things"—Aunt Jemima cookie jars and Sambo salt and pepper shakers, the Pickaninny Peppermints and the Gold Dust twins—prefer selling "seriously derogatory racist stuff," such as slave documents and Jim Crow signs, to other white dealers and collectors, who (according to one account) hawk these items among themselves like pornography in backroom deals.[18] In their new locations, the signs measure the space between their attempts at definition and their failure to define. Clarence Page, a journalist for the *Chicago Tribune,* owns a "Colored Waiting Room" sign that he bought in a memorabilia shop for seventy-five dollars twenty years ago and refuses to sell despite the fivefold increase in its current value. He explains: "This symbol of our past subjugation has become something of a trophy of triumph in our struggle of memory against forgetting. . . . Designed to enforce white supremacy, these old relics possessed by new owners now expose its folly."[19] Marking a place in time as well as space, this sign carries a special charge that made it a privileged object of African American photographers' attention (as the next chapter shows): to own the "Colored Waiting Room" sign is to announce that the wait is over.

Collecting, as Jean Baudrillard and others tell us, is intrinsically an act of resignification. As objects are plucked from one context and repositioned in a different one, they cease to be defined by their function and are redefined in relation to a new set of conditions. It is the collector rather than the producer who determines their meaning by defining the new frame. This displacement from a context of use to one of ownership usually elicits a psychoanalytic reading of a dream of narcissistic plenitude or an anthropological account of Western habits of acquiring objects from vulnerable cultures and transferring them into structures of display that annihilate their original purposes and histories (as well as the manner and meaning of their acquisition).[20] In the contexts of connoisseurship and cultural plunder, collecting is regularly and rightly viewed as a symptom of possessive individualism, whether personal or cultural, but political collections perform a different function.

This function is well named by Whoopi Goldberg, who has mounted her collection of black memorabilia on what she calls her "Wall of Shame." In a calculated shift of context, scattered Jim Crow signs and other testimony to discrimination are gathered together to amass a burden of proof. The wall negotiates a complex temporality. The spatialization of items from different eras assimilates them to a common temporal frame, but the dehistoricization that is a liability of collecting has a productive function here. Without entirely yielding their specific histories, objects in these collections offer them up to a synchronic present that bars the past by so powerfully representing it. These Jim Crow signs retain a monitory function in the service of their new owners: by keeping the past in sight, they ward off its return. They become, in the words of Julian Bond, one of the most passionate and eloquent collectors, "sentinels guarding the past, doorkeepers who prevent our ever returning to it, harsh—if even sometimes beautiful—preservers of the history we have overthrown. . . . They are our common past; silently, they face the future. They have lost the power to define my world; they have taken on the power to create a new one."[21]

Bond's own collection includes only two Jim Crow signs (three if we count the anomalous American Beach sign discussed above), a characteristically tiny percentage.[22] In spite of their scarcity, however, such signs play an important symbolic role in African American collections. By contrast, white-authored catalogues of black memorabilia typically display a strong bias in favor of figural items and either omit the signs entirely or give them a marginal entry under "miscellaneous" or "paper collectibles." It is perhaps unsurprising that the signs' function of exposing racism would make them loaded items for catalogues produced by and seemingly for white collectors, who are driven more by nostalgia than by political witnessing, but with some poetic justice, this function persists when they appear inside this frame.[23] For some of these catalogues (the ones by women are the worst) shamelessly reproduce the power relations of the past. "Which items of black memorabilia you collect is all a matter of taste," explains Jan Lindenberger in her introduction to *Black Memorabilia around the House.* "I personally love it all, but I tend to lean toward the kitchen items. (The smiling mammies in my kitchen brighten my day.)"[24] Her choice and presentation of Jim Crow signs are equally revealing. By selecting and centering an unusually decorative 1940s pair and strategically eliminating the counterparts for whites, the catalogue displays the signs for "colored men" and "colored women" as if they were a tribute instead of an affront. Placed above a pair of mammy and butler candles, the signs construct the colored couple as happy household servants presiding over an entourage of little black children in the form of candles, candy dishes, and Christmas-tree ornaments. This is a plantation fantasy (disguised as miscellany) sufficiently expansive to include a badge of membership in the Ku Klux Klan and a pricey statue of a Klan wizard (his arm detachable to facilitate transportation).

A slightly less egregious instance of the signs' transformation into domestic kitsch appears in Kyle Husfloen's *Black Americana Price Guide,* where the category of "signs" functions as a plausible bridge from theatrical posters to slave documents in the list of items for sale under the rubric of "paper collectibles." There are only two kinds of sign, however, as the visual display makes clear: Jim Crow signs—one set priced between $500 and $1,000 and the second at $40—and advertisements for "Pillsbury's Best" and "O'Baby Chocolate Dairy Drink," a juxtaposition that effectively equates the pair *colored* and *white* with chocolate and vanilla. Even more-reputable catalogues treat the signs as decorative items rather than as historical artifacts. Douglas Congdon-Martin, for example, whose *Images in Black: 150 Years of Black Collectibles* is one of the few catalogs to allocate a couple of pages to "Jim Crow," in a category titled "Flat Art" in the section "For the Home," misattributes the Lenox

Theater's important "Colored Only/No Whites Allowed" sign (see figure 9) to a non-existent Knox Theater because he has not bothered to remove the sign from a frame that crops off the first two letters of the theater's name.

A note on two African American collections, one private, one public, may sharpen the contrast. Although these are not commercial operations, and they therefore inevitably disregard the categories devised for marketing, their emphasis on the power relations that framed the production of domestic iconography is strong enough to warrant comparison. In a wall from the Museum in Black in Los Angeles (Brian Breyé's personal collection), for example, Jim Crow signs are interspersed with Aunt Jemima dolls and advertisements for products such as Black Jeff coal and Gold Dust washing powder under a rod contrived to hold a grinning hobo dangling in the air. The allusion to a lynching transforms the grin—splashed across the wall in virtually every ad—into a grimace. Coercion becomes explicit in the APEX (African American Panoramic Experience) Museum, dedicated to the history of black Atlanta. Here, signs for "White Only" and "Colored Only" are radically displaced from the domestic sphere and replaced in the framework of terror: sole items in an expressionistic setting whose painted patterns and shades of black, white, and grey evoke walls dripping with blood for which the signs, hung beneath gunlike metal rods, appear responsible.

. . .

Despite a shared political purpose, African American collectors are a heterogeneous group, as the last two examples indicate, and the differences among them are both heightened and confused as the field is flooded by reproductions. The noncommercially produced "White" sign at the center of the wall of the Museum in Black, based, like the Jim Crow Museum of Racist Memorabilia, on the decades-long effort of an individual collector, has no counterpart in the APEX Museum, which, like many of the African American history museums founded in the 1980s and '90s, has had to rely on reproductions of the signs, some reconstructed painstakingly from archival photographs, others inexpensive commercial copies.[25] The originals that activists salvaged, their value enhanced by the transgressive acts embedded in their acquisition, have become so rare and consequently precious—worth as much as two thousand dollars when their provenance is known, which is a higher price than most slave documents command—that they are either unavailable or unaffordable to all but the wealthiest collectors, a market increasingly dominated by celebrities (Whoopi Goldberg, Bill and Camille Cosby, Cicely Tyson, Oprah Winfrey, Alan Page, Anita Baker, Sammy Davis Jr., Spike Lee, Magic Johnson, and Juanita Jordan among them), for whom they constitute a badge of membership in a historical community of race.[26]

Because this desire is not confined to celebrities, however, an industry in reproductions has emerged. Some are offered by profiteers who exploit the desire for scarce originals by devising strategies for making recent copies appear old. Their tactics range from the fairly transparent practices of punching holes in metal signs to make them look as if they had been hung on walls and soaking paper reproductions in coffee to turn them brown to higher-tech procedures, such as placing paper in smokehouses or special low-temperature ovens injected with an acidic mixture of gases to accelerate oxidation and aging. Some dealers also capitalize on the early discovery of undistributed or returned Jim Crow signs in company warehouses, shortly after the demand for them declined, by placing phony announcements of hot new warehouse finds in trade journals for antiques.[27]

This industry in fake authenticity, which commands prices lower than certifiable originals but higher than acknowledged reproductions, is driven by the growth of a black middle class with discretionary income to invest in memorabilia, a situation that has led cultural critics such as Gerald Early and Lynn Casmier-Paz to decry what they consider a "bourgeois investment pastime" on the part of a "privileged class."[28] This is not the only class eager to purchase such items, however, and a different kind of product has been devised for buyers of more modest means and aspirations. Although concerns about legislative and social pressure against the dissemination of racist materials have shrouded this industry in secrecy (notwithstanding a widespread belief that it is based primarily in Asia), their inexpensive products, reproductions of mass-produced signs typically priced at fifteen to twenty-five dollars, are easy to find in second-hand stores (indeed, the examples at the beginning of this chapter are readily available versions of these products).[29] Sometimes appearing as minimalist messages without authorizing tags, sometimes in creative reinventions that introduce misspellings and fictional dates, sometimes in multiple variations with differing degrees of specificity, these popular simulacra both attenuate historical accuracy and replenish historical memory, especially in communities with limited access to originals.[30]

Reproductions of segregation signs occupy an important niche in secondhand stores that double as information centers, operated by ordinary citizens turned street educators. Their shops, often located in the heart of the ghetto, function as improvised museums and alternative-history centers, repositories of knowledge both arcane and mundane, meeting places and resource centers that provide a hands-on education in material culture, from segregation artifacts to movie posters, baseball cards, and old copies of *Ebony,* along with local bus and movie schedules.[31] Often history buffs who have gathered their diverse merchandise over many years from many locales and who can recount each item's story in detail, these collector-proprietors also perform the role of organic intellectuals who prod casual shoppers, browsers, kibbitzers, hangers-on, and people who have come in from the rain to wait for buses into an encounter with things whose juxtaposition composes an account of history.

During the prosperous 1990s, the expanding market for black memorabilia could be tapped more directly through a new kind of store designed to meet a new consumer desire. That inexpensive replicas of Jim Crow signs were, for a range of sometimes contradictory reasons, prime objects of that desire is clear in the retailing decisions of one of the most controversial, well-documented, and (for more than a decade) successful of these: Martha's Crib, an Afrocentric art, crafts, and memorabilia store that captured the attention of the national media as well as the Chicago press through its strategies for catering to an African American clientele in urban communities west of Chicago from 1994 to 2005. Uncertain whether Jim Crow signs would offend her customers, its proprietor, Marchel'le Renise Barber, polled them; almost all urged her to produce the signs and asked to be placed on a waiting list to ensure that they would be among the first to own one. Because not only the originals but also *copies* of the signs were by then in short supply, Barber expanded her selection of merchandise by designing her own line: the Martha's Crib Jim Crow Sign Series.[32]

This development is a striking example of historical reversal and continuity: almost a century after Jim Crow signs were produced by and for white businesses, they were being commissioned and designed by an African American business to meet the demand of African American customers motivated, in contrast to the collectors of the 1960s, less to memorialize than to perpetuate their pain. A generation that, as children, was shielded from the signs' wounding force by parents who steered them away from places where the signs were displayed is now seeking out replicas to transmit that wound to their children and grandchildren. Although this impulse to "leave things for the next generation . . . to let our children know that this happened" is a product of the same historical moment that has fueled the recent spate of African American memoirs written for a generation for whom, as Henry Louis Gates Jr. puts it in *Colored People,* the primary reference of *colored* is a box of crayons, it enacts a more aggressive relation to a segregated past whose reconstruction is vulnerable to the hazy glow of memory.[33] The choice of signs is an index of this function: whereas *colored* is the key word in the titles of the printed texts, a tag for an intact and nurturing community that integration undermined, its opposite holds that place in the marketplace of signs. Marchel'le Barber, whose store was dedicated to keeping alive the pain of the past for a generation that had "no sense of history and no sense of hurt," initially planned to reproduce only one or two of the "less offensive" (presumably "For Colored") signs. Her plan changed when an African American man insisted that he wanted to buy a "White Only" sign in order "to hang it in his house outside his bathroom so his teenage son might be able to relate to the experience of needing to go to the bathroom—but not having anyplace he could go." That forged Barber's determination to "go all the way": not only to produce the sign in her Jim Crow Sign Series, but also to hang it outside the bathroom of her own condominium.[34] The disciplining of the body by the "Colored" sign was now administered by a "White" sign in the hands of African Amer-

FIGURE 12. Examples from the Martha's Crib Jim Crow Sign Series.

icans seeking to imprint an endangered dimension of their racial heritage on the nerves and flesh of a younger generation.

In a further ironic twist, the sign's very materiality was altered, along with the racial label it enforced. The "White Only" sign that Barber designed to meet the demand of her customers is, like the rest of her series, openly fake. Barber, who deplores and exposes the practices of unscrupulous dealers who attempt to pass copies off as originals, was scrupulous about marking her signs as reproductions. Although she meticulously imitated the lettering, shapes, colors, and borders of the originals, she stamped her versions "Historical Reproduction" and sold them at only ten dollars apiece (see figure 12). She also stamped them with the name of the store, the copyright symbol, and date. Her signature replaced that of the companies that commissioned and produced the originals: it is not the white sign producers who sign the copies of their signs, but their African American reproducer. As white historical production became black historical reproduction, the date of the ordinance on the originals was displaced by the date of the copyright. Ownership changed hands, but what exactly was now owned? It was not the original object or language, but the copy that was copyrighted, reserving to Martha's Crib the exclusive right to continue to make copies. The copy, apparently, is an original, a form of intellectual property, whose originality resides in its conception and execution as a copy. As a copyrighted copy, however, it makes a different claim on its viewers. The claim to private ownership that is registered by the copyright symbol also marks the copy of the sign with the sign of the published text. As the ordinance that stamped the signs with the weight of the public is replaced by the copyright that stamps them as private property, the signature of the author-producer is severed from the social body, and the sign that was replicated to keep alive an experience of the body takes the disembodied form of a text and a commodity.

With such an attenuated weight of history, what can these signs impress upon the body? One answer might be provided by a closely associated product. For one of the many media stories on Martha's Crib, Barber posed with some of her stock: a variety of figurines, two Jim Crow signs (one from her own line, the other a standard reproduction), and her most controversial product—slave shackles redesigned as jewelry (figure 13). Adapted for contemporary use, the shackles and the signs are similarly designed both to subject contemporary bodies to the burden of the past and to assert a victory over that past by displaying its symbols as trophies or ornaments. Slave shackles are Jim Crow signs' immediate antecedent: as slavery became segregation, the shackles became signs whose control of the body was verbal rather than physical. The photograph translates temporal into spatial continuity: the "Colored Waiting Room" sign that juts at right angles into Barber's chest is connected to the elbow of the forearm that she raises to display the bracelet/shackle in a clench-fisted echo of the Black Power salute in which this narrative culminates. The body is shaped by what it wears: a less historically weighty bracelet would elicit a different modeling gesture (fingers gracefully extended instead of clenched, perhaps). That the link is more than accidental is suggested by its recurrence: Barber used an almost identical gesture to display the shackles in her website advertisement. Her expression is also consistent: the fixed, unsmiling gaze, lips sealed, eyes forward, seems a direct transmission from her ancestors through metal to her flesh. "When I held the slave shackle in my hands for the first time, I got a very chilling feeling. I imagined how my ancestors probably felt being stolen from their homes and taken to a country where they were looked upon with scorn and treated like property."[35] That chill is registered in Barber's frozen posture and face: the shackles design her body as well as the reverse, and Jim Crow signs are embedded in this exchange.

But is it the reproduction of *slavery* or the *reproduction* of slavery that produces the affectless expression and unanimated body that poses with the shackles and Jim Crow signs? The impassivity that expresses the chill of slavery also suggests another mode of alienation in which the copy reproduces the condition of a copy in those it reaches out to touch. Barber's stylized self-presentation—not just her body language, but her designer nail polish, makeup, hairstyle, and jewelry (the shackle/bracelet matched by the chain around her neck)—assimilates the producer to the products she designs. Her blankness and manicured exterior make her look as drained of life as the reproductions on her shelves. Instead of an exchange of painful embodiment, the relation of body to shackles is one of reciprocal disembodiment, which is also a deliberate feature of the bracelet/shackles' design, for the weight of history they carry is tempered not to overtax the contemporary body. The bracelet is designed not to lock, in order to demonstrate that these slave shackles never can enslave; it is also sized to fit comfortably (in small, medium, and large), to slip on and off the wrist easily, and to be lightweight, shiny and visually appealing. Unlike a set of ankle shackles Barber made for home display out of rough textured metal, intended to look worn and old and thus to manifest the historical weight they claim

FIGURE 13. Marchel'le Renise Barber in Martha's Crib. Photograph by Lloyd DeGrane. Courtesy Lloyd DeGrane and *Xavier* magazine.

to carry, the wrist shackles made for bodily display are of polished copper and are made to look attractive, to entice people to buy them. To buy or sell them, however, is to reproduce the profound alienation of human labor that was slavery; the price tag on the bracelet/shackle echoes in a minor key the price tag on the body. To make one's body a prop for the copy of what enforced the conversion of people to property is to place it in this chain of commodities.

Barber attempts to break this chain by securing the commodity's historical meaning. Attached to the last link of the copper chain on the shackle is a coin inscribed with the admonition "Never Forget." The copper chain is intended as a genealogical chain that connects the wearer with her ancestors, removing her from the circuit of commodities and placing her in the chain of history. In the photograph in which the producer models her product, however, the historical exhortation is eclipsed by the other economy into which the coin inevitably inserts her: an economy that rejoins the shackles to the signs. In the spatial logic of the image, these products are contiguous not only in a historical narrative of inscription on the body but also in an economic narrative of that inscription's recirculation as commodity. Sign and shackle are linked metonymically through salient and parallel parts: the coin on the shackle, the price tag on the sign, a bargain copy of the "Colored Waiting Room" sign that Clarence Page refused to part with for any price, are now a packaged and purchasable memory readily available for $22.99. At their outer edge, these crisp geometric shapes—shiny copper circle, bright red rectangle—stand out from their respective frames and reach out to each other in a new signifying chain. Partnered as items for sale, the replica of the sign and the replica of the shackle are implicated in a revised relation to the body. The embodied weight of the racial past becomes the deracinating imprint of the marketplace. A "retailer of revolution" used to be Barber's chosen moniker: "In my own way," she explained, "I am affecting change."[36] Perhaps some unconscious recognition of retailing's effect on revolution found expression in the slip of the tongue (as in the composition of the image): *affecting* change may be what marketing historical ornament is about.

. . .

Retailing history makes it available to anyone. Whereas the expensive original items represent and require a financial and emotional investment that restricts who will buy them, mass reproduction places replicas in general circulation. Barber has insisted on monitoring the uses of her own products by refusing to take phone or email orders, scrupulously guarding against the potential of misuse, but the other reproductions that are on the market travel outside any determinate political or interpretive frame and are as readily available for purchase in redneck as in African American stores. The "White Only" sign demanded by Barber's customers and displayed over her own bathroom to keep the pain of exclusion physically alive is as avidly sought after by whites to display over *their* bathrooms, swimming pools, and recreation rooms to keep the pleasure of entitlement symbolically alive. The meaning of the signs is entirely contextual, and the context of their acquisition as well as of their use spans antithetical constituencies. Inexpensive copies are for sale not only in high-profile racist stores such as the Redneck Shop of the Ku Klux Klan Museum in Laurens, South Carolina, which advertises signs such as "Public Swimming Pool White Only," "Colored Must Sit in Balcony," and "No Dogs Negroes Mexicans," but also in the garden-variety country stores that are a feature of backwoods communities such as Skullbone, Tennessee, whose inhabitants can undoubtedly find them alongside the popular "Equal Rights for Whites" T-shirts, Confederate flags, and Ku Klux Klan crosses. Over the past decade, the Internet has become a primary vehicle for disseminating white supremacist items.[37]

The African American investment in material evidence of segregation has fostered an industry in simulacra that serves opposing camps in opposing ways. This paradoxical effect has been intensified by the fact that signs of white privilege continue to be privileged among African Americans as well as among whites. Both groups want, for antithetical reasons, to preserve the record of white racism and consequently prefer the most blatantly discriminatory signs: indeed, "the most offensive" was Marchel'le Barber's criterion for choosing signs to stock, a yardstick qualified only by her fear of censure by the NAACP.[38] If African Americans wanted primarily "For Colored" signs, they would serve as a way of differentiating black ownership from white in an updated rendition of the racial division the signs themselves imposed. But it is not the Lenox Theater's "For Colored Only/No Whites Allowed" sign that is in most demand at African American stores, but the Lonestar Restaurant Association's outrageous "No Dogs Negroes Mexicans" sign that is a bestseller not only at the Redneck Shop of the Ku Klux Klan Museum, but also at Nightmares and Notions, a ghetto shop in Oakland, California, where it is the hands-down favorite among young African American and Chicano men who buy it to display in their pick-up trucks (see figure 52). A framed copy also hangs on the wall of the director's office at the Museum of African American Life and Culture in Dallas because, in his view, "these things send a message, and the more repulsive, the louder the message," a claim for the verbal field that seconds Clarence Page's claim for the visual field: "The more vile the stereotyping, the more outrageous the bug eyes and fat lips and big hips, the more the item finds itself cherished by some black collectors today. It's a black thing."[39] But a white one too.

In this chapter of their biography, Jim Crow signs depart from their defining frames to enter a mass marketplace that defies racial boundaries in subject matter as well as ownership. The more extreme the language, the more it lends itself to reappropriation—which also runs in both directions, as the display of racial superiority is parodically inverted, and then inverted back again. No sooner did a sign declaring, "Parking for African Americans only/All others will be towed/City Ord 1024" appear on the market, complete with a fictional ordinance number and manufacturer's name that mimic the conventions of Jim Crow signs, than copies of the copy sprang up to vaunt the rights of other minority, but hardly parallel, groups. Alamo Flags Company has offered variations on the template for (among many others) Greeks, Norwegians, Irish, Italians, Australians, Armenians, Serbians, Danes, and Swiss. Printed as much as possible in the colors of the national flag, the model has been deflected from racial to national groups that, however small their numbers in this country, could hardly be construed as oppressed. Indeed, the list has been constructed to occlude culturally sensitive racial and ethnic categories. There has been a "Parking for Mexicans Only" sign, but none for Chicanos; a "Parking for Chinese Only," but none for Asian Americans; a "Parking for Peruvians Only," but none for Latinos; a "Parking for Israelis Only," but no acknowledgment that Jews drive cars at all. The sign for African Americans that gave rise to the others designates the only racial category (and conversely, no African nationalities are named).[40] As soon as the parodic inversion was in place, it was translated into a less volatile form. Other features of the signs changed accordingly: as segregation ordinances became parking authorizations, their numbers evolved from the plausible 1024 on the African American sign to a fanciful 0007 on the Italian sign, a seeming allusion to James Bond, a superhero powerful enough to commandeer that most prized urban possession, a personal parking space. Signs are uncoupled from history, and bodies from identity. As racial difference is diluted into national origin and the struggle over social space devolves to the parking lot, the only bodies that matter are the mobile mechanical ones, stationed under the sign of nationality when it offers an advantage.

It is consequently tempting to call a halt and reserve our regard exclusively for signs authenticated by experts and housed in museums. The tension between the marketplace and the museum, between commercial dissemination and historical preservation, is endemic, social anthropologists tell us, to the biography of objects diverted by the marketplace from their original function.[41] The more potent the objects, the more powerful the pull toward enclaving them. The tools of segregation certainly qualify as highly charged and potent things, and the call to withdraw them from circulation has strong advocates. Perhaps the strongest is Lynn Casmier-Paz: "Preservation requires a museum where history becomes priceless, and painful memories and narratives are suspended behind glass—ostensibly beyond the reach of monetary exchange."[42] As her "ostensibly" seems to register, however, not only does monetary exchange continue to operate outside and indeed to penetrate inside the museum (for how else do objects end up there?), but the parallel between monetary exchange and the flux of memories and narratives unleashed by the circulation of affordable copies, especially of signs that function more as forceful memory triggers than as domestic items designed for whites, also calls into question the possibility and desirability of attempting to suspend history behind glass. The release and exchange of memories in community-based memorabilia stores offers an important counterweight to the authoritative history conserved by museums. As Mary Taylor, co-owner of Aunt Meriam's in Harlem, puts it: "The best things are the conversations." By transforming commodification into conversation, these stores function as *milieux de mémoire,* environments of memory reconstituted by the common touch of objects.[43] The historical meaning of Jim Crow signs does need to be enclaved, but in addition rather than in opposition to the questions and memories provoked by the circulation of copies.

As verbal things, Jim Crow signs occupy an especially delicate position in the trade-off between preserving and disrupting the burden of history. Their commodification does not simply exploit and trivialize the past, as does, for example, the commercialization of the names and faces of Martin Luther King and Rosa Parks; it also advances the destabilizing turn that was always implicit in the written signs by demonstrating that racial markers are neither anchored in the body nor suspended behind glass and beyond change. The intersection of money and race is generative as well as ugly because money is one medium through which the legacy of racial signs can be renegotiated. A more discriminating medium was provided by photography.

1. Charles W. Chesnutt, *The Marrow of Tradition* (1901; Ann Arbor: University of Michigan Press, 1969), 57.

2. James Forman, *The Making of Black Revolutionaries* (Washington, DC: Open Hand Publishing Inc., 1985), 20. For other narratives of defining childhood encounters with Jim Crow signs and regulations, see Sarah L. Delany and A. Elizabeth Delany, with Amy Hill Hearth, *Having Our Say: The Delany Sisters' First 100 Years* (New York: Dell, 1993), 95, 105; Pauli Murray, *Proud Shoes: The Story of an American Family* (New York: Harper & Row), 269–70; Mary Church Terrell, *A Colored Woman in a White World* (1940; Salem, NH: Ayer Press, 1986), 15; Louis Armstrong, *Satchmo: My Life in New Orleans* (New York: Prentice-Hall, 1954), 14–15; Richard Wright, *Black Boy: A Record of Childhood and Youth* (New York: Harper & Row, 1945), 41; Rosa Parks and Jim Haskins, *Rosa Parks: My Story* (New York: Dial Books, 1992); James Forman, *Sammy Younge Jr.: The First Black College Student to Die in the Black Liberation Movement* (New York: Grove Press, 1968), 55; Clifton L. Taulbert, *Once Upon a Time When We Were Colored* (Tulsa, OK: Council Oak Books, 1989), 19; and many of the

narratives included in *Remembering Jim Crow: African Americans Tell about Life in the Segregated South*, ed. William H. Chafe, Raymond Gavins, and Robert Korstad (New York: New Press, 2001).

3. Since Igor Kopytoff put this phrase into circulation (in "The Cultural Biography of Things: Commoditization as Process," in *The Social Life of Things: Commodities in Cultural Perspective*, ed. Arjun Appadurai [Cambridge: Cambridge University Press, 1986], 64–91), it has become a standard concept in cultural anthropology; see, for example, Susan M. Pearce, ed., *Interpreting Objects and Collections* (London: Routledge, 1994).

4. Some intersections between race making and the cultural biography of racist things have been theorized in terms of the uncanny. In "Reification, Reanimation, and the American Uncanny" (*Critical Inquiry* 32, no. 2 [Winter 2006], 175–207), which centers on the "revenge of the black collectible come to life" in Spike Lee's *Bamboozled* (New Line Productions, 2000), Bill Brown derives the "historical ontology congealed within" objects such as the Jolly Nigger Bank, "the most despised and most prized object of black memorabilia," from the ambiguous status of the slave as both person and object (183, 197, 199). In "Jim Crow Signs in Post–Civil Rights American Fiction," a paper delivered at the 2008 meeting of the Modern Language Association and reprised in his forthcoming book *Neo-segregation Narratives: Jim Crow Signs in Post–Civil Rights American Literature*, Brian J. Norman analyzes the "historical uncanny" staged by the representation of Jim Crow signs in post–civil rights fiction. Whereas emphasizing the return of the repressed directs attention to the unconscious dynamics sustaining the traffic in racist objects, *Signs of the Times* charts the ways race is reconfigured through the transformation and circulation of Jim Crow signs.

5. Michel de Certeau, *The Practice of Everyday Life*, trans. Steven Rendall (Berkeley: University of California Press, 1984), xii–xiii, xiv–xv, emphasis in original.

6. Cited by Anthony Ramirez, "Black Collectors Hate and Buy Them," *New York Times*, July 5, 2006. Pilgrim's position extends the critique of commodifying history that was launched by Theodor Adorno and Max Horkheimer in *The Dialectic of Enlightenment* (1947).

7. In his study of signs in public space, David M. Henkin argues that regulatory signs, and the notion of public authority on which they rest, did not develop in New York until the middle of the nineteenth century. See chapter 3 of *City Reading: Written Words and Public Spaces in Antebellum New York* (New York: Columbia University Press, 1998).

8. For some other specifications, see C. Vann Woodward, *The Strange Career of Jim Crow* (New York: Oxford University Press, 1955), 98, 116; Stetson Kennedy, *Jim Crow Guide: The Way It Was* (1959; Boca Raton: Florida Atlantic University Press, 1990), 179–84; Pauli Murray, *States' Laws on Race and Color* (Athens: Georgia University Press, 1997); and Katharine Du Pre Lumpkin, *The Making of a Southerner* (New York: Knopf, 1991 [1946]), 133.

9. Murray, *Proud Shoes*, 268. For the effect of graphic design on the message of presidential campaigns, see Scott Dadich, "What You See Is What You Get," *New York Times*, October 9, 2004, and the responses on October 13–14.

10. Chesnutt, *Marrow of Tradition*, 54.

11. Domingo Faustino Sarmiento, *Travels in the United States in 1847*, 56. cited in Henkin, *City Reading*, 55.

12. See, for example, Victoria Pedersen, "Photography and Modern Movement: Link, Loewy and the Roanoke Station," *Modernism* (Spring 2004), 100, available online at www

.modernismmagazine.com. Critics were well aware of the ways that modernist design contributed to legitimating segregation. Under the title "New N.O. Terminal: Chrome Jim Crow," a story in the *Southern Patriot* (February 1954) comments caustically on the ways that the "gaudy plastic placards—the latest in swank" recast outmoded racial signage in the image of the new.

13. The story of Virginia Beach is related in a 1974 interview with Anne M. Coleman at the Black Archives, History and Research Foundation of South Florida in Miami. The story of American Beach is presented at the exhibit "American Beach: A Haven in the Time of Storm" in Tallahassee, Florida, which includes an interview with MaVynee Oshun Betsch, the great-granddaughter of one of the company founders, who recalls: "We were never told about segregation. . . . We were just so proud that we had our own. It was a black pride thing."

14. Kennedy, *Jim Crow Guide*, 234.

15. See Phyllis Speidell, "Suffolk Man Collects Relics of Racism," *Virginia Pilot*, September 4, 2001, www.ferris.edu/news/jimcrow/links/collector/; Douglas Martin, "Constance Baker Motley, 84, Civil Rights Trailblazer, Lawmaker and Judge, Dies," *New York Times,* September 29, 2005.

16. Brian Breyé, founder of the Museum in Black, interview, Los Angeles, March 2000. Thomas C. Bridge, cited by Sylvia Charmaine in "Dr. Thomas C. Bridge's Live-in Museum," *About . . . Time,* February 1990, 12.

17. Jeanette Carson is cited by Carol Hernandez, "Black Memorabilia Finds Big Demand," *Wall Street Journal* August 10, 1992; Karen Lee Ziner, "Collecting Items of a Hurtful History," *Providence Journal,* www.projo.com/special/black/blk.htm; Dick Friz, "Black Memorabilia & Artifacts Show," *Maine Antique Digest,* September 1997; Mike Karsnak, "Black (Bric-a-Brac) Is Beautiful and Has Educational Value," *Star-Ledger* (Newark, NJ) December 23, 2005, www.ferris.edu/news/jimcrow/links/bricabrac.htm; P. J. Gibbs, *Black Collectibles Sold in America* (Paducah, KY: Collector Books, 1987), 6–8; and Gerald Early, "Collecting 'The Artificial Nigger': Race and American Material Culture," in *The Culture of Bruising: Essays on Prizefighting, Literature, and Modern American Culture* (Hopewell, NJ: Ecco Press, 1994), 160–62.

18. Chuck McDew, telephone conversation June 24, 1997. He also suggested that shame is another motive for the reluctance of some whites to sell racist material to African Americans.

19. Clarence Page, "Collecting Memory," *NewsHour Online*, Public Broadcasting Service, May 30, 1996(www.pbs.org/newshour/essays/page_5-29.html), and "Post–O. J. America Needs to Get Past Symbols," *AZ Republic,* February 12, 1997. In "Buying History: Top Dollars for Collectibles," *BET Week End Magazine* (http://msbet.rocketworks.com/content/life/1412.asp), Angela Dodson notes that a Jim Crow sign from 1931 stating "We Serve Colored Carry Out Only" sold for $805 at an annual black memorabilia show at the Swann Gallery in New York in 2000.

20. The key psychoanalytic account is Jean Baudrillard, "The System of Collecting," in *The Cultures of Collecting,* ed. John Elsner and Roger Cardinal (Cambridge, MA: Harvard University Press, 1994), 7–24. In *On Longing: Narratives of the Miniature, the Gigantic, the Souvenir, the Collection* (Durham, NC: Duke University Press, 1993), 151–69, Susan Stewart also emphasizes the subjective dynamics and dimensions of collecting; her implicit critique becomes explicit when the collector is a member of a Western culture appropriating

artifacts from indigenous cultures. The anthropological critique has been mounted force-fully by James Clifford in *The Predicament of Culture: Twentieth-Century Ethnography, Literature, and Art* (Cambridge, MA: Harvard University Press, 1988), 187–254.

21. Julian Bond, "Collecting Black Americana," *Black Americana Price Guide*, ed. Kyle Husfloen (Dubuque, MN: Antique Trader Books, 1996), vii, ix.

22. Julian Bond, personal communication, January 6, 1998. Out of the thousands of artifacts collected over many years by Phillip Merrill (the owner of Nandy Jack & Co, an organization that researches, collects, and exhibits black artifacts), only one is a Jim Crow sign (telephone conversation, June 23, 1997). James Allen, whose persistence and skill in uncovering relics of the racist past captured national attention through his exhibit of lynching postcards, owns only two Jim Crow signs, although he has been searching for about twenty years (telephone conversation, June 4, 1998). Skip Mason, director of Digging It Up, an African American research and consulting firm in Atlanta, has no Jim Crow signs, which are, in his words, "extremely hard to come by" and prohibitively expensive (telephone conversation, December 9, 1997). Dusty Rose, who advertises "all types of collectible Black Americana for sale" in her Brooklyn shop, confirms that no original signs have been on the market for a long time (telephone conversation, June 12, 1998). Sallie Hurt of ETC Collectibles, who has been collecting black memorabilia for forty years, makes the same observation (telephone conversation, February 27, 1998).

23. For a typology of collectors determined by their motives (nostalgia, investment, liberation, education), see the DVD produced by David Pilgrim of the Jim Crow Museum of Racist Memorabilia. Although Pilgrim does not differentiate these categories along racial lines, it seems clear that the first two motives prevail among white collectors and the second two among African Americans.

24. Jan Lindenberger, *Black Memorabilia around the House* (Atglen, PA: Schiffer Publishing, 1993), 7. Although a particularly egregious example, it is on a continuum with catalogues by other white women. See, for example, Jackie Young, *Black Collectibles: Mammy and Her Friends* (Atglen, PA: Schiffer Publishing, 1991).

25. Florence Davis-Wilson, director of public relations at the Birmingham Civil Rights Institute, noted that the Institute was unable to obtain original Jim Crow signs and used reproductions in its display (interview, July 17, 1997). Even the Black Memorabilia Collectors Association, reluctant to lend its rare originals out for display, commissions copies for its educational exhibits.

26. Phillip Merrill is the source of the figure for researchable signs (telephone conversation, June 23, 1997). Slave papers are rarely priced at more than $1,000 in the *Black Americana Price Guide* and often at considerably less. On the function of the signs as a badge of cultural membership, see Zachary Pincus-Roth, "Next on His Docket: A Supreme Challenge," *New York Times*, April 27, 2008, on the actor Laurence Fishburne. The risks of investing in this cultural membership are dramatized by Spike Lee in his 2000 film *Bamboozled*.

27. I thank Thomas C. Bridge for the tip about the coffee, Dan Williams for the account of the confection ovens, and Rose Fontanella for the clue about the phony warehouse ads. For a broader discussion of "counterfeit antiques," see David Pilgrim, "New Racist Forms: Jim Crow in the 21st Century," Jim Crow Museum of Racist Memorabilia at Ferris State University, www.ferris/edu/news/jimcrow/newforms/.

28. Early, "Collecting 'The Artificial Nigger,'" 155–62; Lynn Casmier-Paz, "Heritage, Not Hate? Collecting Black Memorabilia," *Southern Cultures* 9, no. 1 (Spring 2003), 43–61. See also Julian Bond's response to Casmier-Paz in that volume, 62, and the conversation among Michael Harris, L. Bowery Sims, and Karen C. C. Dalton, "The Past Is Prologue but Is Parody and Pastiche Progress? A Conversation," *International Review of African American Art* 14, no. 3 (1997), 17–30.

29. Although they would not reveal the sources of their merchandise, many of the store owners I interviewed expressed the belief that reproductions were made in Asia. Production centers for other kinds of black memorabilia are located in Japan, Germany, China, England, France, Australia, and parts of Africa, according to Gibbs in *Black Collectibles* and LaCheryl B. Cillie and Yolanda White Powell in *From Darkness to Light: A Modern Guide to Recapturing Historical Riches* (Birmingham, AL: Creative Inspirations, Ltd, 1997). In *Tourists of History: Memory, Kitsch, and Consumerism from Oklahoma City to Ground Zero* (Durham, NC: Duke University Press, 2007), Marita Sturken notes the Asian production of America's favorite memory objects. The vexed relation between history ad memory has generated considerable recent debate. For some assessments, see "Memory and Counter Memory," special issue of *Representations* 26 (Spring 1989), and Andreas Huyssen, *Present Pasts: Urban Palimpsests and the Politics of Memory* (Stanford, CA: Stanford University Press, 2003).

30. On the dangers of inferring historical information from contemporary reproductions, see Richard Jensen about a related case in "'No Irish Need Apply': A Myth of Victimization," *Journal of Social History* 32, no. 2 (2002), 405–29.

31. Some examples of urban stores that double as information centers are Virgil Mayberry's V.J.M. Unlimited, Inc., in Rock Island, Illinois; Dan Williams's Nightmares and Notions in Oakland, California; Mary and Glenda Taylor's Aunt Merriam's in Harlem; and Rose Fontanella's Dusty Rose in Brooklyn.

32. I am grateful to Marchel'le Renise Barber for sharing information about the store, which closed in 2005 in response to the economic downturn that reduced the market for memorabilia. In our most recent conversation (August 19, 2008), Barber also noted that she no longer includes Jim Crow signs in the merchandise she sells at art fairs, where she cannot control the interpretive framework as she could in her own store.

33. Mildred Franklin, former president of the Black Memorabilia Collectors' Association, telephone conversation, December 16, 1997; Henry Louis Gates Jr., *Colored People* (New York: Vintage, 1994). African American interest in Jim Crow signs represents an edgy relation to the "memory markets" that Andreas Huyssen analyzes in *Present Pasts*.

34. Cited in Maureen Jenkins, "Crafting a Positive Image: Store Owner Offers Lessons in History," *Chicago Sun-Times*, December 19, 1997. The request for the "White Only" sign was reported in "The Martha's Crib 1996 Jim Crow Sign Series," an article posted on the store's former website. The sign in her bathroom is described by Lisa Lenoir in "At Home with . . . Shop Owner Marchel'le R. Barber," *Chicago Sun-Times*, December 19, 1997.

35. Quoted in Danielle Hirsch, "Merchant Unshackles Past with Jewelry," *Star* (Chicago), October 1998. See also Nicole Stil, "Shackles Make Debatable Statement," *Chicago Tribune*, December 27, 1998.

36. Cited by Jenkins in "Crafting a Positive Image."

37. The Redneck Shop of the Ku Klux Klan Museum, which opened in 1996, appears to

have survived repeated protests and a lawsuit brought by the Rev. David Kennedy in 2008. On country stores, see Neil Strauss, "Concerts Rock the Tiny Kingdom of Skullbonia," *New York Times,* June 1, 2001; on the Internet, see Pilgrim, "New Racist Forms." I am grateful to Virgil Mayberry and Chuck McDew for information about white interest in Jim Crow signs.

38. Interview with Marchel'le Barber, March 3, 2001.

39. Information about the sign's popularity at Nightmares and Notions is from an interview with its owner, Dan Williams (January 13, 1998). The museum director's claim is cited by Hernandez in "Black Memorabilia Finds Big Demand." Clarence Page's comments are from "Collecting Memory." Similarly, David Pilgrim notes that "signs that have obvious derogatory racist words are the most expensive" (e-mail, February 27, 2003).

40. As of the most recent check, Alamo Flags (www.flagline.com) has dropped the "Parking for African Americans" sign and lists among its offerings only "Country Parking Signs." There are still no African nationalities on its list.

41. Arjun Appadurai, "Introduction: Commodities and the Politics of Value," and Kopytoff, "Cultural Biography of Things," in Appadurai, *The Social Life of Things,* 3–90.

42. Casmier-Paz, "Heritage, Not Hate," 56.

43. Conversation with Mary Taylor, November 10, 2006. Pierre Nora, "Between Memory and History: *Les lieux de mémoire,*" *Representations* 26 (Spring 1989), 7–25. One such conversation involved an African American man in his sixties whose encounter with a reproduction of a "For Colored Only" sign at Aunt Meriam's triggered a memory of bringing the entire football team of Grambling State University to a Louisiana coffee shop for the pleasure of watching the white owner break their dishes after they left (Ramirez, "Black Collectors Hate and Buy Them").

Post-reading Questions

1. How has the writing of American history changed over time?

2. Based on the Gaines reading, how might one define the period from the end of the civil rights movement to the end of the Obama presidency?

3. Why is it important to understand the visual culture of segregation in the United States?

4. What was at the heart of the United States' obsession with creating separate social spheres for Blacks and Whites?

5. Does segregation, whether formal or informal, still exist in the United States? If so, does it have "signs"?

UNIT 3

AMERICAN CULTURE

Because the bodies of people of color and of women are constantly being appraised by others outside their race and gender communities, issues surrounding beauty and aesthetics routinely rise to the surface—and stay there. These issues include valuation of skin tone, hair length, hair texture, body type, and physical endowments. This third unit in *Intersections* invites discussion of these deeply personal and powerful topics.

While American beauty culture keeps women, in general, chasing unattainable beauty standards, these standards are especially hostile to the creation of positive self-images among many women of color. Tamara Winfrey Harris's "Beauty: Pretty for a Black Girl" confronts and explores how the bodies of Black women and girls are seen through the lenses of racial stereotype and devaluation. In this context, Black women's beauty is marginalized as generally transgressive and in need of qualifying—thus the "for a Black girl" caveat.

R. Fleetwood's "'I am King': Hip Hop Culture, Fashion Advertising, and the Black Male Body" explores how the Black male body has been read as something inherently violent and villainous and in need of control through enslavement, segregation, incarceration, or even death. Therefore, when hip-hop entrepreneurs Russell Simmons, Sean Combs, Jay-Z, and others created their own clothing lines that celebrated Black masculinity, they became heroes in the men's fashion game. However, Fleetwood argues that these same moguls were not necessarily fashion heroes for women because they catered to the same types of misogyny that have been pervasive in hip-hop culture at large.

Pre-reading Questions

1. How much does American beauty culture shape the decisions you make on a daily basis?

2. Is there a difference between being called "pretty" and being called "beautiful"?

3. The French translation of "Black is Beautiful" is *Je suis fier d'être Noir* ("I am proud to be Black"). What is the difference between those ideas?

4. Is the current natural hair movement here to stay? Why or why not?

5. What beauty burdens do American women carry? What beauty burdens to American men carry?

Beauty

Pretty for a Black Girl

Tamara Winfrey Harris

Thirty-nine-year-old Heather Carper grew up in Kansas and learned at least one lesson very early: "Black girls were never the cute ones. You could be 'cute for a black girl,' but you were never the pretty one."[1]

To be an American woman of any race is to be judged against constantly changing and arbitrary measures of attractiveness. One decade, being waif thin is in; the next, it's all about boobs and booties. Wake up one morning, and suddenly your lady parts "need" to be shaved smooth and your gapless thighs are all wrong. The multibillion-dollar beauty and fashion industries are dedicated to ensuring that women keep chasing an impossible ideal, like Botoxed hamsters running on the wheel of beauty standards.

But while expectations for how Western women should look have evolved over centuries, one thing has remained constant, and that is black women's place at the bottom of the hierarchy. In 1784, Thomas Jefferson praised the skin color, "flowing hair," and "elegant symmetry of form" possessed by white people, writing that black men prefer the comeliness of white women "as uniformly as is the preference of the [orangutan] for the black women over those of his own species."[2] Stereotypes of black women were designed in part to provide the antithesis to the inherent loveliness of white women, leaving other women of color to jockey for position between the poles of beauty.[3] Old beliefs die hard. Hundreds of years later, in 2011, the London School of Economics evolutionary psychologist Satoshi Kanazawa published a series of graphs and numbers at *Psychology Today*, "proving" that black women are "far less attractive than white, Asian, and Native American women." Because . . . science.

· ·

Moments in Alright

Anala Beavers, age four, knew the alphabet by the time she was four months old, could count in Spanish by one and a half, and never leaves home without her US map. (She knows all the state capitals!) Anala was invited to join Mensa in 2013.[4]

· ·

Neither a Beast nor Fetish Be

The inferiority of black beauty continues to be reinforced partly through popular culture. In allegedly liberal Hollywood, black women are nearly invisible as romantic partners. American fashion catwalks remain so white that former model and activist

Bethann Hardison, who formed the Diversity Coalition to challenge whitewashed runways, was moved to pen an open letter to the industry:

> Eyes are on an industry that season after season watches fashion design houses consistently use one or no models of color. No matter the intention, the result is racism. Not accepting another based on the color of their skin is clearly beyond 'aesthetic' when it is consistent with the designer's brand. Whether it's the decision of the designer, stylist or casting director, that decision to use basically all white models reveals a trait that is unbecoming to modern society.[5]

Black beauty is even marginalized within subcultures that pride themselves on subverting mainstream values, according to twenty-seven-year-old Black Witch,* who is active in pagan, punk, and Lolita fashion communities. Lolita fashion originated in Japan and is inspired by frilly, Victorian-era dress—lots of petticoats and delicate fabrics. Black Witch says that many of her fellow community members see Lolita femininity as at odds with black womanhood.

"They call us ugly. They say we look uncivilized in the clothes," she says. "I once heard a person say, 'I'm not racist, but that looks like an ape in a dress.'"[6]

Increasingly, black women are even absent in our own culture's illustrations of beauty.

"I don't really watch music videos anymore, but I have noticed that white girls are the 'it thing' now," says Liz Hurston,* thirty-four. "When hip-hop first came out, you had your video girls that looked like Keisha from down the block, and then they just started getting lighter and lighter. Eventually black women were completely phased out and it was Latinas and biracial women. Now it's white women. On one hand, thank God we're no longer being objectified, but on the other hand, it's kind of sad, because now our beauty doesn't count at all."[7]

Seeming to confirm Liz's observation, in 2006 Kanye West told *Essence* magazine, a publication for black women, that "If it wasn't for race mixing, there'd be no video girls.... Me and most of my friends like mutts [biracial women] a lot."[8]

In a society that judges women's value and femininity based on attractiveness, perceived ugliness can be devastating. The denigration of black female beauty not only batters African American women's self-esteem, it also drives a wedge between black women with lighter skin, straighter hair, and narrower features and those without those privileges.

Thirty-five-year-old Erin Millender says that the time she felt least attractive was as a teenager. "I went to a very white high school with a very J. Crew aesthetic," she says. "I was brown. I am built stocky. I've always had a butt ... and not a tiny, little gymnast booty either. I was aware of the fact that I did not conform to the beauty standard."[9]

Erin is biracial. Her mother is Korean American and her father is black. Many would see her light-brown skin and shiny curls and note her advantage over black women with darker skin, broader features, and kinkier hair. But Erin says that in school she was teased for "anything that was identifiably black. White kids don't know the difference between various grades of nap. They see frizzy hair and brown skin? That's just nappy hair to them—the same as any other kind of black hair. Brown skin and a big booty gets 'ghetto booty.'"

But at the predominantly black schools she attended before high school, Erin says some black girls targeted her, jealously pulling the long hair that brought her closer to the ideal of mainstream beauty. "Then, after school, in ballet, white girls made fun of my butt."

And the attention of men like West, who fetishize biracial women, is no honor. "[It is] creepy and insulting." Erin says that far too often that appreciation comes with backhanded compliments "implying that I don't really look black and would be less attractive if I did," plus "shade" from other black women, "who assume I think I'm better than somebody."

Black looks are not just erased; features commonly associated with people of the African diaspora are openly denigrated in American culture. (Though it is important to note that blackness is diverse. Black women can be freckled, ginger, and nappy; ebony skinned and fine haired; and every variation in between.)

Get the Kinks Out

Hair is a lightning rod for enforcement of white standards of beauty. And reactions to black women's natural hair help illustrate the broader disdain for black appearance. While black hair can have a variety of textures, most tends to be curly, coily, or nappy. It grows out and up and not down. It may not shine. It may be cottony or wiry. It is likely more easily styled in an Afro puff than a smooth chignon. For centuries, black women have been told that these qualities make their hair unsightly, unprofessional, and uniquely difficult to manage.

Don Imus infamously called the black women on the Rutgers University women's basketball team "nappy-headed hos."[10] In a ubiquitous late-night infomercial for WEN hair products, the host refers to black hair as "overly coarse," assuming that white hair is the baseline next to which other hair is "too" something.

In the 1970s, when veteran investigative reporter Renee Ferguson debuted a short Afro at the NBC affiliate in Indianapolis, she was told that she was "scaring" viewers.[11] Forty or so years later, some young black-female reporters still report being told to straighten their hair. In the summer of 2007, a *Glamour* magazine editor sparked outrage among many black working women when she told an assembled group of female attorneys that wearing natural black hair is not only improper but militant.[12] Even the US military is ambivalent about black women's hair. In 2014, new military grooming guidelines provoked furor among black servicewomen and prompted a letter to Secretary of Defense Chuck Hagel from the women of the Congressional Black Caucus. The guidelines had banned styles traditional for black women without altered hair textures and also referred to some hair (guess whose) as "matted" and "unkempt."[13]

The message that black natural hair is innately "wrong" is one that girls receive early. In 2013, two cases of black girls being punished at school for their natural hair made headlines. Seven-year-old Tiana Parker was sent home from an Oklahoma charter school and threatened with expulsion because her dreadlocks were deemed "faddish" and unacceptable under a school code that also banned Afros. Twelve-year-old Vanessa VanDyke also faced expulsion because of her voluminous natural hair that Florida school authorities found "distracting."[14]

Is it any wonder, after generations in a society that affirms white features while disparaging those associated with blackness, that many in the African American community have internalized negative messages about their appearance and learned that beauty requires disguising, altering, or diluting blackness and that we pass that inferiority complex on to younger generations?

Patrice Grell Yursik, founder of Afrobella.com, does her share of counseling black women scarred by a lifetime of beauty insecurity and parents who could not transcend their own conditioning. She shares a memorable conversation she once had with the mother of a young black child with cerebral palsy. The woman confessed to using double the recommended amount of a caustic chemical relaxer on her daughter's hair in an effort to make it straight. The mother was distraught that despite her efforts, the child's hair held on to its kinks.[15]

"I was horrified. It made me want to cry," says Patrice. "This poor child who cannot fend for herself and cannot physically take care of herself is enduring this burning on an ongoing basis for what? So she can be what? Why are we doing this?"

It should come as no surprise that most black women, rather than wear the braids, twists, Afros, and dreadlocks that black hair adapts to most easily, alter their hair's natural texture chemically or with extreme heat or cover it with synthetic hair or human hair from other races of women.

Let me be clear: black women should be free to wear their hair as they please, including straightened. But as Patrice Yursik urges, "It's really important for us to ask ourselves the tough questions. Why are we in lockstep in relaxing our hair? Why do we all come to the decision that this is something we have to do for ourselves and our children, [especially when] so many of us hate the process and see damage from it.

"Always do what makes you happy, but at least know why it's the thing that makes you happy."

During the "black is beautiful" 1970s, many black women embraced their natural kinks, but that rebellion gave way to assimilation in the Reagan era. The popularity of neo-soul music in the late 1990s and early 2000s, with its iconic faces such as Erykah Badu, Jill Scott, and Angie Stone representing for natural hair, opened the door for a new generation of women to embrace the nap.[16]

The challenge was that many would-be naturals found little support in traditional places for beauty advice, including beauty magazines (even ones catering to black women) and professional stylists. Often, even mothers and grandmothers were of no help; the hair care that many black women learned from their fore-mothers was solely focused on "fixing" or "taming" natural hair, not on celebrating its innate qualities. Many black women had not seen or managed their natural texture in decades. Black beauty magazines such as *Essence* continued to mostly feature models with straightened hair. And, until the recent renaissance, educa-tion for beauticians included little to no training about the care of natural black hair. Stylists were tested only on their ability to handle straightened black tresses.[17]

What is profound about the natural-hair revolution is that it has been driven by everyday black women searching for a way to honor their natural features in spite of all the messages encour-aging the contrary. Finding no support in the usual places, black women created what they needed, forming communities online. Forums buzzed with women offering support and maintenance and styling techniques when family, boyfriends, and employers rejected the natural look. Women with similar hair types learned from one another's trials and errors. Naturals pored through Fokti (a precursor to Flickr) to find photos of cute natural styles on everyday women. Naturals began eschewing the preserva-tives and chemicals in mainstream beauty products and instead searched for natural alternatives. Black women such as Jamyla Bennu, founder of Oyin Handmade, began creating natural prod-ucts in their own kitchens and selling them.

"I didn't come from a family where people had [chemical relaxers]," Jamyla says. "My mom's hair is very loose; it's not like mine, so she didn't have the skills to do the cornrows and stuff like that. I was the Afro puff girl. Although it was always affirmed, there were not a lot of ideas about how to wear my natural hair."

Bennu muddled through, finally beginning to relax her own hair in junior high school. But seeing more natural women in college opened her eyes to new options. "'Oh my gosh, *that's* what you're supposed to do with it! You can twist it. You can braid it.' I stopped perming my hair and have had natural hair ever since."

In about 1999, Jamyla began making hair products for herself "out of general craftiness." She experimented with common ingredients, like honey, coconut oil, and olive oil, that she had grown up using in her beauty routine. And, true to the ethos of the time, she shared her recipes. A freelance website designer, she eventually took a chance and began offering a few of her products online. Today, Jamyla and her partner, her husband Pierre, not only have a thriving online store but a brick-and-mortar retail space in Baltimore. And Oyin Handmade products can be found in select Target and Whole Foods stores across the country.

The natural-hair movement is "an example of women deciding for themselves what's important, what's beautiful, what's natural. . . . Not only how they want to look, but what they want to use to make themselves look that way. It's a really empowering moment in black beauty history and in beauty industry history because it's a kind of user-driven change."

Jamyla, like several other black women, has become a successful entrepreneur through the black beauty renaissance, but she has done so in a way that is uniquely affirming, unlike most consumer beauty brands. When my first box from Oyin arrived in the mail, it included a small container of bubble solution, two pieces of hard candy, and a card that read "Hello, Beautiful."

Jamyla says that approach comes from "myself as consumer, as a feminist, as a person who loves being black, who loves natural hair. I was in a place of pure celebration and discovery, and so was everyone else around me. So were the people with whom I was sharing the product. It didn't even make sense to try to market as if to a deficit or a lack, because I didn't see a deficit or a lack.

"A lot of black women grow up with so much negative messaging around their hair—not only from the marketing, which is, 'Fix it by doing X, Y and Z.'" Jamyla points out that caregivers often frame black girls' hair as a problem from the time they are small. "Sometimes we'll get messages like, 'Oh, this stuff. It's just so hard to deal with.'

"My political feeling is that it is very serious work to love yourself as a black person in America. I think it's an intergenerational project of transformation and healing that we are embarking on together."

Jamyla says that when she found herself with a platform to reach black women, it was important to deliver an empowering message. "You know that this is fly, right? I know you know it's fly, I'm going to echo that to you so that you can feel a little bit stronger in knowing how fly you are."

Now, mainstream beauty and cosmetics industries are playing catch-up in the movement black women began. Not only are homegrown brands like Oyin enjoying broad success, but major cosmetics companies have debuted lines catering to black women who wear their hair texture unaltered. In 2014, Revlon purchased Carol's Daughter, a beauty company with roots in the natural-hair movement.[18] Even Hollywood is taking notice, thanks to stylists like Felicia Leatherwood,[19] who keeps natural heads looking good on the red carpet. Her styling of *Mad Men* actress Teyonah Parris (Dawn) made all the flashbulbs pop at the 2013 Screen Actors Guild awards. Buzzfeed gushed that the actress had "the flyest hair on the red carpet."[20]

"We never thought that would happen," said Leatherwood of the attention-getting coif. And perhaps neither did Parris, when she first did what many black women call "the big chop"—cutting off relaxed hair, usually leaving short kinks or coils. Parris told *Huffington Post*: "I cried. I cried. I was not used to seeing myself like that, I did not want to walk outside.... My [friend] ... had to literally come over to my house and walk me outside because it was such an emotional experience, and it wasn't just about hair. It was what my perception of beauty was and had been for all of my life, and then I look at myself in the mirror and I'm like, 'That doesn't look like what I thought was beautiful.'"[21]

Now the Internet has exploded with not just natural-hair blogs and websites, such as Nappturality, Curly Nikki, and Black Girl with Long Hair, but also fashion sites, like Gabifresh and The Curvy Fashionista, and holistic beauty blogs, like Afrobella, run by black women and including (or catering to) our unique beauty needs.

When Patrice Grell Yursik went natural in 2002, she too went online for guidance and noticed a void of women who look like her tackling broader topics of beauty, including body image, skin care, makeup, and fashion.

"I'm a big girl. My hair is natural. I might have some skin problems. I'm trying to figure out what makeup looks good on me. Nobody was really holistically giving me that."

And so, in 2004, Patrice launched Afrobella. As a beauty blogger, she drew from her own journey to self-acceptance, including coming to terms with her body.

⸱ ⸱ ⸱ ⸱ ⸱ ⸱ ⸱ ⸱ ⸱ ⸱ ⸱ ⸱ ⸱ ⸱ ⸱ ⸱ ⸱ ⸱ ⸱

Moments in Alright

College-educated black women are the most likely group to read a book in any format.[22]

⸱ ⸱ ⸱ ⸱ ⸱ ⸱ ⸱ ⸱ ⸱ ⸱ ⸱ ⸱ ⸱ ⸱ ⸱ ⸱ ⸱ ⸱ ⸱

Fierce, Fat, and Fashionable

For a country with a growing rate of obesity, America is remarkably unforgiving when it comes to fat women. Fat, *black* women have become lazy, comedy shorthand. Want to bring on the cheap laughs? Then trot out an oversized, brown-skinned lady. Even better, despite her fatness and blackness, make her think she is attractive and worthy of amorous attention. (Think Rasputia, in Eddie Murphy's film *Norbit*, or Kenan Thompson's blessedly defunct character Virginiaca on *Saturday Night Live*—hulking, sexually aggressive laughingstocks.)

"My weight has always been at the forefront of things that would weigh me down emotionally and make me feel like I was less attractive than other people," says Patrice Yursik. "I've always been a big girl. When I wasn't a big girl, it was because I was bulimic."[23]

Patrice, though now a Chicagoan, grew up in a well-to-do neighborhood in Trinidad, where her friends and neighbors tended to be light skinned and thin. "I used to have to really psych myself up to go out because I would feel so unattractive next to my friends."

She hid her body under big, shapeless clothes. "I never used to wear sleeveless things. I felt very, very self-conscious of the stretch marks at the top of my arm and the fact that my arms had a little swing to them."

But one day, as she walked across her college campus in warm weather, a classmate, clad in jeans and a little sleeveless top, asked, "Aren't you hot wearing sleeves all the time?"

"I had never thought about it, because it was just my defense mechanism. [But I wondered], 'Why do I feel the need to cover this thing up that is just a part of myself? To try and hide something that anybody could have seen anyway? Why am I trying to hide my arm fat?' I'm a big girl. I get hot, just like any other human being."

That moment began Patrice's transformation into the style maven thousands of women follow. "It was like I started to really come into my femininity and feel more comfortable with whatever that was. I had to define it on my own terms."

It is hard to reconcile beauty insecurity with the woman who took the stage at the TEDxPortofSpain event in 2013. Standing on stage in a leather motorcycle jacket and long fuchsia skirt, a halo of burgundy kinks surrounding an impeccably made-up face, there is no doubt why Yursik is sometimes called the "Godmother of Brown Beauty." She is fierce. But the message she delivered that day was even stronger: all women can be beautiful on their own terms. It is a notion that she says underpins the black beauty revolution, which allows African American women, even those with kinky hair, large bodies, brown skin, and broad features, "a place at the table."

Many black women have been liberated by that lesson.

Heather Carper says she feels beautiful more often now than when she was a kid in Kansas. She says part of her evolution from "pretty for a black girl" to beautiful woman involved the realization that attractiveness is not as narrowly defined as mainstream culture would have women believe. Her mother once told her, "When you appraise art, you look for color and texture. With your skin and your hair, you will never lack either."

"The view of what makes you pretty is very dictated to you when you're younger. Whether it's the media or your peers, there is a whole lot of looking for external validation for what's pretty. You're just kind of checking in with everybody: 'Is that pretty? Is she pretty? Is this outfit pretty?' Part of getting older is that you stop checking in so much about whether what you like is cool with everyone else. You know, it may not ever be cool. But you know what? I like it. My beauty falls into that, too."[24]

Patrice says, "I always knew that there was something different about me, and I used to want to hide that difference when I was younger; to assimilate, to blend in. As I grew older, I realized: Why am I going to fight what I am? I am made to be a beautiful woman on my own terms, why not just embrace that and be that?

"Am I going to hate myself forever . . . or am I going to be free?"[25]

Beauty: Pretty for a Black Girl

1. Heather Carper, interview by the author, August 13, 2014.

2. Thomas Jefferson, *Notes on the State of Virginia,* ed. William Peden (Chapel Hill: University of North Carolina Press for the Institute of Early American History and Culture, Williamsburg, Virginia, 1954).

3. Collins, *Black Feminist Thought,* 98.

4. Dahvi Shira, "Anala Beavers Is a 4-Year-Old Genius," *People,* July 27, 2013, http://www.people.com/people/article/0,,20721049,00.html.

5. Bethann Hardison, "Open Letter to the Fashion Industry," September 5, 2013, http://balancediversity.com/2013/09/05/balance-diversity-2/.

6. Black Witch, interview by the author, September 17, 2014.

7. Liz Hurston, interview by the author, phone, August 17, 2014.

8. Carmen Van Kerckhove, "Kanye West: Mixed Race Women Are 'Mutts' and Exist Solely for Music Videos," *Racialicious,* November 20, 2006, http://www.racialicious.com/2006/11/20/kanye-west-mixed-race-women-are-mutts-and-exist-solely-for-music-videos/.

9. Erin Millender, interview by the author, August 20, 2014.

10. "Rutgers Players Describe How Imus' Remarks Hurt," CNN, April 10, 2007, http://www.cnn.com/2007/SHOWBIZ/TV/04/10/imus.rutgers/index.html.

11. Renee Ferguson, "A Dilemma for Black Women in Broadcast Journalism," *Neiman Reports*, Summer 2007, http://www.nieman.harvard.edu/reports/article/100240/A-Dilemma-for-Black-Women-in-Broadcast-Journalism.aspx.

12. Moe, "'Glamour' Editor to Lady Lawyers: Being Black Is Kinda a Corporate 'Don't.'" Jezebel, August 14, 2007, http://jezebel.com/289268/glamour-editor-to-lady-lawyers-being-black-is-kinda-a-corporate-don't.

13. Karen Grigsby Bates, "Congressional Black Caucus Urges Rethink of Army Hair Rules," NPR, April 11, 2014, http://www.npr.org/blogs/codeswitch/2014/04/11/301509842/congressional-black-caucus-urges-rethink-of-army-hair-rules.

14. Clare Kim, "Florida School Threatens to Expel Student over 'Natural Hair'," MSNBC.com, November 26, 2013, http://www.msnbc.com/the-last-word-94.

15. Patrice Grell Yursik, interview by the author, August 15, 2014.

16. Felicia Leatherwood, interview by the author, August 19, 2014.

17. Ibid.

18. Tonya Garcia, "L'Oreal USA Purchases Carol's Daughter to Reach the Multicultural Market," Madame Noire, October 20, 2014, http://

madamenoire.com/480079/loreal-usa-purchases-carols-daughter-to-reach-the-multicultural-market/.

19. Felicia Leatherwood interview.

20. Heben Nigatu, "Teyonah Parris Has the Flyest Hair on the Red Carpet," Buzzfeed, April 10, 2014, http://www.buzzfeed.com/hnigatu/teyonah-parris-has-the-flyest-hair-on-the-red-carpet.

21. Chanel Parks, "Teyonah Parris Cried over Her Natural Hair: It Didn't Look Like 'What I Thought Was Beautiful,'" *Huffington Post*, July 15, 2014, http://www.huffingtonpost.com/2014/07/15/teyonah-parris-natural-hair_n_5587721.html.

22. Philip Bump, "The Most Likely Person to Read a Book? A College-Educated Black Woman," *The Wire*, January 16, 2014, http://www.thewire.com/culture/2014/01/most-likely-person-read-book-college-educated-black-woman/357091/.

23. Patrice Grell Yursik interview.

24. Heather Carper interview.

25. Patrice Grell Yursik interview.

"I am King": Hip-Hop Culture, Fashion Advertising, and the Black Male Body

Nicole R. Fleetwood

From leather Louis Vuitton suits to fat-laced or no-laced Adidas athletic shoes to tight spandex shorts, African medallions, baggy Tommy Hilfiger jeans, and oversized hooded sweatshirts, hip-hop fashion has provided the visual markers for a larger cultural movement that has transformed popular music and international youth cultures in the last decades of the twentieth century. Since the 1970s, hip-hop music has been associated with a broader set of cultural practices, including a social presentation that is aggressive, defiant, and yet composed; a resignification of language, dance trends, graffiti art, and fashion. Aside from the music itself, fashion continues to be the most profitable and recognized of the practices affiliated with hip-hop culture.

Black fashion and style are interwoven into many studies of black cultural history and criticism. Yet they remain arenas that have been underresearched in terms of their significance to blacks' cultural and material histories and the social and psychic formation of black subjects. In her study of black dandyism, Monica Miller explores how style, namely fashion, has been integral to the formation of black diasporic identities since slavery. Miller analyzes the relationship among black stylization, the performativity of blackness, and black diasporic identities.[1] Miller looks at black selffashioning through the history of racial subjugation that heightens the stakes and risk involved in such practices. According to Shane White and Graham White, the historical development of a style among black everyday subjects in the United States as a "public presentation of the black body" is rich with seemingly ordinary acts of defiance, pride, self-articulation, but always with the risk of white disapproval and violence. White and White recount an early twentieth-century anecdote from Benjamin Mays's autobiography in which Mays was hit in the face in a public space by a respected white man because Mays was "'trying to look too good.'"[2] Mays's self-fashioning was read by his white perpetrator as stepping out of the subjugated place relegated to blacks during Jim Crow segregation.

Robin Kelley argues that twentieth-century history abounds with examples of everyday stylistic and fashioning practices among blacks that offered a challenge to systems of inequality. While it was often the case that black everyday subjects were not using style as an overtly political stance, Kelley in his influential study "The Riddle of the Zoot Suit" considers the cultural politics of 1940s young, working-class black males whose fashioning and public presentation affronted middle-class sensibilities. Kelley argues that these zoot suiters "sought alternatives to wage work and found pleasure in the new music, clothes, and dance styles of the period."[3]

The post–civil rights era marked an important shift in black fashion and style, largely because of aesthetic changes in black hair and fashion. The influence of black freedom struggles, especially the Black Panther Party's coifed Afros and black leather jacket, and the African-inspired fashion of the Black Arts movement, provided alternative imagery for black self-presentation. Political and aesthetic shifts as a result of these movements spurned many racially identified fashion trends throughout the latter decades of the twentieth century. Looking at changes in black fashion in the post–civil rights 1970s, Richard Powell reads the portraiture of Barkley L. Hendricks, whose works in the 1970s "introduced a new subject to painted portraiture: young, urbane blacks whose claims to pictorial posterity resided neither in deeds nor dictates but in their clothes, carriage, and color." The figures in Hendricks's painted portraits of the era are not iconic subjects of dominant history. Instead they are blacks whose sense of self-presentation relies on a self-conscious fashioning of the body that signals racial alterity, confidence, and self-possession. Many of the black men who are the subjects of his portraits are dressed in wear that can be read as racially inflected, platform shoes, hats with large brims, sunglasses, and long trench coats with upright collars. Powell notes that Hendricks's subjects appear to acknowledge being watched, "being the objects of countless spectators."[4] Hendricks's work of the era documents some of the key elements that presaged the development of hip-hop fashion, attitude, and social presentation.

Jamel Shabazz spent much of the late 1970s and the 1980s documenting young black and Latino subjects affiliated with the emerging cultural movement now ubiquitously and globally known as hip-hop. In over 10,000 images from that era Shabazz focused on the fashion, style, and posture of a wide range of children, teens, and young adults whose presentation of their stylized bodies in public spaces established many of the visual signs associated with the early movement. The interplay between the photographer, the camera, and the photographic subject exudes in his work through the deliberate, determined, and yet often playful poses, facial expressions, and stares of those photographed. Yet, as Kalefa Sanneh explains, Shabazz's idealized portraits are not based in the canonical documentary tradition of photographing human dignity in struggle, but based in the tradition of street glamour, urban black culture, and attitude as a way of life. Sanneh quotes Shabazz:

> I took very few candid shots. . . . I would approach a person and say, "Can I take your picture?" They'd say, "How do you want me to stand?" So I would give them a stance, a pose, and the pose added flavor to it. I'd put them up against a wall that matched their shirt, or find a fence that matched their hat, or back them up in front of a fly car.

Sanneh emphasizes the ability of Shabazz to capture the emergent subjects. For him, part of what makes Shabazz's practice so fascinating is that he would document for the approving eye of his subjects. He worked with them to produce idealized images of urban black style and life. Sanneh writes:

> When Shabazz returned to the same spot, days or weeks later, to share the prints with his subjects, they were invariably pleased—not because he'd captured some essential truth, but because his camera was telling a lie they wanted to believe. They'd never looked so good.[5]

The looking good in early hip-hop documented by Shabazz was a strategic and playful performance of visuality that signals codes not aligned with dominant cultural norms of fashion, beauty, and social demeanor. The subjects of Shabazz's camera redefine the flâneur based on the aesthetics and social conditions of postindustrial urban black life.

In *Number 2 Train* (1980), Shabazz photographs two young black men posing for his camera on a New York subway train whose interior walls are covered in graffiti and tags. One subject stands with arms held out to the side in a familiar hip-hop gesture that asserts readiness. The subject directly faces Shabazz's camera. His expression is both playful and confrontational. The face along with the position of his arms can be read as posing "What?," a black vernacular question that can have many interpretations, including "Why are you looking at me?" Or even more precisely, "I know I look fly. What do you have on me?" Representin' in the black vernacular sense of the b-boy of the day, he is dressed in a white-striped Izod, white jeans, and Adidas tortoise-shell sneakers with thick, red shoelaces. His outfit is made complete with Cazal glasses and a black Kangol. The second subject leans, one foot balanced on the train seat, in crisply ironed khaki pants, matching socks, and white leather shoes. He wears a camel-brown leather jacket, a white bowler hat tilted to the side, and a gold chain. His slight smile and dress are representative of a young, urban, sophisticated street mack with legacies in blaxploitation aesthetics and pimp mythology. Together, the young men in *Number 2 Train* reflect the various style and aesthetic influences on hip-hop fashion and the performative utterances of the hip-hop fashioned body. Connecting contemporary urban youth culture to the history of black style as self-presentation of racial differentiation, Regina Austin writes, "Today's B-boys with their baggy jeans, reversed baseball caps, fade haircuts, rap music and cool poses are the modern-day descendants of the zoot suiters of the 1940s."[6]

Like black fashion in general, scholars have paid very little detailed analytical attention to hip-hop's fashion system and the rapid growth throughout the 1990s and 2000s of hip-hop fashion companies often owned by young black entrepreneurs and entertainers. The trends and visual cues of hip-hop fashion have been taken at face value as a method of identifying individuals and groups associated with the movement. When early hip-hop fashion has been discussed, it is quite often through the lens of subculture theory and fashion is relegated to one of many practices that mark (and oftentimes romanticize) the cultural movement as distinct from normative American culture.[7] More recent discussions of hip-hop fashion, in journalism and cultural criticism, have framed consumption among hip-hop practitioners through pejorative terms of capitalistic excesses and material greed. Austin writes about how black consumption practices are labeled as socially deviant behavior; she argues,

> the efforts of young enterprising artists and media types of the Hip-Hop Generation to generate markets with their ingenuity have provoked an outcry against the commodification of black culture. In late capitalism all cultures are turned into commodities, not just black American culture. Black American culture is always already in the public domain where it is ripe to be ripped off by anyone paying attention.[8]

Neither the paradigm of black subcultural authenticity or black deviant consumption attends to the complex interplay of the social performance of looking good in black vernacular culture; the resignification of visual and

Figure 4.1. Jamel Shabazz, *Number 2 Train*, 1980. Courtesy of the artist.

fashion signs; the symbolic, material, and sometimes obsessive quest for wealth accumulation; and the development of an industry to mass-produce fashion goods associated with hip-hop. Central to the evolution of hip-hop fashion and its transformation into an industry is the fixity of the black male icon of hip-hop. Examining the significance of urban male fashion and the iconic, racialized, adorned male body of hip-hop's material and visual culture offers insight into the relationship among materiality, representation, and consumption in black popular culture. Embedded in representations of the fashioned black male body of hip-hop is the interplay between a highly stylized and reproducible racial alterity, nationalism, and hypermasculinity. By racialized alterity in the context of urban fashion and black masculinity, I mean how the black male body signifies within and outside of black communities a form of coolness through racialized and masculine difference and a diaphanous "outlawness" that maintains an affective quality even as it functions as a highly reproducible and mass-marketed commodity.

This chapter examines the emergence of a hip-hop fashion system and its strategic uses of urban, young black male iconography to frame the black male figure of hip-hop as possessor of a new American dream and inheritor of the legacy of Americana.[9] Using writings on fashion and the fashion system by Roland Barthes, Diane Crane, Fred Davis, and Dorinne Kondo, I reorient fashion studies away from (white) women's wear and femininity to analyze black male fashion, the industry that supports it, and the interplay of masculinity, desire, ambivalence, and national identity. Dorinne Kondo's influential study of Japanese businessmen fashion examines the relationship between masculinity, race, and nationalism in fashion codes. Kondo argues that "[c]lothing can have a political edge as signifiers of subcultural style and as components of ethnic/racial pride," while simultaneously reinscribing problematic codes of nationalism and essentialism.[10] In considering the racialization and masculine construction of hip-hop clothing, I also critique notions of subcultural authenticity by focusing on the strategic production and performance of racial authenticity through hip-hop fashion wear. Authenticity is a highly racialized and complex term in American culture. John Jackson, in his ethnographic study of racial authenticity and racial sincerity, argues:

> To talk exclusively in terms of racial authenticity is to risk ossifying race into a simple subject-object equation, reducing people to little more than objects of racial discourse, characters in racial scripts, dismissing race as only and exclusively the primary cause of social domination and death.[11]

In the context of blackness and masculinity, authenticity imbues the subject with a mythic sense of virility, danger, and physicality; in representations of hip-hop, authenticity most often manifests itself through the body of the young black male who stands in for "the urban real." Focusing on the production of racialized and gendered wear in hip-hop fashion, I examine the visual advertisements of several hip-hop fashion companies with attention to how authenticity, masculinity, and nationalism are retooled and ad/dressed through black masculine street fashion.

Hip-hop fashion, like the music, flourishes on the "mixing" of elements as diverse as high-end couture with found artifacts, tagging (or brand-naming), and sports apparel. Tricia Rose explains that hip-hop—as a style based in referentiality and reflexivity—thrives on appropriation and redefinition, which is the essence of "mixing," the musical technique that is at the root of the cultural movement.[12] Hip-hop fashion also regenerates itself through the same process. The ever-changing trends, many of which appropriate upper-class status symbols that have been coded as whiteness and privilege, such as luxury car insignias and European fashion designers, are the equivalent of the musical practice of sampling. In *Hip Hop America*, cultural critic Nelson George cites Dapper Dan, a Harlem designer who in the 1980s custom-made clothing that appropriated branding and design elements of high-end labels like Gucci and Louis Vuitton. Dapper Dan's Boutique had a clientele of black Harlem gangstas, athletes, musicians, and local residents. As rap became more established and profitable, Dapper Dan designed much of the clothing worn in early music videos and concerts.[13] Kobena Mercer argues that this process of mixing is fundamental to the development of black diasporic practices in his analysis of black hair style:

> Diaspora practices of black stylization are intelligible at one "functional" level as dialogic responses to the racism of the dominant culture, but at another level involve acts of appropriation from that same "master" culture through which "syncretic" forms of cultural expression have evolved.[14]

Because of these diasporic practices and the interplay between various forms and discourses in black cultural practices, hip-hop fashion and music complicate simplistic cultural models that posit authenticity against appropriation, or originality against commercialism.

Hip-hop culture, particularly fashion and the referencing of fashion in lyrics, often defies ways of understanding subcultural practices as inevitably incorporated into mainstream society through forms of commercialism and commodification that destroy or disempower the authenticity of the cultural practice studied. Noel McLaughlin, in his study of rock music, masculinity, and fashion, argues that authenticity is also a much-bandied term in studies of popular music and intensifies in discussions of music and blackness:

Indeed, the performative possibilities of black performers have been over-looked by a more general rock discourse that has validated black music as the authentic expression of racial "essence," and a key aspect of this has been the longstanding "necessary connection" forged between black people, black culture (clothes and performance styles) and music-making: between blackness, the body, rhythm and sexuality.[15]

The significance of appropriation, the performance of success/excess, and the preoccupation with looking good that are performative enactments at the heart of the hip-hop fashion system challenge the aura of authenticity that cloaks much of hip-hop's earliest musical and clothing styles and grassroots cultural practices. The "syncretic" process by which an aesthetic of racialized alterity blends with the quest for material wealth and financial success is most clearly evidenced in the visual invocation of Americana (and its aesthetic of red, white, and blue) by hip-hop fashion designers. These symbols of patriotism incorporated into hip-hop fashion and consumer goods work together with notions of urban black masculine alterity to create a character who is at once an ultra-stylish thug and the ultimate American citizen. His embodiment is most realized in the manifestation of the hip-hop mogul, a turn-of-the-millennial phenom. Christopher Smith defines the hip-hop mogul as an elite social position that developed at the end of the twentieth century made up of primarily young black male entertainers who became successful entrepreneurs by selling a variety of products, ideals, and values associated with hip-hop. Smith writes,

> In a time of imminent technological dislocation in the recording industry, all these men became famous for turning the relatively segmented market for urban music into a sprawling mainstream empire of life-style based merchandise spanning fashion, restaurants, soft drinks, film and theatrical production, and personal services.[16]

The successes of hip-hop moguls in the fashion industry rely on their ability to signify racialized and gendered specificity through the marketing of the urban black male icon while appealing to a wide range of young consumers of various races.

The Development of an Industry

The relationship between hip-hop music, specifically its lyrics, and fashion is mimetic. Clothing acts as the visual identifier of the sound, and articles of clothing, specifically brand names, are cited frequently in hip-hop lyrics. One of the most notable and documented examples of the exchange between the music and the clothing style—the visual, material and auditory signs—is Run-D.M.C.'s popular 1986 song "My Adidas," along with the wearing of the sports shoes in the rappers' music video, concerts, and public appearances. Nelson George relays how Russell Simmons, then manager of Run-D.M.C., negotiated a deal with the owners of the German-based company Adidas. "Within a year, Adidas and Rush Management had negotiated a $1.5 million deal with the rappers to market Run-D.M.C. sneakers and various accessories."[17] Run-D.M.C., it is important to note, is considered the first major crossover rap group to win large audiences of young white people, in addition to core urban black fans.[18]

This deal among Adidas, Run-D.M.C., and Rush Management serves as a defining moment when hip-hop fashion moved from the incorporation and redefinition of existing trends to actually designing and marketing products as *hip-hop fashion* on a mass scale, that is, beyond the custom boutiques like Dapper Dan's Boutique and other similar small enterprises located in centers of hip-hop culture, like Harlem and Brooklyn. The affiliation between the product and the rap group is significant because it set the stage for other rappers to endorse retail products. It marks an important transition of the localized cultural practices associated with hip-hop into a growing culture industry.

By the early 1990s the relationship among hip-hop musicians, their lyrics, and major apparel companies had grown more intermingled, as large retail companies realized the economic potential of tapping into hip-hop culture. According to journalist Marc Spiegler, Tommy Hilfiger was the first major fashion designer who actively courted rappers as a way of promoting his clothing label. Spiegler, writing in 1996, contends,

> Over the past few years, [Biggie] Smalls [aka the Notorious B.I.G., now deceased] and other hip-hop stars have become a crucial part of Hilfiger's open attempt to tap into the urban youth market. In exchange for giving artists free wardrobes, Hilfiger found its name mentioned in both the rhyming verses of rap songs and their "shout-out" lyrics, in which rap artists chant out thanks to friends and sponsors for their support.[19]

Hilfiger's success convinced other large mainstream American fashion design companies, like Ralph Lauren and Calvin Klein, to tailor lines to the lucrative market comprised of hip-hop artists and fans. This targeting of hip-hop markets by large mainstream fashion companies like Ralph Lauren and Tommy Hilfiger is part of what Laura Kuo argues is the commoditization of hybridity in the fashion industry during the 1990s. Kuo describes how multiculturalism gets marketed in fashion of the decade through what she calls "commoditized hybridity"—the conflation of "race, class, gender, sexuality, ethnicity, nation, and culture within a totalizing logic of neoliberalism."[20] Kuo's analysis of the advertising campaigns that marketed difference to increase its consumer base is in line with another industry trend that Paul Smith analyzes occurring during the same period in fashion. Smith argues that designers like Lauren and Hilfiger (Hilfiger being the focus of much of his analysis) adopted an industry practice of "mass customization" of designer fashion as a response to economic globalization in the late twentieth century.[21] Through mass customization, the good life symbolically represented in clothes by Lauren and Hilfiger became attainable to a broader section of consumers.

The 1990s also saw another crucial shift in hip-hop fashion production, as the market continued to expand through the popularity of the music and the visibility of the artists in music videos, commercial endorsements, and other venues. Black designers, many having created locally for black urban communities throughout the 1980s, acquired success and recognition nationally for their urban gear targeted at hip-hop communities. As stated earlier, much of hip-hop's early fashion trends (like Run-D.M.C.'s Adidas and LL Cool J's Kangol hat) began as appropriations of existing cultural goods and products. With the growth of young urban black designers and entrepreneurs, then, fashion trends were created and targeted now specifically at hip-hop markets. One of the first black designers to gain national attention and success in this market was Karl Kani, who has received significant recognition and praise from the fashion industry and business magazines, like *Black Enterprise*.[22] In the mid- and late 1990s, Kani's success resulted from the appeal of his clothes beyond urban black hip-hop fans, a shift that brought profit to many hip-hop clothing companies. Journalist Tariq K. Muhammad writes, "His trademark style, which includes baggy jeans and oversized casual knits, found an unexpected white suburban audience eager to mimic black urban fashion." In examining the roots of Kani's popularity, Muhammad employs a typical schema used to analyze hip-hop that reinforces notions of authenticity about black cultural practices in which blacks create and whites consume. The success of Karl Kani opened the door for several other black designers and marked the expansion of a lucrative market. By 1998 the fashion company FUBU [For Us, By Us], founded by four young black male designers, made $350 million in sales.[23]

The success of designers like Kani, FUBU, and Moshood in the 1990s has much to do with the in-roads that black fashion designers and models made in fashion centers like New York City during the last half of the twentieth century, especially during the disco era. Stephen Burrows, Willi Smith, and Scott Barrie were a few of the designers whose clothing was embraced in the 1970s. These designers were trained in fashion schools and apprenticed within the design world. Their work, like most fashion, was targeted at women's wear. Burrows, who graduated from the Fashion Institute of Technology and is a three-time Coty Award winner, was known for designing work that spoke directly to disco culture and music. In a review of his spring line in 1977—at the height of disco—fashion critic Nina Hyde described him as "a master of the sexy feminine look, whether in chiffon, crepe or jersey, and even in chamois. He uses elasticized or drawstring waistlines and drawstring necklines, partly for comfort but also 'so that the clothes work differently for each woman'" (quoting Burrows).[24] One recurring feature of his oeuvre is particularly relevant for how it speaks to black fashion and visual culture largely and directly to the development of hip-hop fashion a generation later: the visibility of seams and cuts in his design.

> Sociologically, Mr. Burrows captured a moment—presaged it, even—that being the moment of Gloria Gaynor and all of the 3 a.m. revelry attending it. Fashion history has ascribed to Halston the look of the disco years, but Mr. Burrows's clothes caught the messiness of that time more instinctively. Unlike Halston's, his lines were never quite as clean or refined. He worked in matte jersey and cut chiffons with uneven hemlines. His colors were bright to the point of assault. The necklines on his sequin halters billowed and sloped. His signature was lettucing, a technique that made a hem or the edges of a wrap dress, say, look like the crinkled tops of a carnation.
>
> The most distinctive element of Mr. Burrows's clothes is that they looked as if they left the house around midnight to wind up the next afternoon a crumpled heap on some bedroom floor at an address the wearer was probably not all that familiar with 24 hours earlier.[25]

I cite reviews of Burrows's designs in some detail here because of certain aesthetic elements in his work that recur in hip-hop fashion a generation later. The aesthetic of visible seams is a recurring "stitch" in black visual and cultural practices. The visible seam is a technique and a look that resurface in hip-hop clothing such as the designs of Karl Kani and FUBU in the 1990s. Much of their clothing incorporated bold or contrasting stitching that highlighted t-shirts, jeans, and sometimes shoes. Their lines were also known for asymmetrical contours and patterns often as stitch work on pants pockets, sweaters, or the back of shirts and jackets. These hip-hop fashion designers would often work with Black Nationalist and pan-Africanist symbols and colors to signify racial differentiation through their fashion.

While hip-hop fashion lines began with fashion designers who specialized in clothes for hip-hop musicians and fans, the hip-hop fashion industry soon merged with the music industry as the hip-hop musician/producer turned fashion designer and business entrepreneur, that is, the hip-hop mogul, emerged. In Smith's analysis of the hip-hop mogul as cultural icon and business powerhouse, fashion is just one of the areas of capitalist and cultural expansion for this entrepreneur. He emerges as one of the successes of the continuous expansion of popular and entertainment cultures and the rise of the New Economy, marked by deindustrialization, technological advances, and the rise in the service industries. The most celebrated are Russell Simmons, Sean Combs, and Jay-Z, all having established very successful fashion lines that topped the market in profits during the past decade.

Among the first to establish his multiplatform reign in the areas of hip-hop cultural production and dissemination is Def Jam Records co-founder Russell Simmons, the same businessman who negotiated the deal between Adidas and Run-D.M.C. With his creation of the hip-hop clothing company Phat Farm in 1992, the production of the music and the creation of its fashion trends were inextricably linked. Simmons, one of the most successful entrepreneurs of hip-hop culture, opened up the possibility for the cultural producers of the music to become also producers of its fashion trends.[26] The number of rappers and hip-hop groups who have established clothing lines since Simmons's initial success is too long to list here; 50 Cents Eminem, Nelly, OutKast, and Pharrell are just a few. By the first decade of the twenty-first century, the companies were so numerous that in many respects a clothing line became just another venue of celebrity promotion and an extension of the rapper's lyrics and public image. Hip-hop cultural industries, like multinational retail companies in the mid-nineties (GAP and Abercrombie and Fitch, for example), successfully turned profits on branding a lifestyle.

Phat Farm apparel invokes the discourse of Americana while playing with and remaining bound by the trope of black male as public threat, or the menacing "hoodie"-wearing black thug of postindustrial American visual culture. Simmons's Phat Farm line makes for an interesting case study of how fashion becomes a venue for branding and marketing the hip-hop lifestyle and demonstrates the reproducibility and desirability of the hip-hop b-boy as a commercially viable marker of the cultural movement. Part of the company's success rests in Phat Farm's ability to market its line as mainstream American culture, while simultaneously incorporating notions of subcultural authenticity. Simmons, who remained closely involved with the development of Phat Farm's fashion products in the 1990s, was quoted as proclaiming that t-shirts "'are gonna make me richer than records ever did.'"[27] Influenced by the successful marketing and design of fashion moguls Tommy Hilfiger and Ralph Lauren in hip-hop communities, Phat Farm employs the red, white, and blue of the American flag in clothing patterns and the company's logo. In the selective advertising campaigns—geared toward hip-hop and young adult magazines and billboards in urban settings—Phat Farm, as representative of many hip-hop fashion companies, seeks new sites of coolness through a reappropriation of the aesthetics of Americana. These campaigns exploit cultural nostalgia for a mythic national past while re-envisioning urban b-boys and those who want to be such hipsters as the native-born sons and inheritors of "the America" of myth.

While the urban black male who represents hip-hop fashion stands for alterity and difference from mainstream fashion and society, he is bound by the restrictive visual codes of this particular fashion system and the normative ideology of American capitalism and nostalgia. Fred Davis argues that fashion distinguishes itself from style and custom through its compulsion for change; he also argues that change in fashion is necessarily cyclical. According to Davis the cycle of fashion moves from cultural producer (such as fashion houses or independent designers) to elite consumers or small group-identified populations to mass markets to the death of the trend. While change is essential to fashion, originality and creativity are subjugated to familiarity with styles for retailers and consumers.[28] Diana Crane, in her study of the sociology of clothes and gender, expands this analysis to examine how social norms discipline fashion and the fashioned body.[29]

The trends of the larger hip-hop fashion companies exemplify the normative and commercial prerogative toward modesty as it also defines itself by its visibility and distinction from other fashion styles. For instance, a simple, quite mundane, item produces much of the wealth in hip-hop fashion: baggy, oversized jeans. Tommy Hilfiger built his fashion empire on this seemingly understated article of clothing. New lines by emerging designers often test the market by branding jeans (often competing lines are manufactured by the same sweatshops) and selling them selectively at street markets, in regional boutiques, or showrooms. Like most styles produced by the fashion industry, hip-hop clothing trends change each season; yet, oversized designer jeans, hooded sweatshirts known as "hoodies," athletic shoes and boots have remained staples throughout the past two decades. In this same period and through these conservative trends, the hip-hop fashion industry has secured itself as a force to be reckoned with in apparel. As the industry grew throughout the 1990s and 2000s, the market moved toward a level of homogenization exemplified by the popularity of hip-hop styled jeans. Apart from denim and seasonal colors, the more popular hip-hop fashion styles are based on reproducing the three colors of the American flag in patterns and fabrics that both reference and redefine the nation and patriotism. What distinguishes the articles of clothing is the company's label placed strategically on the products. Wearing a hip-hop fashion line is a method of demonstrating one's affiliation with a particular rapper and whose line one supports as a customer, similar to supporting a favorite athlete by wearing the jersey of the sports star.

Like popular sports and the music itself, hip-hop clothing style is virulently and heterosexually masculine and designers cater to male teenagers and young adults. This is not to say that women do not exist in hip-hop fashion or music, but that the industry promulgates itself on the fetishized body of the young black male. Until the later establishment of fashion lines for women and girls in hip-hop—like Baby Phat (the feminized division of Phat Farm), Jennifer Lopez's fashion lines JLo and Sweetface, Eve's Fetish clothing line, and Beyoncé's Dereon, hip-hop designers almost solely made clothing for males or created unisex articles and accessories, in part because female fashion is a much more difficult and risky industry to enter. More significant, though, is the emphasis on the racialized and masculine body in hip-hop culture. When hip-hop fashion companies like Phat Farm create apparel for females, the line is branded as something distinct from its trademark male line. In Phat Farm's case, Baby Phat has as its logo a silhouette of a stationary domestic cat with a curvy tail. This clothing line is highly sexualized, consisting of club clothing, such as tight-fitting body suits, miniskirts, and revealing lingerie. The marketing of Baby Phat has centered around the image and style of Russell Simmons' now ex-wife, model Kimora Lee Simmons, who has modeled for the line since its inception and is an executive in the company. Kimora Lee is the face of the line and represents an unattainable fantasy for many of the line's female consumers to marry into hip-hop royalty. Phat Farm, with its relaxed style of baggy jeans, oversized sweaters and head gear, can be seen as an extension of Simmons's fashion style and personality (he is known for his casual dress, which always includes a Phat Farm baseball cap or hat), while Baby Phat embodies Simmons's (now ex-) wife, the iconic, mixed-race (Asian and black), runway model, whom Simmons at one time described as his trophy. The racial and gender signification in these articles of clothing is most clearly exemplified in a Phat Farm t-shirt sold in the early 2000s; the t-shirt included a large imprint of Kimora's face and was targeted at young men, further highlighting that the figure of the female body exists to accessorize that of the male.

The more recent and ancillary female fashion lines in hip-hop have received much less attention and have been less profitable.[30] For example, the rapper Eve's Fetish line has been relaunched multiple times with different partnerships over several years but without being able to establish itself as a force in the fashion industry.[31] Of note is the controversial male rapper Nelly who has been the subject of much debate and protest among black women because of his representations of women in his music videos; Nelly has been moderately successful with his women's clothing line Apple Bottom, designed with the intention, according to marketing materials, of "liberating the natural curves of a woman's body."[32] These lines geared toward women and girls have had modest popularity among young urban consumers but have not had the national appeal or success of male hip-hop fashion lines. This, I believe, in many respects has to do with the cultural impact of the black masculine iconic figure that centers hip-hop style and culture. Many women who participate as consumers and rappers in hip-hop identify with the signs of heterosexual masculinity in hip-hop fashion. Imani Perry argues that some female hip-hop artists, practitioners, and consumers choose to wear what is perceived to be masculine fashion, like baggy jeans and athletic shoes, as a response against the codes of white and racialized femininity. Perry writes, "Even as black Americans maintain a separate sexual aesthetic, white female standards of beauty still haunt black women, so that some African American women have chosen more masculine outfitting as a counter-hegemonic move."[33] Thus, the racialized alterity of the black male icon in hip-hop fashion is also consumable and wearable by women and girls in hip-hop.

The consumption and performance of a racialized masculinity and success (material and sexual) are linked inextricably through hip-hop fashion. The declaration of success/excess is reiterated in the lyrical play of rappers. For example, Notorious B.I.G.'s "Big Poppa" analyzes and romanticizes the seduction and decadence of this condition: "Money, hoes and clothes all a nigga knows / A foolish pleasure, whatever / I had to find the buried treasure / So grams I had to measure / However living better now / Gucci sweaters now."[34] The growth in the hip-hop fashion market is one more example of the seemingly unlimited possibilities of capitalism to make a profit from cultural movements, no matter how dissident.[35] The diversification of hip-hop culture into various successful industries is also a result of the maturation of the cultural movement after more than two decades of growing from the local to the national to the transnational.

Marketing Hip-Hop Americana

The growth of the hip-hop fashion industry and the spectacle induced by what has been framed as another hip-hop gold mine are seen in the coverage and advertising in hip-hop magazines, most notably *Vibe* magazine, founded by music producer Quincy Jones in 1993. From the late 1990s throughout the first decade of the twenty-first century, as the hip-hop fashion industry grew, *Vibe* magazine moved to incorporate more fashion into its content, not just through advertisements. The "V Style" and "V Fashion" sections of the magazine—consisting of theme-based fashion shoots that often include top models, musicians, and other celebrities—began to take up a significant portion of the magazine's pages. In the October 2001 edition of the magazine, the two sections occupied twelve pages and showcased designers as diverse as Gucci, Ralph Lauren, Helmut Lang, and Mecca USA. In *The Fashion System*, Roland Barthes outlines the relationship between "real" (my quotation marks)—or material—clothing, image clothing as in photographs and illustrations in magazines, and written clothing, or the language used to describe articles of fashion. "V Style" and "V Fashion" are particularly interesting because of their incorporation of narrative into fashion; the sections produce written clothing that, according to Barthes, "endows the garment with a system of functional oppositions (for example, fantasy/classic), which the real or photographed garment is not able to manifest in as clear a manner."[36] *Vibe*'s fashion spreads place the body of hip-hop in a state of constant leisure and play. The highly stylized fashion photography in the magazine often reinterprets music videos and rap lyrics. These "functional oppositions" arise in *Vibe*'s fashion sections, in part because of the inaccessibility of realizing these fantasies for most of its audience—teenagers who are in some way bound by parental, financial, and legal constraints. Dorinne Kondo analyzes the relationship among desire, identity, and fashion advertising:

> Within our regime of commodity capitalism, it is hardly surprising to find powerful articulations of identity in a domain whose business is the figuration of idealized objects of desire: advertising. Designed specifically to promote identification and provoke object lust, consciously deploying techniques to pull on issues resonant for their audience, ads—particularly fashion ads—become privileged sites for the examination of subject formation.[37]

The magazine served as a central site, along with music videos, for transmitting messages of the fashioned, and predominantly masculine, body of hip-hop (often through visual fantasies of material wealth and sexual excess) at the turn of the millennium.

A Phat Farm advertisement in the October 2001 issue of *Vibe* occupies two of the most expensive pages in the front of the magazine. The advertisement is seemingly simple. In close focus is a young dark-skinned black male in a gray sweat suit. In the center of his chest and on his left thigh is the "Phat Farm" logo in red and white block letters. His hands are in his pockets and the hood of the sweatshirt covers his head. The hoodie frames his features and the photographic lighting emphasizes his high cheekbones, bald scalp, polished skin, broad nose, forehead, and slightly puckered full lips. The model does not meet the spectator's gaze. Instead, he looks down and off to the side, outside of the spectator's line of vision. Behind him, a young Latino walks toward him with his hands in his pockets; he looks off to the side, in the same direction as the other model's gaze. His head is angled upward, while the black male's head is slightly tilted down. The approaching model wears ubiquitous baggy blue jeans and a plaid blue shirt with "Phat Farm" scripted above the breast pocket. He also wears a large blue casual jacket with the company's name again above its breast pocket. While he is clean-cut and carefully groomed, his clothes are referential of the uniform of the Crips gang, particularly the uniformity of the color blue by which the gang is identified. The two models are on a picturesque autumn lawn replete with auburn leaves. They both have anticipatory glances on their faces as they look outside of the spectator's line of vision. A large two-story brown shingled home serves as the backdrop with a peaceful sky above. Next to the Latino model is a graphic of the Phat Farm logo—a large letter *P* encapsulated by two slightly curved lines on each side. The ubiquitous motto of the company, "Classic American Flava," resides underneath the *P*. In the corner of the advertisement, as a small graphic, is the Phat Farm *P* again but this time in a layout reminiscent of the American flag with red and white stripes.

The Phat Farm advertisement invokes an aesthetic of suburban sublime oddly in harmony with the markers of an urban, youthful, racialized code. The suburban house with its colorful leaves on the lawn is not foreign territory for the urban young men in the photograph; instead, they exist in this space as its normative occupants. They *belong*. The black male model in the hoodie references the trope of the urban black menace so clearly visualized in the ghetto action films of the early 1990s and contemporary music videos.[38] Yet, here in this setting of suburban bliss, he is so clearly not

Figure 4.2. Advertisement as it appeared in *Vibe*, October 2001. Courtesy of Phat Farm, LLC.

a threat. He stands reflectively—at peace—with hands in pocket, looking with a reflective gaze. The Latino model, whose fashion symbols evoke gang identification, no longer signifies fear or intimidation; instead he walks with his body open toward the camera and a wistful gaze on his face. Although they employ the racialized and youth-based codes of visual threat in post-industrial US culture, here on the lawn in peaceful suburbia they occupy a place of tranquility and belonging. They are *together* here in this American dream. Their clothed bodies have become incorporated into the American sublime—the pastoral—the belief in mythic destiny and unlimited success. The Phat Farm tag line "Classic American Flava" is crucial to the *refashioning* of their bodies in the advertisement. Applying Barthes' concept of written clothing, language produces meaning that:

> conveys a choice and imposes it, it requires the perception of this dress to stop here (i.e., neither before nor beyond), it arrests the level of reading at its fabric, at its belt, at the accessory which adorns it. Thus, every written word has a function of authority insofar as *it* chooses—by proxy, so to speak—instead of the eye. The image freezes an endless number of possibilities; words determine a single certainty.[39]

"Classic American Flava" reinforces the image and the positioning of the two young males as inheritors of American wealth and destiny. At the same time, the use of "flava" in exchange for "flavor" implies a racial and stylistic rewriting of the American dream. The tag line invokes American privilege and dominance while subverting the normative whiteness and history of exclusion that these concepts connote.

Fred Davis's notion of ambivalence in contemporary fashion is useful here for analyzing the merger of normative icons of Americana with nonnormative or underrepresented (in the realm of fashion) bodies. For Davis, ambivalence—like change—is the basis of the regeneration of fashion styles. He writes: "As for fashion specifically, while it must of necessity work within the broad parameters of a relatively well established and familiar clothing code, it turns for fresh inspiration to tensions generated by identity ambivalences, particularly those that, by virtue of cultural scripting and historical experience, are collective in character."[40] The role of ambivalence is central to the success of hip-hop fashion marketing campaigns and is what makes the Phat Farm advertisement decipherable. Kuo considers such ambivalence a key to the marketing of commoditized hybridity. She argues that such advertising

> operate[s] on the ability to hold two contradictory beliefs. This disavowal of difference—*I know very well* that all people are not equal in the United States due to racism, labor exploitation, homophobia, classism, sexism, and so on, *but nevertheless*, I believe that everyone is equal and can be "one"—is structured on the dual recognition of: (1) racial inequality and (2) the multicultural promise that enables the political meanings of these photographs to circulate in the first place.[41]

Using Kuo and Davis, the visual salience and cultural value in the Phat Farm advertisement has precisely to do with the history of exclusion of these racialized bodies from the material and symbolic registers of American success and the good life, such as the suburban enclave.

This high level of self-consciousness about evoking the rhetoric of Americana while reinventing "the nation" emerges explicitly in Phat Farm's post–September 11, 2001, advertising campaign. In the April 2002 issue of *Vibe* magazine, Russell Simmons addressed his customers and his mythic hip-hop nation directly through a full two-page advertisement that consists of Simmons, dressed in Phat Farm clothing, standing in front of the Phat Farm rendition of the American flag. Text with his signature accompanies the image; the quote reads:

Ten years ago we found Phat Farm,
a brand born out of the
Hip-hop lifestyle—
a lifestyle others did not acknowledge.
But one that became bigger than
their ability to suppress.
Today we stand in front. [in larger, bold and italicized font]
We are humbled and give thanks to those
who support us in the pursuit of
a new American dream.

In the post–September 11 era, Simmons is even more explicit in invoking nationalism, possessing the symbols of Americana, and framing consumerism in patriotic terms. Simmons constructs race on nationalistic terms as a performative engagement with social and symbolic signs and through participation in certain practices as a consumer. He argues that hip-hop fashion becomes a shared language for the imagined nation as envisioned by hip-hop entrepreneurs.

The audiences targeted by hip-hop fashion advertisements show the contradiction in commoditized hybridity marketing as Kuo discusses. It has been widely acknowledged and discussed (possibly overemphasized) that by the early 1990s white young males made up the largest demographic of consumers of hip-hop cultural products. Thus, Phat Farm, in appealing to an audience beyond urban racialized fans, reframes the b-boy and gang-identified tropes of visual culture and domesticates them by setting the models in the milieu of hip-hop fashion's more lucrative consumer base—middle America, the suburbs.

The media coverage of one of the most public and successful hip-hop moguls, Sean Combs, demonstrates the ambivalence between the signs of hip-hop fashion and ambitions of hip-hop fashion designers and entrepreneurs. Combs and his highly publicized personal life, including trials for criminal wrongdoing, previous romantic involvement with Latina superstar Jennifer Lopez, and series of successful television shows and other offshoots of hip-hop culture, come to stand in for his clothing line. His representation as an above-the-law, resourceful, and refined thug overshadows the industry recognition that he has received for his clothing company. Most notably, Sean Combs was the first black designer to be nominated for the prestigious "Perry Ellis Award for Menswear at the American Fashion Awards."[42] Yet, in a February 2002 series covering New York's Fashion

Figure 4.3. Advertisement as it appeared in *Vibe*, April 2002. Courtesy of Phat Farm, LLC.

Week, the *New York Times* featured Combs and his well-received clothing line, Sean John, with a headline reading "A Fashion Statement: Hip-Hop on the Runway." Journalist Guy Trebay writes:

> A clue to Mr. Combs' ambitions came Thursday, when he appeared, along with Terry Lundgren, the president of Federated Department Stores, to ring the opening bell at the New York Stock Exchange. Some on hand remembered that the last time Mr. Combs appeared publicly downtown was to hear his acquittal in criminal court on charges of carrying a concealed weapon in a nightclub. He was wearing a suit on that occasion last year, and he wore an even nattier one of chalk stripes from Versace this week, as he spoke about the importance of giving New York economic support.[43]

Trebay's comments invoke the language and imagery of black criminality and illegitimacy; in doing so, these racialized invocations overshadow the success of Combs's entrepreneurial venture and fashion contributions. For Trebay, Combs's fashion line is newsworthy in how it reflects upon normative ideas about black masculinity, specifically the specter of the black deviant thug who is always a public threat and an illegitimate participant in the wealth and success of American capitalism.[44]

At the same time, hip-hop moguls capitalize on the media's twin representations of their entrepreneurial successes and their signification of black masculine alterity. In a 2009 billboard advertisement for Combs's cologne, King, an offshoot of his fashion and accessories line, Combs's body stands in for the former of these representations. The larger-than-life image runs eighteen stories alongside a high-rise building in New York City's Times Square. Sean Combs poses in evening wear with black slacks, a white dress coat, and a black bow-tie. Combs stands relaxed, confident, and intent, looking out over the cityscape. In his ear is a large diamond, reflective of the waning era of bling-bling. Under his image, scaled much smaller, is a bottle of the cologne being advertised. Next to the cologne reads, "I am King" with the signature logo of his fashion company, Sean John, in scripted letters—a signature of authentication. Above the poster is a larger inscription of the logo. Combs is dually dressed as the embodiment of American success and establishment and as racially inflected other.

A few blocks away from Combs's advertisement is another larger-than-life image of a hip-hop entrepreneur turned fashion designer. On the side of the building that houses MTV and VH1 channels, one of the most popular sites for tourists and youth in New York, is a billboard for Jay-Z's Roca Wear clothing line. The advertisement is a profile shot of Jay-Z performing with a microphone held to his mouth. Jay-Z, one of the most prolific and critically acclaimed rappers of the past two decades, is applauded by hip-hop fans for his ability to stay connected to the mythic and material "streets" of hip-hop as he has become one of the wealthiest individuals in popular music of the early twenty-first century. Jay-Z's image is moody and mysterious. His face is obscured in shadow and dark lighting. His head is tilted down and sunglasses cover his eyes. His dress is unimportant here; he is dressed in a gray button-down that is only partially seen. His hand reaches out as if penetrating the two-dimensional plane of the photograph and hovers above the crowds and passersby on the streets of Times Square. These twin billboards—Combs dressed in evening wear and the signs of the cultural elite, Jay-Z a "lyrical god" of the street—represent the interwoven messages marketed through hip-hop fashion and advertising.

Underlying this dual representation is a dialectic that places authenticity in hip-hop cultural in productive tension with the pursuit of capitalism—a dialectic that has existed as long as the art form itself. As the industry has grown, hip-hop entrepreneurs like Combs and Simmons have become conscious

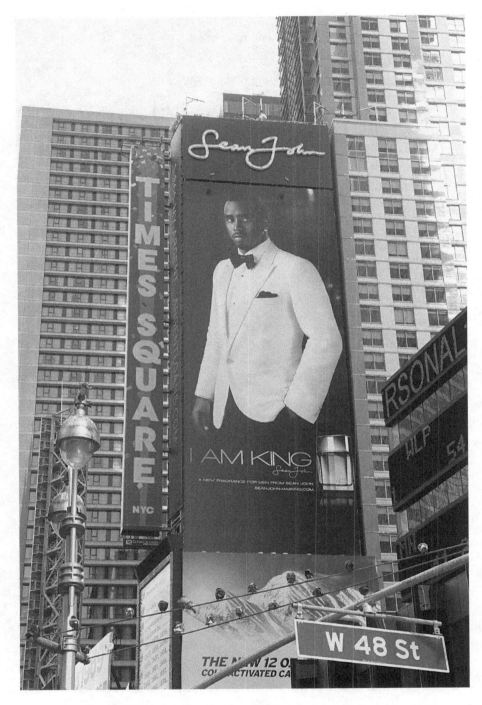

Figure 4.4. "I am King" advertisement, Times Square, New York, September 2009.
Courtesy of Tracy Collins.

Figure 4.5. Roca Wear advertisement featuring Jay-Z, Times Square, New York, September 2009. Courtesy of Tracy Collins.

about aligning their fashion companies with American cultural and national symbols while, at the same time, promoting their clothing as based in the realness or authenticity of the urban streets. Many hip-hop entrepreneurs perform the authenticity of their clothing as b-boy gear by wearing their labels routinely in public and simultaneously articulating their desire to have their line become incorporated into mainstream fashion. In a 1999 article journalist Nancy Jo Sales quotes Simmons's reaction to a buyer from a major department store who shows little interest in carrying Phat Farm apparel:

> "I'm talking to that [name deleted] who does the buying for [name of shopping mall chain deleted]," he sputters, "and she says, 'Oh'—he makes his voice high and phony—'we just don't want any *jeans stores* in our shopping center.' Now, what does *that* mean?" He's frowning, waiting.
>
> "Means she doesn't want a lot of little ghetto niggas runnin' up in there," he says.[45]

This exchange, as reported by Sales, brings to the fore what Simmons must do in order for T-shirts to make him richer than records, his stated ambition. Simmons' response to the buyer articulates the anxiety of hip-hop fashion producers who having capitalized on a niche market find themselves bound by the niche that they helped to create. The drive to turn a profit from hip-hop cultural production and the desire to create the visual markers of urban coolness in turn bring questions of credibility and an interrogation of the authenticity of the product and producer. By 2004, the success of Simmons' twin-fold goals—to signify hip-hop authenticity and to become extremely wealth through selling fashion goods—manifested in the purchase of his fashion empire, including the Baby Phat trademark, for $140 million by Kellwood, a camping and conservative apparel company known for moderate-price fashion items geared toward women.[46] In the same article, Sales quotes Andre Harrell, a black music producer and Simmons's good friend, expounding on the impact of the hip-hop industry on American culture and economy: "This is not about a moment. . . . This is way past a moment. This is Americana; this is a cultural change."[47] Harrell's grandiose statement announces to a larger public who fears a change in power from white male hands to black male hands that change has already occurred. Harrell explicitly claims American myth and legacy for the hip-hop community, specifically its black male entrepreneurial leaders, as he actively constructs a new narrative for "Americana." They are the new "forefathers" in Harrell's framework for understanding hip-hop's impact. We are to understand his proclamation as continuing, while reinventing, the legacy and "greatness" of America. Harrell's statement can be read within what Hazel Carby calls the legacy of "race men" who consider the work of race and nation building in the United States as (black) men's business.[48]

"Black Style Now" as Hip-Hop Fashion's Past

As hip-hop fashion companies have grown larger and more diversified in goods produced and marketed, they have moved away from racial or culturally specific language in marketing their brands. In an article about hip-hop fashion, Leslie E. Royal writes, "To further widen their appeal many urban designers are moving away from using the label 'urbanwear' and moving toward 'contemporary' or 'metropolitan,' says Ellzy of the Fashion Association."[49] This is an obvious move to deracinate the lines and simultaneously have them reflect consumable difference. Herman Gray writes of this tension throughout black masculine visual and material cultures: "Self representations of black masculinity in the United States are historically structured by and against dominant (and dominating) discourses of masculinity and race, specifically whiteness."[50] Gray's analysis applies to the instability of authenticity or "realness" in hip-hop music and visual culture, given that these categories are shaped in terms of competition among hip-hop markets and entrepreneurs, corporate marketability, and white audience reception. The success of hip-hop designers and entrepreneurs to absorb hip-hop fashion into mainstream fashion apparel and, more significantly, dominant narratives of success and difference as depoliticized and individualized can be seen on multiple fronts.

Hip-hop fashion companies that developed after an established market had been secured have moved away from the conservative fashion apparel on which companies like Phat Farm and Roca Wear built their fortune: hypermasculine apparel, namely baggy jeans, oversized outerwear, caps, and t-shirts. Pharrell Williams, a well-known hip-hop producer and musician whose musical experimentation pushes hip-hop beyond the hard-edge representations of black masculinity that have proliferated since the late 1980s and the rise of gangsta rap, started two fashion lines in the mid-2000s. Williams's Billionaire Boys Club and Ice Cream combine hip-hop fashion with Japanese animation, skateboarding style, and science fiction and target consumers who are interested in the purchase of hip-hop as hybrid culture (as distinguished from hip-hop as representative of an "authentic" urban street or thug culture). Williams very self-consciously distinguishes his fashion sensibility from earlier hip-hop fashion lines. In an interview, he expresses his distaste for "bling" and what he describes as bright and loud clothing (i.e., racially inflected colors and patterns). Marking his difference from the visual icon of black hypermasculine alterity, Williams states,

> I was a kid who wore Vans and Vision Streetwear, bad T-shirts, plaid pants and weird haircuts. But I admired Rakim. He was the best rapper, and stylistically he was about big gold chains, classic sneakers and customized Dapper Dan threads [the clothier to old-school rappers]. Billionaire Boys Club has some eighties influences—some of it reminds me of what LL [Cool J] used to wear when I was a kid. Ice Cream is more about skate couture.[51]

For Williams, old school hip-hop fashion becomes one of many influences of an aesthetic that signals "commoditized hybridity," not simply as marketing strategy but as the fashion wear itself. Williams's references to hip-hop are not in terms of its authenticity but one of many elements for a new urbane self-fashioning. It is an example of a twenty-first century relationship to hip-hop in which hip-hop's past is rendered palatable and even somewhat kitsch. No longer does the black male icon of hip-hop signal threat. Instead audiences interpret the posturing as a performance of racial alterity, of self-conscious differentiation based on familiar tropes of race.

Another sign of hip-hop fashion's incorporation into mainstream fashion industry is the self-conscious historicizing and institutionalizing of hip-hop's fashion history and its impact by key figures in hip-hop. In fall 2006 the Museum of the City of New York hosted a wildly popular exhibition titled *Black Style Now*. The show's brochure describes it as

> dynamic and diverse, bold and colorful. It's street style and it's high fashion. It's sexy, soulful, athletic, and it's all about attitude. BLACK STYLE NOW explores how black style has evolved in New York City and how the hip-hop revolution has turned fashion on its head. Hip-hop—today America's most important cultural export—has made black style big business, bringing attention to black designers and claiming a huge market of consumers—black and not—who have been eager to buy the latest in BLACK STYLE NOW.

The promotional material contains hyperbolic statements about hip-hop including "today America's most important cultural export." The show becomes a reflection on hip-hop fashion by hip-hop fashion companies with the sponsors of the exhibition including three of the largest hip-hop fashion companies, Academiks, Roca Wear, and Sean John. The exhibition was wholly celebratory of black style innovation and, more important, commercial success, with almost no critique of the culture of excess and material consumption.

In reviewing the show, Eric Wilson notes that black fashion designers of an earlier era, like Stephen Burrows, have received more attention due to the prominence of hip-hop fashion companies and the black hip-hop moguls who own these companies. However, Wilson questions the credibility of hip-hop moguls as designers, writing:

> If that has changed [recognition of black designers], it is mostly a result of the runway arrivals of hip-hop artists and record producers like Sean Combs and Russell Simmons, who are not really designers but entrepreneurs building clothing brands from their outsize personas, capitalizing on a style born of black street culture, and not so different from, say Donald Trump's constructing a brand on the culture of the boardroom.[52]

Interviewing the two curators—Michael Henry Adams and Michael McCollom—Wilson writes that the curators worked to expand the vision of the exhibit beyond its conception by the staff of the museum:

> The two men said senior museum administrators envisioned a crowd—pleasing display of youth styles that started in the streets and became an exuberant worldwide uniform. They did not want the show to fully explore thornier issues behind the mass market embrace of hip-hop looks—specifically, whether styles based in criminal subcultures perpetuate antisocial attitudes.[53]

The success of hip-hop fashion has hinged on the tension it produces as performance and promotion in authenticating "the urban real" while mass marketing commodifies a new reading of "Americana" and "American"-ness. While the popularity and success of hip-hop fashion companies are in every way a manifestation of advanced capitalistic processes in which the development of niche markets and the marketing of lifestyle brands continually fuel capital's expansion, the phenomenon is also an example of the rich and complex history and practices of hip-hop culture. Throughout much of the movement's history, its cultural producers have courted capitalism and promoted consumption through the marketing of difference. The late twentieth century trend to refashion "Americana" as cool and racialized through hip-hop clothing provides another lens to view black masculine investment in the legacy, wealth, and myth of nation. As significantly, these recent strategies to reclaim "America" have increasing significance given hip-hop's growing transnational marketability. Wilson quotes Sarah Henry, the deputy director and chief curator of the Museum of the City of New York, "Black style has become American style and arguably world style. . . . The hip-hop revolution has transformed the way the world dresses."[54] The re-fashioning and promotion of the new and cool America performed through the black male b-boy and produced by the hip-hop mogul are manifesta-tions of globalization and the marketing of youthful and racialized alterity as a stylized and reproducible commodity.

1. Monica L. Miller, *Slaves to Fashion: Black Dandyism and the Styling of Black Diasporic Identity* (Durham, NC: Duke University Press, 2009), 4–6.
2. Shane White and Graham White, *Stylin': African American Expressive Culture from its Beginnings to the Zoot Suit* (Ithaca, NY: Cornell University Press, 1998), 2, 153.
3. Robin D. G. Kelley, *Race Rebels: Culture, Politics, and the Black Working Class* (New York: Free Press, 1994), 163.
4. Powell, *Cutting a Figure*, 128, 130.
5. Kelefa Sanneh, "Fine and Dandy," *Transition* 12, no. 4 (2003): 123.
6. Regina Austin, "'A Nation of Thieves': Consumption, Commerce, and the Black Public Sphere," in *The Black Public Sphere: A Public Culture Book*, ed. The Black Public Sphere Collective (Chicago: University of Chicago Press, 1995), 239.

7. For more on subculture studies, see Dick Hebdige, *Subculture: The Meaning of Style* (London: Routledge, 1979), Stuart Hall and Tony Jefferson, *Resistance through Rituals: Youth Subcultures in Post-War Britain* (London: Hutchinson, 1976), and Ken Gelder and Sarah Thornton, eds., *The Subcultures Reader* (London: Routledge, 1997).

8. Austin, "A Nation of Thieves," 243.

9. Roland Barthes, *The Fashion System*, trans. Matthew Ward and Richard Howard (Berkeley: University of California Press, 1983).

10. Dorinne Kondo, "Fabricating Masculinity: Gender, Race, and Nation in the Transnational Circuit," in *About Face: Performing Race in Fashion and Theater* (New York: Routledge, 1997), 16.

11. Jackson, *Real Black*, 15.

12. See Rose, *Black Noise*.

13. Nelson George, *Hip Hop America* (New York: Penguin Books, 1998), 158.

14. Kobena Mercer, "Black Hair/Style Politics," in *The Subcultures Reader*, ed. Gelder and Thornton, 430.

15. Noel McLaughlin, "Rock, Fashion and Performativity," in *Fashion Cultures: Theories, Explorations and Analysis*, ed. Stella Bruzzi and Pamela Church Gibson (London: Routledge, 2000), 269.

16. Holmes Smith, "Hip-Hop Moguls," 61.

17. George, *Hip Hop America*, 158–59.

18. See William Eric Perkins, "Rap Attack: An Introduction," in *Droppin' Science: Critical Essays on Rap Music and Hip-Hop Culture* (Philadelphia: Temple University Press, 1996).

19. Mark Spiegler, "Marketing Street Culture: Bringing Hip-Hop Style to the Mainstream," *American Demographics* (November 1996): 29.

20. See Laura J. Kuo, "The Commoditization of Hybridity in the 1990s U.S. Fashion Advertising: Who is cK one?," in *Beyond the Frame: Women of Color and Visual Representation*, ed. Neferti X. M. Tadiar and Angela Y. Davis (New York: Palgrave Macmillan, 2005), 31–47.

21. See Paul Smith, "Tommy Hilfiger in the Age of Mass Customization," in *Popular Culture: A Reader*, ed. Raiford Guins and Omayra Zaragoza Cruz (Thousand Oaks, Calif.: Sage Publications, 2005), 151–58.

22. The magazine has featured Karl Kani in at least four articles in four years, and in 1996 the magazine labeled his company "BE Company of the Year."

23. See Tariq K. Muhammad, "From Here to Infinity: A Hip-Hop Clothier with Mainstream Appeal, Karl Kani Is Poised to Become the Fashion World's New Wunderkind," *Black Enterprise* 26, no. 11 (June 1996): 140–47; and Leslie E. Royal, "Hip-Hop on Top: We Look at the Elements and Top Designers that Have Helped Urban Fashion Skyrocket, and Predict Where the Industry Is Headed," *Black Enterprise* 30, no. 12 (July 2000): 91–94.

24. Nina S. Hyde, "Springing Softly Burrows: Stephen Burrows' Flair for the Sensual," *Washington Post*, November 11, 1977, D11.

25. Ginia Bellafante, "A Fallen Star of the '70s Is Back in the Business," *New York Times*, January 1, 2002, B1.

26. As a part of a larger trend toward the increasing visibility of black male figures in American popular culture, this transition of rappers to designers runs parallel with a number of rap stars becoming film actors and directors.

27. Nancy Jo Sales, "Hip-Hop Goes Universal," *New York* 32, no. 18 (May 10, 1999): 25.

28. Davis enumerates the fashion process as 1) Invention; 2) Introduction; 3) Fashion Leadership; 4) Increasing Social Visibility; and 5) Waning. See Fred Davis, *Fashion, Culture, and Identity* (Chicago: University of Chicago Press, 1992), 137.

29. Diana Crane, *Fashion and Its Social Agendas: Class, Gender, and Identity in Clothing* (Chicago: University of Chicago Press, 2000).

30. The exception to this would be Jennifer Lopez's lines in the early part of the 2000s, which received a great deal of attention and branched out into perfumes and other accessories. However, by 2009, she was reportedly halting production of at least one of her clothing lines due to lackluster sales and interest. See Julee Kaplan's "Jennifer Lopez Exits Apparel in the U.S.," *Women's Wear Daily*, June 24, 2009, http://www.wwd.com/markets-news/jennifer-lopez-exits-apparel-in-the-us-2187085 (accessed October 29, 2009).

31. See "Eve Re-Launching Fetish Clothing Line," *World Entertainment News Network*, May 17, 2004; Julee Greenberg, "Eve Gives Fetish Another Try," *Women's Wear Daily* 126 (June 14, 2007): 9.

32. See Apple Bottom official website, http://lifestyle.applebottoms.com/company.asp (accessed October 29, 2009).

33. Perry, *Prophets of the Hood*, 157.

34. Notorious B.I.G., "Big Poppa," *Ready to Die* (Bad Boy Records, 1994). Lyrics transcribed by author.

35. See Thomas Frank, *The Conquest of Cool: Business Culture, Counterculture, and the Rise of Hip Consumerism* (Chicago: University of Chicago Press, 1997), and Thomas Frank and Matt Weiland's *Commodify Your Dissent: Salvos from the Baffler* (New York: W. W. Norton, 1997).

36. Barthes, *The Fashion System*, 14.

37. Kondo, *About Face*, 158.

38. For more on the ghetto action film and its relationship to hip-hop, see Watkins, *Representing*.

39. Barthes, *The Fashion System*, 13.

40. Davis, *Fashion, Culture, and Identity*, 26.

41. Kuo, "The Commoditization of Hybridity," 36.

42. Royal, "Hip-Hop on Top," 94.

43. Guy Trebay, "A Fashion Statement: Hip-Hop on the Runway," *New York Times*, February 9, 2002, B4.

44. For a more detailed profile on Combs's impact on mainstream fashion and his ambivalent embrace by the fashion industry, see Michael Specter's profile, "I Am Fashion: Guess Who Puff Daddy Wants to Be?" *New Yorker*, September 9, 2002, 117–27.

45. Sales, "Hip-Hop Goes Universal," 28.

46. Sally Beatty, "Kellwood to Buy Urban-Style Label Phat Fashions," *Wall Street Journal*, January 9, 2004, A9.

47. Sales, "Hip-Hop Goes Universal," 24.

48. Hazel V. Carby, *Race Men* (Cambridge: Harvard University Press, 1998).

49. Royal, "Hip-Hop on Top," 94.

50. Herman Gray, "Black Masculinity and Visual Culture," *Callaloo* 18, no. 2 (1995): 401.

51. George Epaminondas, "Pharrell Williams: Interview," *InStyle* 15, no. 3 (March 2008): 291.

52. Eric Wilson, "Who Put the Black in Black Style?" *New York Times*, August 31, 2006, G1.

53. Ibid.

54. Ibid.

Post-reading Questions

1. According to the author, how does popular culture affirm the beauty of Black girls and women? How does it deny it?

2. What can women do to affirm the beauty of other women?

3. How did Simmons, Combs, Jay-Z, and other entrepreneurs affirm Black men through their clothing lines? Why was this affirmation necessary?

4. Why does the author make the distinction that Simmons, Combs, Jay-Z, and others are entrepreneurs rather than designers?

5. How do global perceptions of African American beauty differ from American perceptions?

UNIT 4

CONTEMPORARY MOMENTS

This final section of *Intersections* examines more recent American history and culture and also places it in a larger global context. For generations moving forward, there will always have been an African American president and first lady. That image holds fast, regardless of the (im)permanence of Obama-era policy. The historical profiles of Barack and Michelle Obama illustrate the interplay of race, gender, and class in shaping their professional trajectories and their respective legacies.

"From Chattel to First Lady" is a historical summary of Black women's history in the United States and pushes against the stereotypes of Black women discussed earlier in this collection. While not an easy road to travel, the story of Black women's rise from property to Pennsylvania Avenue does elicit in the reader a sense of awe for just how far Black women have come. Making clear the connection between Michelle Obama and the community that raised her, Marsha J. Tyson Darling points out Michelle Obama was not born into the wealth that she enjoys today but rather emerged from the true richness that comes from self-awareness and a service ethos shaped by her community.

In "Everything His Father Was Not," Heidi Ardizonne explores how former president Barack Obama's parenting of his daughters, Sasha and Malia, played concurrently with his performance as father at the national level. Giving sage advice and calming crying babies, Obama was seen as nurturing—nurturing the nation's children and soothing some of the nation's deepest historical and racial wounds. Barack Obama's first and subsequent presidential election gave him a visibility that was unmatched in the country. It also allowed him to be read as the antithesis of the stereotypical, dysfunctional Black father.

Author Dionne Rosser-Mims places freedom seeker Harriet Tubman, civil rights activist Charlayne Hunter, human rights activist Malala Yousafzai, and the more than 200 kidnapped Nigerian school girls in a larger continuum of women who have either fought for freedom or have suffered the dire consequences of trying to improve their lives socially, economically, and politically. The chapter illustrates how race, gender, and political structures combine to empower or disempower women.

Rosser-Mims argues that *all* women can learn from the battles for empowerment that women of color have waged in the name of improving opportunities for themselves, for other women, and for their communities.

Pre-reading Questions:

1. What was it about Barack Obama's presidential candidacy that drove voters to the polls in 2008 and again in 2012?

2. What was it about Michelle Obama that made it possible for people to see her as a first lady?

3. With the election of a Black (male) president achieved in the United States, why does the election of a woman president prove to be so challenging?

4. Why are strong Black fathers "noteworthy"?

5. What stereotypes do women in general—and Black women in particular—have to battle in order to participate in politics?

FROM CHATTEL TO FIRST LADY

Black Women Moving from the Margins

MARSHA J. TYSON DARLING

ONLY THE BLACK WOMAN CAN SAY, "WHEN AND WHERE I ENTER, IN THE quiet, undisputed dignity of my womanhood, without violence and without suing or special patronage, then and there the whole *Negro race enters with me*" (Cooper 1892, 31).

This quote is taken from a speech delivered to black clergymen by Anna Julia Cooper in 1886, a tumultuous year following the Civil War. In "Womanhood: A Vital Element in the Regeneration and Progress of a Race," Cooper, an admired public speaker, expressed black women's sense of a pursuit of self-discovery. She eloquently captured the relationship between the advancement of *Negro* women and the uplift of the *Negro* race. Cooper, and many other black women, might not have imagined that within two generations of their active agency to transform social relations in America that a majority of the nation's voting electorate would elect and re-elect a black man to lead the United States as its president, and that a black woman from working-class roots would stand and act at his side as First Lady.

INTERSECTIONALITY, COMPOUNDING DISCRIMINATIONS, AND BLACK WOMEN'S "HERSTORY"

This essay is a discourse on the journey of the black woman from chattel to First Lady. The cumbersome, slow, thorny road that black women have traveled from being someone's personal property (chattel) to First Lady has required an active tradition of black women's self-help agency and mutual assistance, and far-reaching social and political changes across the nation.

Indeed, recent surveys of black Americans who lived through or were directly affected by Jim and Jane Crow segregation confirm that few imagined that Americans would elect a black president in their lifetimes. First Lady Michelle Obama is no shadow of her husband. She was an accomplished lawyer before she met Barack Obama, and she continues active personal agency in her work to advance projects that she considers important and socially transformative, especially the crisis of obesity in the nation and the connection between food, diet, and health.

As important as Ivy-educated Michelle Obama is to our nation and to the discourse on black women's "herstory" in this narrative, the opportunities she has acted on were out of reach for most black women in her mother's and grandmother's generations. Indeed, it was the powerful and transformative social forces that reshaped American society that enabled Michelle Obama's self-help aspirations. Because it is important to engage a perspective that assesses intergenerational social transformation of black women's herstory, this essay examines important social thresholds in black women's journey from chattel to First Lady. This chapter begins by examining the manner in which socially constructed ideas and stereotypical stigmas about black women have, over time, become corrosive barriers to the social advancement of black women as a group. Then, it briefly notes the active self-help traditions and transformative social forces that have helped many black women connect upwardly mobile personal aspirations with progressive outcomes. Next, it focuses on First Lady Michelle Obama and the social forces, stereotypes, and personal agency and self-discovery that have enabled a working-class girl to move from the margins toward the center, where life-affirming options, privileges, and immunities exist. And finally, it concludes by situating this historical moment and Michelle Obama in society's larger context.

All women and girls experience their lives through socially constructed multiple and intersecting identities. They belong to more than one community and have more than one identity in their social relationships within various patriarchies. A social science methodology that exposes how multiple and intersecting discriminations affect women's and girls' lived experiences is particularly useful. Intersectional analysis is such a theoretical approach in that it identifies the intersection and operation of the racial, ethnic, economic, sexual, cultural, age, caste, ability, and gendered dimensions of multiple and compounding forms of discriminations against women and girls. Intersectionality also exposes how the convergence of multiple discriminations in the lives of women and girls operates to subjugate and marginalize them (Darling 2010b, 91–106).

Intersectionality is not a new paradigm for delineating multiple, intersecting, and compounding identities, especially identities marked for discrimination, subordination, and marginalization. Over the past several decades, black feminist theorists have enjoined intersectional analyses in providing discourses regarding critical race feminism. Intersectionality emerged as an essential component of the critical race theory discourses espoused by feminist women of color who sought to render the multiple discriminations experienced by indigenous women, women of color, and racialized women more visible. Intersectionality has helped to denote the marginalizing racial, ethnic, class, and sexual aspects of gender discrimination. It has also been instrumental in promoting advancement and equity for marginalized women and girls of color (Collins 2000b, 404–20; Crenshaw 1991, 1241–99).

Considering that black women and girls lead lives at the intersection of blackness, femaleness, and often poverty-all of the time—it is important to keep the theory of intersectionality in the forefront of our thinking and analysis because too often black women's multiple burdens have been missing from public debate and scholarly discourse. It should also be noted that direct and derivative white privilege, patriarchal fundamentalism, and internalized self-hate are among the continuing threats to black women and girls actualizing racial and gender equality and class advancement.[1]

STEREOTYPES OF BLACK WOMEN IN THE AMERICAN CULTURAL IMAGINATION

Although oppressions should not be ranked hierarchically, some burdens are unique to black women in the United States. The multiple, intersecting, and compounding discrimination and marginalization of black women and girls that continue to stymie their social progress derive from powerful racist and misogynist stereotypes and social metaphors that have been repeated intergenerationally.

Some of the derogatory and degrading ideas and stereotypes that have had the greatest impact on black women's lives have become icons in the American cultural imagination. Many have an enduring place in the white imagination, and some, such as "wench," "Jezebel," "Sapphire," and "Welfare Queen," have become part of U.S. popular culture and black vernacular. Beliefs about black women as property, as evil seductresses, as possessing an unrestrained sexuality and unclean genitals, often have been used as a rationale for sexual assault and rape.

Sexualizing black women and girls in racist and overtly misogynist ways assures that some members of dominant groups will target them for sexual assault. It also means that assault on or violence against marginalized black women and girls is often dismissed or excused, and the violated are blamed for "causing" or "deserving" the violence. Such is the power of negative stereotypical stigmas to complement marginalizing private action against black women and girls (Jewell 1993, 35–54).

On the other side of the impact of negative stereotypical stigmas directed toward black women and girls is that notions of white male decency and white female virtue increase. White culture is presented as civilizing, tolerant, and uplifting of black people, even references to white men as rapists (except in abolitionist literature) have been largely muted. A focus on white people's contribution to the moral propriety of black people helps to sustain skin-color privilege for all whites. Hence, white-skin privilege exists in direct proportion to the actions, ideas, and stereotypical images and slogans that are created by white racial and gender dominance.

Stereotypes are powerful servants of thought and action because they pose answers to the unasked queries about social order and ranking. Stereotypes are always offered as an answer and never the question about why social subjugation continues to occur. In reality, racial, gender, class, and ethnic stereotypes almost always serve to camouflage and naturalize social dominance and oppression. While stereotypes can be negative or positive, racist and misogynist stereotypes continue to maintain patriarchal and white-skin privilege in U.S. society. Some stereotypes, often repeated intergenerationally, have assumed a life of their own, and many people hold them as truth. In fact, some stereotypes are so powerful that they function as icons in our culture. As representations of ideas, beliefs, and even stereotypes, icons can appear without an accompanying explanation and still be tremendously effective in conveying social meaning.

Racist and misogynist stereotypes continue to maintain multiple and intersecting racial, gender, and class discriminations against black women and girls and simultaneously posit inferiority and dysfunction as static qualities that are expected of them. So pervasive is this legacy that one frequently hears white people and foreigners express surprise when they interact with a black woman or man who acts outside the learned social boundaries established by racial, gender, and class stereotypes. Furthermore, while such stereotypes blunt the racial and cultural knowledge capacity of many whites, racist, misogynist, and classist stereotypes often operate to undermine and even destroy self-esteem in black females. This is especially true if the stereotype denigrates a black woman's capacity for intelligence and moral sensibility. Hence, such stereotypes help to maintain the discriminations that enable the marginalization of black women and girls.

The stereotypes about black women that are focused on here are derived from historical relationships laden with racial betrayal and sexual exploitation. In that historical narrative, the most destructive stereotypes have reduced black women to an object (or "a thing"). A "thing" is not a sentient human being. Denying black women's humanity while sexually and materially exploiting their persons was a betrayal encoded into the social dominance practiced by many white males. Then, as now, oppressive choices and decisions that created and sustained betrayal, inequality, and marginalization required an explanation. The marginalizing portrayals and representations of black women as "wench," "Jezebel," "Mammy," "Sapphire," or, more recently, "pathological," "Baby Machine," "Welfare Queen," and "whore" have sought to undermine personal agency as well as compassion for black women and girls.

SLAVERY, BLACK WOMEN, AND THE EUROPEAN AMERICAN CULTURAL LANDSCAPE

Discrimination is created by dominant social groups that impose social barriers on black women's lives: poverty, lack of healthcare, poor education, sexual violence, substandard housing, and poor diet, as well as police violence in poor communities. Marginalizing stereotypes are tools for presenting negative images that further the political, economic, social, and even cultural work of opposing social progress and discouraging civil rights agency for certain segments of society; in this chapter, black women. The incongruity between most black women's lives and the stereotypes of passivity, ignorance, uncontrolled anger, and sexual licentiousness endure despite a reality that is far afield of the illusion. While these stereotypes tell us little about the actual lived experiences of most black women, they signal the persistence of significant social barriers to their entitlement in the United States.

One starts with the fact that black women live in a society that values people of Western European descent. Black women occupy a social space at the intersection of blackness and femaleness, and since most have been and continue to be poor; they have been pushed to the margins of society because of the intersection of their race, gender, and class. Perchance, add lesbian or transgender sexual orientation and the stigmatizing discriminations that black women and girls experience are multiple and compounding. Of course, age is always an important qualifier of social status. Hence, since black women derive no skin-color privilege that lifts them beyond the diminished social status accorded to all women under patriarchy, and since most black women are poor, there is little if any social reward accorded black women in a society dominated by all men and light-skinned or white people.

For centuries, the oppression of black women has been intensely physical, psychological, and spiritual as a direct result of chattel slavery. The system of chattel slavery developed in the last half of the seventeenth century by English colonial slaveholders was based on the "absolute authority" of slave owners over the life or death of enslaved women and men. The enslaved had no *human right* to life. A colonial Virginia statute proclaimed that slave owners who killed a "slave" were exempt from felony charges. The argument that planters took care of the enslaved because they had paid money for them has three weaknesses. First, the record shows that some planters also worked white indentured servants to death, so why presume that Africans captured for the taking, or birthed and reared on plantations—and lacking any of the cultural "value" accorded white Christians coming from Europe—would have fared any better? (Heilbroner and Singer 1999, 40).

Second, the fact of the law's passage is instructive, because resistance to enslavement and its arduous labor-intensive work was an ever-present reality, and violence, even death, was a means to control captive African men in particular. Third, the statute unequivocally supported the emerging doctrine of "absolute authority." It is important to note that Atlantic economy slavery developed away from any of the institutions, customs, traditions, or customary obligations formed in Europe's social evolution that might have served as checks and balances, restraining some of the authoritarian excesses of slave owners, who answered to no one. Taking authority a step further, at about the same time that the Virginia House of Burgesses led the way in crafting "absolute authority" as slavery's operating doctrine, slave owners in the British North Atlantic colonies established in law that black enslavement would extend across generations (Higginbotham, Jr. 1978, 19–60).

By law, the bodies of enslaved women, and especially their wombs, were the key to the intergenerational transmission of enslavement for all of the children born to them. Racial and sexual slavery *evolved*—that is, captive black women performed agricultural and reproductive work, as quite literally enslaved women's wombs became *capital*. Enslaved women's wombs were put to "work," undergoing pregnancy for as many of their fertile years as possible. "Breeding babies" reproduced a slave labor force for free, as by law an infant's status rested entirely on the status of one's mother. While the evidence is more scant than the frequency of its occurrence, it is clear that some enslaved black women resisted the intentions of slave owners to treat them as "breeding machines" (Schwartz 2006, 9–32, 67–106).

As students of history know, captive women and rape and coerced sex go hand in hand. Treated as sexual prey from the moment of capture, enslaved women and girls were victims of sexual coercion or violence. Slave owners largely controlled the paternity of pregnancies of enslaved women. The wombs of enslaved black women became part of an agricultural production process—black women were stereotyped as a "wench," which is a tool, a unit of production. Enslaved black women were compelled to bear children sired by captive black men and mulatto children sired by white men. For at least two hundred years, such were the conditions of racial and sexual slavery for black women, puberty-aged girls, and their children (Morgan 2004; Roberts 1997; Jennings 1990, 3, 45–74; 2001, 1619–50; Follet 2003, 510–39).

Of course, there were instances where white males developed genuinely caring relationships with enslaved black women. Some white men who had mixed-race children with enslaved black women, freed the woman, and raised their biracial children. Some white men manumitted and married enslaved black women, and sometimes a white man purchased the freedom of an enslaved woman from another man in order to marry her. However, we should question to what extent consensual relationships between men and women, free and slave, within the context of slavery were ever really possible. It was the power that white males held over black people in such settings that went largely unchecked by other whites. Such a system of extreme social dominance seldom generated consensual relationships.

Even though slave owners crafted a social order that worked to their advantage, moral issues emerged that required a response. The issue of sexual "licentiousness," namely, sex outside Christian marriage, in an age of professed fervent Christian morality disturbed many individuals, especially those in the pulpit. Second, the issue of interracial sex between white men and their "slave" women, evidenced by the increasing numbers of light brown babies being born, also bore directly on Christian marriage. To complicate matters, many of the mulatto babies born to captive black women were sired by white men of property who were married to white women. Some married white Christian women anguished over the threat that the presence of captive African and captivity-born black women posed to their husbands' sexual loyalty. But white women were themselves in no position to curtail male lust for their concubines. Consequently, many white males, both married and single, continued the sexual behaviors that pleased them—after all, white wives and black or mulatto concubines were all white male property (Omolade 1994, 3–18).

Ever accustomed to answering to no one in slavery's system of "absolute authority" over captive Africans, slave owners came under moral pressure from white and free black abolitionists. Abolitionists used every available means: newspapers, broadsides, speeches, books, articles, and by the nineteenth century, autobiographies to attack the institution of slavery. The issue of moral impropriety/fornication emerged as abolitionists began providing the funds to publish the narratives of black women who had escaped slavery. Scathing in their indictment of the rampant sexual abuse of enslaved black women and girls by white men in the South, the few black women's narratives that were published exposed, through first-person accounts, the horrors of the sexual abuse and violence they had experienced and witnessed (Jacobs 1861, 26–29; Sterling 1984, 18–31).

White men were called upon to answer the moral challenge to their virtue. They denied any moral impropriety, insisting that they were governing over Christian wives and promiscuous, sex-crazed slave women who would not let them be good Christian men. They called the enslaved women "Jezebel," an evil seductress invoked from biblical teachings (White 1985/1999, 27–61; Jewell 1993, 55–71). Further seeking to quell allegations of conduct unbecoming of moral Christian men, slave owners offered an image of the quintessential female servant/slave, "Mammy," as a counterpoint to Jezebel. Mammy was a dutiful, hard-working, self-sacrificing black woman who was committed to serving her white "family" at the expense of her own children; even as that "family" maintained its belief in her innate racial inferiority. Asexual, unattractive, and "ugly" by white standards of beauty, never sassy or a seductress, sometimes fat or obese from eating well in the big house, a great cook who toiled without a fret, she was always docile and loyal. Thus, many slave owners sought to assert that her role in their lives posed no threat at all to their moral sensibility or to white Christian marriage.

"Mammy," Jezebel, and Sapphire

"Mammy" has become the dominant racial and sexual stereotype and cultural icon of black women in American society dating from the slavery era. In the early twentieth century, Hollywood films packaged the stereotype of an idyllic slavery South—*Birth of a Nation*, *Song of the South*, *Show Boat*, *Imitation of Life*, and the all-time blockbuster, *Gone with the Wind*, which cast Hattie McDaniel in her Oscar-winning portrayal as Mammy. With the advent of television in the 1950s, *Mammy* moved into American living rooms. Although "tweaked" a bit, she is still with us on television today. Mammy's pictorial representation—head scarf covering unkempt or "ugly" hair, obese, asexual, and always smiling while cooking—remains as it has been for decades, as "Aunt Jemima" (Bogle 1992, 9–18).

The Jezebel and Mammy stereotypes stood in stark contrast to a system of production based on at times the brutal sexual exploitation of black women's bodies and wombs. During the same decades that black women's slave narratives were published, some Virginia slave owners engaged in the business of "breeding" slaves for sale (Baptist 2001, 1619–50). Mean-spirited measures held slavery in place: physical brutality—whippings which sometimes resulted in death, the withholding of food, especially in relation to obtaining sexual compliance from captive women, selling family members away from each other as punishment, and other controlling behaviors. As the decades passed, the numbers of black captives fleeing into the dark of night increased—though many more black men ran away than black women who would not leave their children behind.

In addition to Jezebel, slave owners invented "Sapphire," the out-of-control, wild-with-anger black "thing," who could only be subdued with physical force. Those outside slavery's domain were shocked and horrified when enslaved black women who had escaped bared their backs to reveal the scars of repeated beatings. The illusion of southern tranquility and docile, primitive slaves ran headlong into the reality that slavery was a system of racial and sexual exploitation held in place by sustained physical and sexual violence.

Black men who watched their mothers, sisters, wives, lovers, daughters, and other female relatives and friends indiscriminately raped or coerced into having sex with white men were not likely to have blamed the black women and girls around them. Indeed, some of these enslaved black men lost their lives, or were crippled or maimed attempting to prevent the sexual abuse of the vulnerable women and girls whom they cared for (Northrup 1853). While enslaved black men scoffed at white men's constructions of Jezebel and Sapphire stereotypes, the persistence of these stereotypes has continued to exert a colonizing influence on black popular culture.

For decades now, stereotypes of an oversexed, uppity, and in-your-face black woman—the "black bitch"—have trickled from the wider American culture into black popular culture and song. The "black bitch" is Sapphire renamed, and she is invoked to explain why black women and girls have to be treated roughly. Only aggression and violence, not compassion or love, works. In real time, misogyny (Jezebel, Sapphire, and the "black bitch"), like racism, provides stereotypes that transfer the blame for group oppression onto the victim. This misogynist message represents black women as fallible, sexually tainted, even fallen women who have made unwise choices based on individual preferences; it is the women who have created their bad situations.

BLACK WOMEN FROM SLAVERY TO FREEDOM-SELF-HELP AND MUTUAL AID

Free black women worked in the only jobs available to them: washing, sewing, cooking, cleaning, nursing, and caring for other people's children. Even during the twentieth century, the majority of black women were relegated to service jobs. More prosperous free black women were able to acquire an education, often at colleges such as Oberlin College in Ohio, which opened its doors to blacks in the nineteenth century. Educated black women worked as teachers, or started businesses, such as catering, bakeries, hair salons, boarding houses, millineries, and dressmaking. Black women also participated in mutual aid societies; they paid dues to benevolent associations for burial benefits and initiated their own educational and benefit organizations. Some supported philanthropic efforts to assist those in need, especially blacks on the run from enslavement. Many were avid antislavery proponents, and some assisted with the Underground Railroad, and many helped to institutionalize independent black churches. Some black women even helped strengthen the development of African Free Schools in northern cities. In some instances, they used their earnings to operate their own businesses, including boarding houses (precursors to inns and motels), and established societies, schools, and colleges to educate black girls and women.[2]

Claiming freedom with the Civil War behind them, black women looked to a future ripe with promise, but soon confronted southern *de jure* (by law) and northern *de facto* (by custom) racial segregation and disfranchisement as white opposition to black progress. A number of middle-class black women mobilized to strengthen black communities and create advancement opportunities for black women and girls. The creation of the organizations and institutions that comprised the black Women's Club Movement:

the Bethel Literary and Historical Association (Washington, D.C.), the Colored Women's League (Washington, D.C., 1892), the New Era Club (Boston, 1895), the National Federation of Afro-American Women (Boston, 1895), the National Association of Colored Women (NACW, Washington, D.C., 1896), the Northeastern Federation of Women's Clubs, the National Council of Negro Women, the Phillis Wheatley clubs and homes, and the Working Girls' Home Association was spearheaded by Ida B. Wells-Barnett, Mary Church Terrell, Josephine St. Pierre Ruffin, Mary McLeod Bethune, Jane Edna Hunter, Margaret Murray Washington, Anna Julia Cooper, and other black women who sought to provide leadership outlets for professional black women and race uplift (Clark-Lewis 1994, 51–95; Giddings 1984, 57–117; Higginbotham 1993, 1–88; Hunter 1997, 74–97; Jones 1985, 142–46; Terborg-Penn 1998, 1–80).

BLACK WOMEN FROM SEGREGATION TO CIVIL RIGHTS

Black women's organizations worked to promote the educational, economic, and social advancement of black people, including women and girls during the very same decades in which racial and sexual segregation were the ugliest (for instance, by 1930 official reports confirmed that over 3,000 black men had been lynched primarily in the South). A generation of young black girls watched their mothers, older sisters, aunts, and older woman friends help sustain and strengthen black institutions and organizations while also promoting self-help goals. Such was the "stuff" of self-discovery that spurred some black women to ask and expect more of American society. The generation of young black women and men who stood with Dr. Martin Luther King, Jr., grew up watching black adults engage in self-help activities as "race uplift." In the post–World War II years, as the Supreme Court's *Brown* decisions in 1954 and 1955 struck a decisive blow at the *Plessy* doctrine of race-based segregation and exclusion, increasing numbers of black women and men dared to act on rising expectations for their lives (Collier-Thomas and Franklin 2001, 21–41; Gilkes 2001, 15–60).

While helping to sustain themselves and their families in the twentieth century, black women confronted pervasive racist and misogynist stereotypes about their bodies—especially their skin color, hair texture, lip shape, buttocks size, sexuality, intelligence, and moral values. Some fell prey to the sustained hate that a virulent racism imposed on black women's lives—what Professor Melissa Harris-Perry describes as the "crooked room," which robbed them of a sense of an affirming set of positive possibilities. Many others found a way to live affirming lives and teach the generation they were rearing to create a better future for themselves and their communities. Many also taught the young that if opportunity presented itself, they should work for change. The black women who predate Michelle Obama were raised by black women and men whose active agency sustained them through poverty, discrimination, and institutional marginalization.[3]

The Obamas, Fruits of the Great Society

Barack and Michelle Obama and their generation are beneficiaries of social transformations that have produced enormously transfiguring changes in American society over the past fifty years. These transformations did not come easily; long-standing barriers to the exercise of civil rights and access to educational, economic, and political opportunities were a constant struggle. Barack and Michelle were children during the tumultuous struggles that created the social changes that in their teenage years enabled both to earn scholarships to attend America's premier educational institutions. This meant access to still greater portals of opportunity for achievement, entitlement, and power.

Barack and Michelle Obama have enjoyed fulfilling work and financial prosperity beyond what their parents might have imagined as possible. They have enjoyed successful professional advancement and upper-middle-class family life in America. Like so many other black folks, who now enjoy the fruits of the great society, Barack and Michelle were able to pass through "opportunity's doors" when those doors swung open.

Barack Obama's parents were privileged in terms of their educational background and as such were part of the middle class. Barack's mother attained a doctoral degree in anthropology and his father earned a master's degree in economics. Yet both Barack and Michelle came from modest economic circumstances and were raised by parents who lived in a generation that witnessed changes in their access to civil rights and social equality. We can be sure that those parents whispered to them, "Yes, you can!," as they began to find their way. Barack and Michelle are among those who have used educational advancement, smart career choices, political savvy, and a changing political climate to fashion a reality for themselves that is hardly reminiscent of America's dark racial past. The ascent of Barack and Michelle to fame, fortune, and real political power suggests a new direction for American race relations. Michelle's place in this new era suggests not just a shift in the gendered dimensions of race relations in the United States, as Michelle's journey from margins to mainstream has been interesting to observe.

MICHELLE OBAMA—BLACK WOMAN FROM THE MARGINS TO THE MAINSTREAM

As Barack Obama sought and achieved the presidency in 2008, many also focused on Michelle Obama. So who is Michelle Obama? How does she represent herself and how is she represented by others? And how much of those representations derive from the legacy of how racism and misogyny have intersected to demean black womanhood in the United States? What has Michelle been up against, especially in terms of the American media, and how has she responded? What has she done to meet customary expectations as First Lady? What is her impact on America and on black women and girls? In what ways has she sought to "connect" children in marginalized communities with powerful people and institutions, and what has been her self-described motivation for attempting to reach black girls?

Born on January 17, 1964, to Fraser Robinson III and Marian Robinson, Michelle LaVaughn Robinson is the younger of two children. Michelle's researched genealogy reveals that she is descended from Melvinia (a mother at the age of fifteen), an enslaved black woman who lived in the mid-nineteenth century and who gave birth to a mulatto child fathered by a white man on a 200-acre plantation in Georgia. Growing up in a working-class family surrounded by an extended kinship network, Michelle and her older brother, Craig, received many of the core values that have remained with them over time: hard work, persistence, stick-togetherness, sacrifice, aspiration, self-help, being charitable, and obligation/reciprocity.

While these affirming self-worth values are not unique to the black working class, it is important to mention them because racist and even classist representations of working-class people of color often deny that these values are important to identity development among those who are poor. In Michelle's words:

> I was raised in a working-class family on the South Side of Chicago, that's how I identify myself, a working-class girl. My mother came home and took care of us through high school. My father was a city shift worker who took care of us all his life. We were so blessed, my brother

and I, because we had everything you needed. It had nothing to do with money, but we had two parents that loved us, a father that had a steady job all of his life. We had a strong external family unit, I grew up with grandparents and uncles and aunts. People didn't go to college, but you had Christmas dinner together. You know, they were just this huge, strong support system. The neighborhood that I lived in wasn't wealthy, but it wasn't crime-ridden, so you could play in the streets, and there were gangs, but there weren't gangs that would keep you from going to school. (Scherer and Gibbs 2009; Newton-Small 2008)

When Michelle reflects on who helped define her other than her quiet, steady father who used family monies to help both Craig and Michelle attend college, she says of her upbringing:

But in terms of whose stories stay in my head, it's my mother's, my aunts', my neighbors', my teachers' from growing up on the South Side of Chicago. I mean the people who really moved me were the people that I knew in my life: my mother, the teachers that I had. I mean, I have real strong memories of great teachers that I had in grammar school, the teachers who told me that I was smart, who pushed me to skip a grade, who challenged me with tough projects. Those are really the people. Those are the stories that really guide me. Those are the folks that I'm trying to make proud. (Scherer and Gibbs 2009)

Michelle graduated from Chicago public schools and went on to undergraduate studies at Princeton, where she graduated with a Bachelor of Arts in Sociology in 1985. Michelle's sixty-four-page senior honors thesis, "Princeton-Educated Blacks and the Black Community," offers insights into being black, female, and working class at a prestigious white university. Michelle noted,

Earlier in my college career, there was no doubt in my mind that as a member of the Black community I was somehow obligated to this community and would utilize all of my present and future resources to benefit this community first and foremost. My experiences at Princeton have made me far more aware of my "Blackness" than ever before. . . . I sometimes feel like a visitor on campus; as if I really don't belong. . . . These experiences have made it apparent to me that the path I have chosen to follow by attending Princeton will likely lead to my further integration and/or assimilation into a white cultural and social structure that will only allow me to remain on the periphery of society; never becoming a full participant. This realization has presently made my goals to actively utilize my resources to benefit the Black community more desirable.

In addition to her studies, Michelle spent time working with kids in a free literacy program (Robinson 1985, 2–3).

Michelle took her interest in progressive social change with her to Harvard Law School, where she participated in demonstrations that pressed Harvard to recruit more minority professors and students. Harvard law professor Charles Ogletree remembers Michelle Robinson as exerting practical energy in working to recruit black undergrads to Harvard Law School. After graduating, Michelle was hired as an intellectual-property lawyer at Sidley Austin, a prestigious Chicago firm. After meeting and falling in love with Barack, a junior lawyer she mentored, Michelle left her position at Sidley Austin to work in public service, initially working for the Chicago mayor's office, followed by working to build Public Allies, a new charity. After successfully helping to anchor the organization financially, Michelle moved on to work as an associate dean of students at the University of Chicago, and then to serving the university as the vice president of external relations. In both positions, she worked to connect the university to its undergraduates and to improve the university's relations with local communities (Wolffe 2008; Newton-Small 2008).

As the quotes above make clear, Michelle Obama sees her past in her personality and makeup. It is a past filled with loving and affirming adults who also challenged her towards high achievement. Michelle recounts how little she knew or understood the world of privilege and opportunity that existed where she grew up on the South Side of Chicago: "There but for fortune go I." A major goal for Michelle Obama is that she has "made" something fine of herself and is ever concerned to promote children's self-discovery. Her self-image is confident, positive, and affirming about being black; she is affectionate and emotionally secure. She is committed to helping her daughters navigate from childhood to young adulthood, and she seeks to empower others, especially children in marginalized communities. That's how Michelle Obama sees and understands herself.

When it comes to how others see and represent Michelle Obama, answers reflect the complicated legacy bearing on black women's lives. The accomplished, professional black woman in American society is not something new. The tradition of black women's active agency outside the confines of family life is long-standing. Professional black women in earlier generations were usually educated at historically black colleges and universities (HBCU). Michelle Obama received her education when the walls of Jane and Jim Crow segregation were beginning to crumble. While Michelle attended Chicago's segregated public schools through high school, unlike her black female predecessors, she received her undergraduate and professional training at Ivy League universities. This allowed her to assume a professional "place" in the white world previously only imagined by black folks accustomed to living professionally active but segregated lives within the confines of black communities.

Despite Michelle's achievements, she still encounters white perceptions of her that harken back to America's legacy of black women-hating. Specifically, her assertiveness—a quality highly prized in her corporate law firm and in her role at the University of Chicago—often has been interpreted as black women's "bitchiness" by some in the white media. There have been several caricatures of Michelle Obama dating to Barack Obama's 2008 bid for the White House. Not surprisingly, a tradition of negative stigmas and hate imaging of black women has also given strength to sustaining hate speech toward black women who step out of "their place." Those voices attack Michelle's *persona* and not just her *ideas*; they represent her as "the bitter, anti-American, ungrateful, rude, crude, ghetto, angry Michelle Obama." These are words that strike not only at Michelle's ideas about what needs to be done in the nation, but also her concern on behalf of those in the United States who have been marginalized or left behind. Depicting her in such a negative light is an attack on *her* working-class roots and her concern for the humble folks who in their poor circumstances are so often invisible and ignored. Reflecting the ways in which many Americans have learned to renounce black women's voices, in 2008 Michelle was dismissed by many as just an *angry black woman* (Gibbs 2008).

Conservatives have accused Michelle Obama of "whining" and preaching a "Gospel of Misery," and radio star Hugh Hewitt noted that when she says that "before we can work on the problems, we have to fix our souls," his response is "whenever someone from the government comes to you and says, 'we have to fix your soul,' be very afraid. No one believes outside of the hard-core left that government can fix your soul." Rejection words have been accompanied by images of Michelle as threatening and out of step with the American character. The "black bitch" is Sapphire descended from her nineteenth-century creation as the aggressive, threatening woman whose person, and not just her ideas, should be assaulted. During the 2008 campaign, the white media wasted no time invoking a menacing image of Michelle Obama. That spring, the *National Review* pictured Michelle Obama on its front cover calling her "Mrs. Grievance," accompanied by the text, "Michelle Obama embodies a peculiar mix of privilege and victimology which is not where most Americans live" (Gibbs 2008).

Then, in July 2008, the cover of *The New Yorker* represented the Obamas as dangerous, flag-burning militants. Michelle is represented with a very large Afro hairstyle, reminiscent of how Angela Davis appeared on FBI wanted posters during the Black Power Movement. Michelle is standing in what appears to be the Oval Office, exchanging fist-banging greetings with Barack under a picture of a much sought after al-Qaeda "terrorist." Michelle is toting a large shell capacity assault weapon strapped to her back, and she is wearing military style pants stuffed into above ankle combat boots. Barack is represented as unbecoming in his place in Western civilization; an "alien," he is clad in the tunic, turban, and sandals easily associated with Muslim men. Decried by some as racist and misogynist, *The New Yorker* cover stirred old portrayals of black women and men as radicals who pose a threat to America. At a time when many Americans wished for Osama Bin Laden's murder, and some questioned Barack's pedigree, to suggest a similarity between al-Qaeda and the Obamas served to intensify not diminish racial and cultural fears of them. The Secret Service reported record numbers of death threats against the Obamas, and some whites brought ropes tied into nooses and explicitly racist posters to political rallies. Melissa Harris-Perry has aptly noted that *The New Yorker*'s representation of Michelle emerged from an ideological perspective about her, in which "anger was an easy default framework for interpreting Michelle."[4]

Amidst the clamor over Michelle's occasional forthrightness during Barack's 2008 campaign, *Time* magazine's Nancy Gibbs commented that Michelle's "speeches can sound stark and stern compared with her husband's roof raisers. He's about the promise; she's more about the problem.... She goes further, worrying out loud about the country's lack of fairness, the corrosive cynicism of its citizens and how Americans spend more time talking about what we won't do, what won't work, what can't change than about what is possible." Gibbs noted that some commentators are uncomfortable and angry at Michelle Obama's concern for the voiceless on the margins. They also seemed angry that Michelle has an assertive voice and uses it, which is something white men and some white women in positions of authority do frequently, but they assert their agency in a society where the legacy of racial stereotypes does not trigger animus towards their assertiveness. So, while Michelle Obama sometimes received praise for her candor in the 2008 campaign she also received opprobrium, especially by the right wing, for stepping out of her "place" as a black woman (Gibbs 2008).

MICHELLE OBAMA AND THE COMPLICATED LEGACY OF BLACK WOMEN'S LIVES

Not surprisingly, a number of black women commentators have focused on the ways in which Michelle Obama will surely challenge the racist and misogynist legacies that have followed black women in America. In *Newsweek* in November 2008, several months after the controversial and negative portrayals of Michelle Obama on the covers of the *National Review* and *The New Yorker*, Allison Samuels, an African American reporter, noted that Michelle has a chance to counter the negative stereotypes about black women:

> *Usually, the lives of Black women go largely unexamined. The prevailing theory seems to be that we're all hot-tempered single mothers who can't keep a man, and according to CNN's* Black in America *documentary, those of us who aren't street-walking crack addicts are on the verge of dying from AIDS. My "sistafriends" are mostly college educated, in healthy, productive relationships and have a major aversion to sassy one-liners. They are teachers, doctors, and business owners.... Yet, pop culture continues to hold a much unevolved view of African-American women. Black women still can't escape the stereotype of being neck-swirling, eye-rolling, oversexed females raised by our never married, alcoholic mothers.... These images have helped define the way all black women are viewed, including Michelle Obama." (Samuels 2008)*

But the nation's First Lady has responded to the racist misogyny that has attacked her persona in at least three significant ways. First, she has challenged and redefined conventional expectations of the First Lady so well that some journalists have taken note: "As a political spouse, she is somewhat unusual. She isn't the traditional Stepford booster, smiling vacantly at her husband and sticking to the script of carefully vetted blandishments.... She travels the country giving speeches and attending events" (Wolffe 2008). Further, Michelle has learned to protect herself by carefully choosing which media outlets she will be interviewed by, photographed by, or profiled by using first-person quotes she supplies.

In an interview in which Michelle was asked about how she felt about public perceptions of her, she reflected: "I'm pretty much who I've been for a long time. So that, I just think that people have the opportunity to see all of who Michelle Obama is over a longer period of time. And, hopefully, they like what they see. And I think they actually—to the extent that they saw all of me—liked what they saw then . . . because if it weren't the case, I don't think Barack would be President" (Scherer and Gibbs 2009). Michelle's oversight of the East Wing is vitally important to her sense of connecting vision with action: "I think that's where the relationship between the East and the West Wing matters. . . . The issues I've selected are important to me personally, which is the start . . . it is also important that these are issues that are going to potentially have some kind of traction with the West Wing" (Scherer and Gibbs 2009).

Michelle has become known as a leader in her own right—spearheading Let's Move!, an effort to combat childhood obesity by focusing on healthy eating choices and physical fitness in our schools (M. Obama 2011, 138–40). In addition, the First Lady travels to speak on behalf and advocate for military families, noting "when our troops go to war, our families go to war. We can do a greater service if we can ensure that while those folks are fighting on behalf of our country that their houses aren't being foreclosed on, that they have health care, that their kids have good schools to go to" (Rogak 2009, 100). Further, she cares deeply about supporting and encouraging volunteerism.

In the same interview in which reporters prescreened questions (at her request), Michelle Obama focused on her work to reach out to children, especially girls. Commenting on her decision to invite successful, high-profile women such as Alicia Keys to join her visiting local schools and then having the children at the White House, Michelle Obama has sought to create a bridge that reduces the divide she knows exists between the lives of many children and powerful people and institutions:

> *And I just feel like through the small things that we can do here at the White House with messages of encouragement, we can start exemplifying the importance of building those bridges, in real meaningful ways, so that when young people come here, they don't have to come here and be something they're not. They can come here and be who they are, and the folks here will listen. And we can go out and be ourselves and listen*

in their communities as well. . . . Well, how powerful would it be for
young girls to come into this space and hear from other really powerful,
impressive, dynamic women and to have that conversation go on here
in the White House? (Rogak 2009, 100)

Choosing what she will wear and how she wears it is still another way in which Michelle Obama has chosen to control what happens with her image, while also distinguishing her own sense of style. In the spring of 2009, the *New York Times* reported that contrary to tradition or the expectations of editors-in-chief, Michelle Obama chose what she would wear, how she styled her hair, and what, if any, makeup she used when she appeared for the photo shoots that put her on the covers of *People, Essence, Vogue, More,* and *O Magazine.* A *New York Times* reporter noted the First Lady's efforts at image control:

Vogue Magazine, *the fashion world's chronicler of first ladies, bedecked*
Hillary Rodham Clinton in black velvet and Laura Bush in blue silk;
but not Michelle Obama. She insisted on choosing her own dress (a
sleeveless, magenta silk number) and using her own hair and makeup
stylists for the glossy photograph which splashed across Vogue's *March*
cover. . . . Indeed, the First Lady is methodically shaping her public
image, and in ways that extend far beyond fashion. . . . By focusing on
her domestic persona and harnessing the fascination with her family,
the First Lady and her communications team have emerged as the key
architects of one of the most remarkable political transformations in
years. Only ten months ago, Mrs. Obama was described as an angry
black woman by some conservatives and as a liability to her husband.
(Swarns 2009)

The First Lady has worked assiduously to craft a public persona on her own terms rather than through the lens of those whom she feels may not really understand her. In her comments to MSNBC, Michelle noted, "We certainly don't want to spend the next four or eight years in the White House trying to live up a persona that isn't true. I want to be able to be me." (Rogak 2009, 81). Michelle Obama relates her philosophical view on accessing self-discovery on one's own terms as a woman:

One of my personal philosophies and it didn't come from this experi-
ence, it just came over life, is that in life you're got to make choices that

make sense for you, because there is always going to be somebody who'll
think you should do something differently. So you might as well start
with what you like and what you care about, what your passions are,
what makes sense. That's my message to women . . . find your space. . . .
If you're comfortable in the choice and it resonates with you, then all of
the other stuff is just conversation. . . . As women we don't make choices
that have meaning to us. And when those things fall apart, you have to
have yourself to fall back on. . . . You have to own the choices you make.
(Scherer and Gibbs 2009)

Embedded in Michelle Obama's statement is a message about her decision to make choices that she finds personally fulfilling regardless of how others attempt to control her. While it is a message that any number of professional women might offer, it is particularly important coming from the most visible woman in the United States—and it is a message coming from a black woman whose sense of self-direction is nothing short of compelling.

While Michelle Obama has had her detractors and critics, she also has millions of admirers, including African American women's blogs such as Black Girls Rock, Sisterlicious, and That Black Girl Group. Contributor Felicia Jones wrote of her: "Michelle Obama will be the hero my little girls have been looking for. The hero doesn't have to shake her booty or point her finger to get noticed and respected. My little girls finally have a 'role model.' Michelle will have to work to please everyone—an impossible task. But, for many African-American women like me, just a little of her poise, confidence and intellect will go a long way in changing an image that's been around for far too long" (Samuels 2008; Harris-Perry 2011, 269–77). Clearly, Michelle Obama is already building her legacy. Whenever and how she enters our lives as Americans, she immediately challenges and helps to transform negative stereotypes of black women because her level of visibility is a beacon to the generation of young girls on their way to womanhood.

PROGRESS AND CONTINUING CHALLENGES FOR BLACK WOMEN

Black women have endured unique burdens, which Harris-Perry describes as occurring in "America's crooked room," a place "for most black women . . . filled with distorted images, presenting many opportunities for shame and disaster" (Harris-Perry 2011, 299). Despite the barriers to self-discovery, notable numbers of black women hail from a tradition of organized self-help, and professional black women like Michelle Obama are not only the beneficiaries of progressive social reforms but are themselves social reformers. Today there are thirteen black women serving in the U.S. House of Representatives, one each representing the District of Columbia and the Virgin Islands, and 240 in state legislatures. Seven black women (Charlene Mitchell in 1968, Shirley Chisholm in 1972, Margaret Wright in 1976, Lenora Fulani in 1988 and 1992, Isabell Masters in 1992 and 1996, Monica Moorehead in 1998 and 2000, and Cynthia McKinney in 2008) have been candidates for presidents; one black woman, Carol Moseley Braun, has served in the Senate; and a black woman, Condoleezza Rice, served as secretary of state in the George W. Bush administration. Clearly a number of professional black women have made gains that have served to fulfill personal aspirations, and at the same time change the face of leadership in the nation. That is the good news: that some black women are able to engage in self-discovery, help empower others, and challenge long-standing, demoralizing negative racial and gender stereotypes (Smooth 2010, 14–18).

Needless to say, the majority of black women remain poor and marginalized. Unwed black mothers are still a target not only of the conservative media, but also of the conservative, largely male-controlled black media. On the one hand, black communities are hard-pressed to help care for the increasing numbers of children being raised by single, poor mothers or grandparents. Nearly 60 percent of black families are headed by black women, and 3.7 million black children live in poverty. On the other hand, with so many absent fathers, poor black mothers and grandparents are the principal resource for their children's survival (Cooper 2008, 83–87).

Many of the absent fathers are incarcerated. As the Bureau of Justice statistics indicate, in 2006 black men comprised 37 percent of the male prison population in the United States (compared to 35 percent of white men and 21 percent of Latino men). Black women are approximately 48 percent of incarcerated women (compared to 33 percent of white women and 15 percent of Latina women) (Johnson 2003, 19–49). In addition, health-care disparities are a significant issue for all women of color. The intersection of race, gender, and class translates into the reality that poor black women are at far greater risk than white women to die from diabetes, AIDS, cancer, cardiovascular disease, and complications in pregnancy. Also, in terms of health insurance, approximately one-third of uninsured black women live below the poverty level and are between the ages of eighteen and twenty-four (Morris 2008, 173–77; Schulz and Mullings 2006, 3–17).

Black women-hating is too often a theme playing in the background of American society. It has become a hot-selling commodity in which representing black women as a "thing" to be insulted, disrespected, conquered, abused, and abandoned is widespread, especially in much of black male hip-hop music. Black women-hating sells music and enriches primarily white record and music video producers, as well as black male rappers. Presented and often defended as entertainment, this co-optation of black popular culture is a major avenue of oppression. Young black feminists and their male allies are challenging misogynist images and messages aimed at destroying black women, and especially the capacity for working-class black love and black solidarity. Their challenge to internalized hate is to decode the messages that fuel black colonization and oppression. Thus, it is essential that they bring a message that hate is not a sustainable self-determination, especially for a people long colonized by systemic hate (Davis 1995, 127–42; Morgan 1999, 74–78; Pough 2007, 889–92; Rose 1994, 146–85).

CONCLUSION

Black people have been a colonized social group for most of the nation's history. When social groups are oppressed, individual members in those groups are often deprived of human and civil rights and they are often powerless to exercise the few rights that they do have. The intersecting discriminations, particularly those borne by poor black women and girls, compound over time to trap many on the margins of society where their needs for respect, compassion, kindness, and opportunities for personal development and the exercise of meaningful personal agency go unmet. Since those who are physically dominated and marginalized seldom control the production of information, the root causes of their marginalization remains largely invisible.

Self-discovery has never been easily attained for black women in U.S. history. For centuries, colored, Negro, Afro American, African American, and black woman have referred to a quantifiable percentage of blood that comprised one's racial pedigree—the nation's "one-drop rule." "Race" has been powerful in its authority to determine one's relationship to social death (slavery and racial segregation). But it turns out that race is just an *idea*, an illusion that has spawned an ideology that has recently been deprived of any scientific legitimacy. Scientists at the Human Genome Project (HGP) have reported that there is no gene for "race," and further, that we are all descended from an African woman ancestor. It seems quite likely that in time the remarkable findings of the HGP will alter the intellectual and social landscape of our nation. But while "race" is being discounted as a genetic marker transmitted across generations, the reality of racism and the persistence of its impact on many people's lives remains. One can only hope that having elected a black man and black woman to our highest office, U.S. society is signaling that even though the road is long and winding, strewn with impediments and hazards along the way, we are nonetheless moving forward.

Notes

1. Elsewhere, I have written on the statutory, legal, political and social burdens borne by women of the African diaspora, dating from being transported as captives to the North Atlantic British colonies to the present. See Darling, 2010a, 389–402.

2. For example, Francis Jackson Coppin (1836–1913) graduated from Oberlin College and founded the Institute for Colored Youth, later renamed Cheyney State College in Pennsylvania. See Hine, Hine, and Harrold, 2008.

3. See Rodgers-Rose 1980, 15–41, and Harris-Perry 2011, 28–97 on the social construction of a "crooked room" surrounding black women's lives in the United States.

4. See, "Cover," *New Yorker*, July 21, 2008, July 21, 2008, http://archives.newyorker.com/?i=2008-07–21, and Harris-Perry, 2011, 276.

"EVERYTHING HIS FATHER WAS NOT"

Fatherhood and Father Figures in Barack Obama's First Term

HEIDI ARDIZZONE

[T]he Barack Obama I know today is . . . the same man who drove me and our new baby daughter home from the hospital ten years ago this summer, inching along at a snail's pace, peering anxiously at us in the rearview mirror, feeling the whole weight of her future in his hands, determined to give her everything he'd struggled so hard for himself, determined to give her what he never had: the affirming embrace of a father's love.[1]

—MICHELLE OBAMA, 2008

If I had a son, he would look like Trayvon [Martin].[2]

—BARACK OBAMA, 2012

"ARE YOU OKAY, BABY?" THE FORTY-FOURTH PRESIDENT OF THE UNITED States coos at the baby fussing in his wife's arms; her back is initially to the camera, obscuring her face and the child. "Oh, no! Oh!" he laughs, as the fussing escalates to loud cries. In a video released by the White House just before Father's Day, 2011, the Obamas are chatting with a small group of mostly white families who laugh sympathetically with their attempts to soothe their temporary charge. As the First Lady starts to return the now loudly unhappy infant, the mother asks instead for a photo with the president. He obligingly reaches out to pull the child against him, and she immediately falls silent, much to the delight of onlookers. Michelle Obama turns to stare in half-outrage as her husband smugly grins back, patting the contented baby's back with a practiced hand.

Much circulated on the Internet and boasting over a million views among the top two copies posted to YouTube,[3] this "crying baby" video both

Figure 1. President Obama comforts a crying baby; this still shot taken from a different angle than the video discussed. (Pete Souza, White House Photographer, June 15, 2011.)

captured and reconfigured the baby kissing photo-op that every political campaign seeks for its candidate. Moreover, it featured a twist that made Barack Obama supporters (and some critics) melt: his immediate success, where his wife had failed, in quieting the child. The apparent soothing nature of the president's touch, dubbed "magic" by several news organizations and bloggers, might have reflected the "Magical Negro" critiques of Obama's political opposition.[4] But here it is his fatherhood on view.

This crying baby video is only one of hundreds of stories and images of Barack Obama with children that have circulated in mainstream press and online communities during the four years of his first term in the White House. Obama is particularly adept at interacting with children, comfortable in the modern role of the nurturing father, whether to his own daughters or to the younger members of audiences at political events. Photographers consistently capture him actively engaged with children: crouching down, leaning in close, making faces.

Obama's reputation as a "baby whisperer" is grounded in his own experience as a father. The looks he exchanges with his wife in the "crying baby" video are all too familiar to partnered couples who share, if not completely equally, the burdens of late-night feedings and capriciously fussy babies. Images of him holding, talking with, or otherwise interacting with children evoke his relationship, past and present, with his own children. And actual images of the Obama family were everywhere during his campaign and first years in office. In the vast majority of these family photos, Obama is in close

Figure 2. The Obama family on election night, 2008. (Carol M. Highsmith Archive, Library of Congress, Prints and Photographs Division.)

physical connection with at least one of his daughters: carrying them when they are young, holding a hand, touching a shoulder, bending down to listen or talk. In both contexts he is performing fatherhood: Obama-as-father and Obama-as-symbolic-father are closely linked.

Obama's performance as a father has also played a role in his political career. His public interactions with children are part of his own self-representation and the political image-making of his campaigns and White House press. Although little academic attention has been paid to this aspect of his presidency, media coverage and popular interest place great emphasis on his role as "father in chief." Obama's ability to embody the nurturing father is particularly significant; visual and textual representations of Obama depict a modern father with a deep connection to his own family and a genuine ease with children. At the same time, these images resonate against a complicated pattern of expectations for fatherhood, for black men and their families, and for dual career couples and parenting. Obama's real and symbolic position as the first First African American father evoke the absence of other black men from the (African) American family:[5] absent fathers and endangered (or dangerous) black boys.

Beyond the frames of images of the happy, healthy, functional Obama family stands a crowd of supposedly "dysfunctional" families that they are not and black men whom he is not. The grim statistics of those men and boys disproportionately unemployed, dropped out, imprisoned, or killed, challenge post-election declarations of America as post-racial. Not only has performing fatherhood become a significant aspect of Obama's political identity, then, but his political fatherhood operates in a crossroads of tensions around economic success and family structures, the shifting and contested expectations for American fathers, and the particular pressures on and scrutiny of African American families in the twenty-first century.

AFRICAN AMERICAN FAMILIES AND PHOTOGRAPHY

In a voice-over against photo and video montages of the new First Family, which introduced a 2009 interview with the president, Harry Smith of CBS News summarized the importance of Obama's fatherhood.

> *Maybe it was on Election Night when we first realized that not only would there be a new president, but also a new First Family . . . a family with young children. Along with the role of commander-in-chief and leader of the free world, Barack Obama would be First Dad. So yes, there would be a swing set. And yes, there would be a dog. He is everything his father is not.[6]*

This idealized family picture, with the heterosexual, married couple and their two beautiful biological daughters, a swing set in the yard, a dog running around it, is marred only by the shadow presence of the other father Smith evokes: the father who was not there. Similarly, visual studies scholars have argued that photographs and images contain more than the objects and figures they capture. The literal images within the photograph's frame enter into a relationship with memory, identity, and cultural ideologies. They prompt the viewer to think, reminisce, remember, and reimagine both what is inside and outside the boundaries of the image (Barthes 1981, 53–57; Raiford 2011, 1–28; Romano and Raiford 2006, xi–xxiv). It is in this sense that I consider the absent presence of missing fathers, and eventually sons, in visual and other representations of the Obama family, and Obama's symbolic fatherhood especially. Before examining these absent figures, however, I begin with the significance of depictions of the First Family as they are usually defined: father, mother, daughters.

Commentary on Obama's campaign and early presidency has evinced a particularly "deep fascination" with the Obamas (Ogletree 2011, v). More children's books had been written about Obama before the end of his first year in office than about any other recent president (Nel 2010, 334–35).[7] WorldCat lists over 3,000 non-juvenile books with Obama as the subject, virtually all of them published since 2008. The vast majority of adult books examine his political development, emerging policies, and historic significance. Many, however, also or exclusively focus on his personal story and life.[8] Moreover, popular magazine and news stories, photoessays, and interviews provide a collective "celebration of his own role as father and husband" (McElya 2011, 185). The book sales and family focused articles suggest that the U.S. public is eager to know more about the man whose candidacy and presidency seemed so unlikely for so many reasons.

Lisa Belkin, in the *New York Times* magazine, attributes this popular interest to "a generation of parents obsessed with parenting" who would therefore already be interested in parents coming into the White House.

> *We are intrigued by the first family not only because their children are adorable and so excited about getting a puppy and meeting the Jonas Brothers but also because our president seems to be such a good father. (Belkin 2009, MM9)*

For many who praise his parenting, understanding Obama as a "good father" seems to be the key to understanding him as a man and a politician. His family life perhaps promises to reveal more about him than his political actions. Belkin warns here that Obama's political leadership style might also be "fatherly" and Americans' expectations of him might, to their detriment, become more the expectations for a father, not a president. For others, Obama's fatherhood operates on a different plane from politics. As Fox News' Neil Cavuto put it, "Policies can be debated, but this man's commitment to fatherhood cannot" (Cavuto 2012). The implications or contradictions of fatherhood for the president's particular political views or policies is beyond the scope of this essay, other than to note the many, many times he has cited his daughters as the inspiration or motivation for specific legislation, general political statements, or his very decision to enter politics (Sarlin 2012). Here, I focus on the social and cultural ramifications of Obama's performance of fatherhood: What does it mean to be a "good father"? What does it mean for a black, married, heterosexual father of two young black girls? What does it mean for the president for the United States?

These questions have a social history as well as a visual history. They also convey the hope that this American and black family represent for a better racial future for the nation (Schwarz 2011, 138–55).[9] Barack Obama's positioning as the culmination of African American struggles for civil rights is reflected in his own references to the nation's "better history," to his inauguration as representing the "long time coming . . . change."[10]

But in the context of a century of African American family portraits, Obama family photographs come into conversation with a longer movement of struggle for upward mobility, inclusion, and equality. Whether created for private display or public exhibition, these portrayals collectively countered popular stereotypes of laziness, sexual deviance, and inferiority. In both historical and contemporary contexts, black fathers and black families have been sites of external criticism, scrutiny, and public policies, as well as internal tensions (Baskerville 2002, 695–99; Connor and White 2007, 2–8). These family photographs presented a silent illustration of the ongoing collective claim to social equality: Americanness without the erasure of blackness. Drawing on middle-class conventions of family structure and gender roles within it, the images highlighted heterosexual married couples and their children (Gaines 1996, 195–213; Mitchell 2004, 108–72, 218–40). Most relevantly, generations of African Americans have used the visual racial text of photography to emphasize their ability to fit American gender and family norms, and therefore their suitability for full citizenship.

At the turn of the twentieth century, W. E. B. Du Bois and Booker T. Washington both used family photographs that conveyed these dynamics in remarkably similar ways, despite these leaders' very different approaches to addressing racial inequities in the U.S. Both Washington's use of photographs in his *A New Negro for a New Century*, and Du Bois's set of albums brought to the 1900 Paris Exhibition's American Negro Exhibit, emphasized heterosexual marriage as the basis of the family unit, women's roles as wives and mothers, and men's ability to provide for their wives and children (Ross 2004, 66–68; Smith 2004, 44–63). As professional photographers, artists, advertisers, social scientists, and activists, African Americans in the early- to mid-twentieth century continued to rely on this particular definition of family, and a presentation of gendered parental and marital roles (Ross 2004, 1–3, 12–13; Summers 2003, 1–15). For these generations, personal presentation through respectable dress and behavior as well as professional and social accomplishments was a political statement.

African American family photographs of the early- to mid-twentieth century also employed similar photographic conventions to those Du Bois and Washington used in their highly public presentations. For example, Caroline Bond Day collected hundreds of family photos throughout the 1920s as part of her data for an anthropological study of "Negro-White Families" (Ardizzone 2006, 106–132; Day 1930, 3–11). Although Day took many individual portraits herself, most of the hundreds of photographs she included in her study were personal family photos her subjects lent to her. Their emphasis on presenting the "functional black American family" followed consistent patterns across generations and families. Women with carefully coiffed hair and stylish gowns or dresses. Mothers holding their children. Fathers standing behind the family unit. Girls and boys in formal dress, clean and unrumpled. Men in military uniform. Backgrounds revealing an ample porch, a well-furnished room, artwork, automobiles, houses. Handsome. Beautiful. American. For Day's families, their black ancestry was not always obvious in their physical appearance, but she claimed political and social identities as "Negroes" for them and for herself.[11]

Like Caroline Bond Day and her subjects, Barack Obama has not always been accepted or recognized as unambiguously black. Throughout his short political career, Obama's public and social identity has been clearly marked, as the essays in this volume attest, by his biracial ancestry and his identification as both black and mixed. He has also been shaped by his experiences as a brown-skinned boy raised by white Americans in Hawai'i, then Indonesia, then as a black man in the United States, and as the husband of Michelle Obama, an African American woman.

Scholars and pundits alike have made much of this slippery, contested terrain of Obama's racial identity, focusing on his own family and background: Obama has been heralded as symbolizing a multicultural global society and a post-racial turn for the United States by virtue of his multiracial ancestry. At the same time, these experiences and connections (the Muslim Kenyan father, an Indonesian stepfather, and a childhood spent mostly in Hawai'i and Indonesia) are seen as incompatible with American citizenship and identity. In this context, Obama's racialization as black places him back within a familiar and very American context. His earlier experiences and writings emphasized his multiracial identity, and he continues to acknowledge this ancestry and celebrate his multiethnic extended family. But he has increasingly identified as black, culminating in the public announcement of his choice to only check "Black, African American or Negro" rather than add one or more additional categories in the 2010 federal census.[12] As black or African American, Obama becomes a more familiar other for white American voters.

While his family of origin has marginalized Barack Obama, the First Family further solidifies his identity as, or at least with, African Americans. His marriage to an African American woman, and their co-parenting of two beautiful young black girls, performs important political work for a candidate and president whose identity is so unexpected and difficult to simplify into a sound bite. Framed together they are a visually black family, and Barack Obama becomes unambiguously black. Their darker, slightly varied skin tones shade his into a shared palette. Beautiful. Handsome. Black. American (Schwarz 2011, 139).[13]

Obama's wife and children further normalize him for some who see his African Muslim father and his Hawaiian birth as marginal or even incompatible with American identity.[14] A descendent of slaves, raised by two black parents in a working-class home in Chicago, Michelle Obama's family background and connections root him, through her, to mainstream African American history and culture. At times, this role became conscious and explicit. In a popular campaign speech, she playfully acknowledged her own doubts about the man who had to ask her out several times before she said yes:

> I've got nothing in common with this guy. He grew up in Hawaii! Who grows up in Hawaii? He was biracial. I was like, okay, what's that about? And then it's a funny name, Barack Obama. Who names their child Barack Obama? (Slevin 2007, C01)[15]

By naming all the ways her husband appears outside the frame of Americanness, Michelle Obama consciously sought to address and counter those fears. Also navigating her own path through the images of her as an angry black woman and a radical, she was adept at reassuring her audiences that her husband was worthy of her, and their, attentions, despite his atypical name, his unusual pedigree, and his non-continental American birth. It was the same message that she gave in her speech at the Democratic National Convention, cited at the top of this piece. There she invited the nation to picture her husband slowly driving her and their newborn daughter home for the first time, "feeling the whole weight of her future in his hands . . . determined to give her what he had never had."[16] Sandwiched between a recitation of the campaign's progress from Iowa and the future election, this vignette promised the same concern and determination to the country under the care of Malia and Sasha's father. The girls joined their mother on stage, and their father appeared on a screen behind them. Barack, Michelle, Malia, and Sasha: the ideal American family unit.

NURTURING FATHERS, PRESIDENTIAL FATHERS, AND ABSENT BLACK MEN

Michelle and Barack Obama were hardly the first presidential couple to bring their children to the White House. Fatherhood and the presidency have a long entwined history: most presidents have also been fathers (Quinn-Musgrove and Kanter 1995, xxiii, xxiv). Other presidents married strong women, were closely invested in their children's lives, and struggled with raising children in front of cameras while dealing with overwhelming national crises and international turmoil. First Families—especially those with young children growing up in the White House—have always been a source of interest to the American public.

Nor has Obama been the first sitting president to focus on fathers and fatherhood in politics or in policies. The 1965 Moynihan report famously linked African American urban poverty to the "pathology" of female-headed households and urban violence and crime to fatherless families. In the context of Lyndon Johnson's War on Poverty, extended in many ways by Richard Nixon, national success became linked to family structure and gendered parenting in federal policy and the racial rhetoric surrounding it. Such associations between blackness, poverty, and absent fathers, continued to shape federal welfare policies of the 1990s and early twenty-first century, perhaps most notably the 1996 welfare reforms under the Clinton administration (Cott 2002, 221–23; Roberts 1998, 145–62). Clinton also introduced the President's Fatherhood Initiative, which emphasized the importance of American men as active and present fathers within a "healthy marriage," in order to address poverty, education, and national values. Clinton followed up with a Responsible Fatherhood Initiative in 2000, focused on promoting employment to boost enforcement of child support payments. George W. Bush continued the RFI, building on the Texas Fatherhood Initiative he claimed credit for as governor. During his term as president, Bush's father-focused policies emphasized faith-based and marriage-based initiatives, many of which Obama has continued. These fatherhood initiatives have had explicitly race-based rhetoric and policy goals, often aimed at black families and fathers (Weaver 2012, 297–309). In 2009, Obama also created a Task Force for Responsible Fatherhood and Healthy Families. These programs, part of a growing "fatherhood responsibility" movement of the 1990s (Gavanas 2004, 247–66), signaled a turn for Obama's performance of political and social fatherhood. In this context, Obama's success at fatherhood also serves to further distance himself from the bad fathers that pervade popular images of black men in the United States, including his own absent father.

Over the same four or five decades of increasing federal attention to fathers as a key to solving economic and social problems, the model of the male breadwinner father has declined in American society. In the wake of economic need for most households to have two incomes and feminist shifts in women's roles, the "nurturing father" or the "involved father" has emerged as a new model (Kellan 2008, 1172–75; Lewis 2001, 152–54; Marks and Palkovitz 2004, 113–29). This is not to say that the good provider husband and father, paired with the stay-at-home wife and mother, has disappeared: it still describes the economic division of labor of approximately one quarter of American households since 2000 (Kreider and Elliot 2010, 7–8). Compatible with an array of employment patterns, nurturing fathers might also be breadwinners, part of a dual-career couple, or stay-at-home dads. The expectation that fathers, regardless of their economic role in the household, should see their primary role as the caretaking of their children, prioritizing an emotional relationship with them, emerged in the 1970s and 1980s (Coltrane 1996, 3–7, 51–83; Lamb 1987, 3–17). The male-breadwinner/female-homemaker couple also survives as an ideology: a set of ideas about gender, work, marriage, and parenting, which define an ideal against which other practices might be judged (Cott 2004, 3, 93; Cunningham 2008, 300–302). But recent work emphasizes the increased obstacles posed by labor downturns, even before the 2008 economic crises that preceded Obama's election and quickly eclipsed his campaign priorities to shape his presidency (Williams 2008, 488). The attention to Obama as a father also coincides with the aftermath of an economic crash that led to increased unemployment and underemployment, overrepresented in traditionally male jobs. Regardless of the specific economic and political issues he has faced in office, however, the president sits at the crossroads of rhetoric about the problems of black fatherhood and changing expectations for the behavior of men who are present in their children's lives.

Married in 1992, with their daughters born in 1998 and 2001, Michelle and Barack Obama reflect this shift and the lingering significance of the breadwinner ideal in their co-parenting style. When the girls were very young, Michelle Obama also worked full time and felt the burden of the "second shift" of unpaid domestic and child care work that falls to the vast majority of employed American mothers (Hoshchild and Machung 1989, 238–49, 415–23). And both have been honest about the difficulties she faced, working full time and raising two young girls.

Both Obamas are also unapologetically modern in their understanding of the gendered and ungendered nature of parenting. As his rising political career increased time away from home, she made a series of sacrifices to her career in order to offset his absences. This resulted in a very traditional-looking division of labor, but the meaning they give to it is hardly traditional. While avoiding the label "feminist," Michelle Obama is very clear that she expects her husband to participate in the most mundane aspects of parenting as well as remain emotionally connected to the family despite his grueling schedule. And she understands her willingness to take the role she has as situational, not gender-determined: "someone has to be focusing on the kids—and that's me. But it could easily be him. There's no reason why the nurturing has to come from Mom—it just has to be there" (Salvatore 2008, 3).

While the division of labor with the children is clearly quite traditional, Obama continues the model of the nurturing, involved father. He phones or video-chats with his daughters from the road, schedules family time, even coaches Sasha's soccer team. "The president manages to strike a balance between leading our country and spending time with his family," Ron Kirk told *Jet* magazine, "and that is something we all can learn from."[17] Kirk further specified that Obama's example of "active" fathering was particularly pertinent for African American men, a qualification Obama would probably agree with. "I resolved many years ago that it was my obligation to break the cycle," he explained in his 2008 Father's Day speech. Being "a good father to my girls" would become his priority.[18] And, as we have seen, the definition of good fatherhood has expanded.

During his first term in office, Barack Obama has been very outspoken about the problems he sees facing families in the United States, especially in the black community. While scores of sociological studies challenge a direct association of "single mother" with "dysfunction," Obama himself has been quick to identify "missing" fathers as the source of many other problems. His "More Perfect Union" speech cited "a lack of economic opportunity among black men, and the shame and frustration that came from not being able to provide for one's family" as contributing to "the erosion of black families."[19]

His controversial 2008 Father's Day speech before the African American Apostolic Church of God in Chicago went even further. After praising the important work that fathers were doing, he also chastised the "too many fathers" who were "missing from too many lives and too many homes. They have abandoned their responsibilities, acting like boys instead of men. And the foundations of our families are weaker because of it."[20] Such statements have earned mixed responses. Most criticisms focus on his failure to identify or directly address the contexts for those failures: the sustained patterns of discrimination and racism, poverty and lack of resources, opportunities, and support. And, add Mark and Roger McPhail, "the fundamental contradiction of being on the one hand denied one's personhood, and on the other expected to be a 'man'" (McPhail and McPhail 2011, 680).

Still, Obama's focus on responsible, engaged fatherhood within black communities has also garnered widespread support. *Jet* magazine published a story titled "America's Favorite Family Man: How Obama is Restoring the Image of African American Males," which highlighted Obama's consistent messages to fathers to be more active and more nurturing, but also emphasized the significance of his own marriage and parenting as a model for black men.[21] Juan Williams also wrote approvingly about the speech and praised the father in chief as a "national treasure . . . the fact that he is a good father who leads a black family is even more important because the rate of absentee fathers in the black and Hispanic community amounts to a national crisis (Williams 2011, 488).

His hard stance on absent fathers appealed to conservatives who otherwise found little in his policies to approve of. The *National Review*, for example, praised Obama's Father's Day message the following year. Noting that the president was "now in a unique position to shape black attitudes toward marriage and fatherhood," the magazine cited his speech approvingly: "We need fathers to realize that responsibility does not end at conception. We need them to realize that what makes you a man is not the ability to have a child—it's the courage to raise one" (Currie 2009, 27–28).

Images of Obama as a father also range from neutral to assertively pro-Obama. There is a wealth of negative, anti-Obama imagery, some of it horrifically racist. However, his fatherhood rarely comes up in more mainstream attacks. There are some exceptions, of course. Bishop Harry R. Jackson, for example, criticized Obama's recent public support of same-sex marriage, quite predictably given Jackson's connections to the anti-gay rights Family Research Council. And Jackson particularly scolded Obama for failing to act as a proper father by teaching his daughters the moral arguments against homosexuality. Instead, Obama had allowed the roles to be reversed, letting himself be swayed by the girls' acceptance of their friends' same-sex parents. Despite this criticism of Obama's failure to maintain his most basic "father knows best" authority, Jackson carefully couched his comments in praise for the president "as a family man." He admired the "healthy family practices" that the First Family models, and called Obama "the nation's father in chief."[22]

It is also worth noting Kevin Williamson's mocking comments that Obama's failure to have biological sons suggested a failure of his masculinity and leadership abilities (Williamson 2012). Written during the second election cycle, Williamson's satirical point was to compare Obama unfavorably to Republican presidential nominee Mitt Romney, who had five sons and far more grandsons than granddaughters. Through a combination of allusion to the biblical patriarchs and evolutionary psychology, Williamson concluded the Romney was clearly biologically the superior man and leader. The target of the joke was not only Obama, who had won the damning label of effeminate before for his quiet tone, his intellectualism, and his liberalism. The target was also femaleness itself. In the logic of the humor, sons were clearly superior to daughters.

But, in the run-up to the 2008 election, the girls' age and their gender probably helped their father's image as safely domesticated husband and father. Sasha (Natasha) and Malia Obama were seven and ten, respectively, when they attended their father's 2008 inauguration. In a gender analysis of presidential children from Lyndon Johnson to Chelsea Clinton, Lori Cox Han concluded that daughters garnered "an overwhelming amount" of the media coverage, relative to sons (Han 2004, 160). Those daughters, however, were significantly younger than the sons and six of them married while their fathers were in office. As many news reports noted, Amy Carter at nine and Chelsea Clinton at twelve were the closest in age to the Obama daughters in recent history. In the twentieth century, only the Kennedys had younger children when they moved into the White House.[23]

Sasha is now eleven; her father recently won a new round of praise when he announced he is assistant coach for her basketball team (Cavuto 2012; Simon 2011). Malia has since reached fourteen, a tall slender athletic girl who is not yet allowed to date. Nor is she likely to, if her father follows through on his recent jokes that a second term in the White House will allow him to keep her surrounded by "men with guns" and allow him to intimidate prospective dates by meeting them in the Oval Office.[24] Video and photographs of the family at their late-hour 2012 election night appearance provided visual evidence of how much the younger Obamas had grown in the four years of their father's first term.

On a personal level, Barack Obama does not seem to experience his lack of sons as a lack at all. When asked about the possibility of sons, which he has been on several occasions, he has never expressed a desire for one, although he acknowledges that boys are "generally" different from girls "in some ways."[25] The question implies the same assumption as the Williamson piece: that sons are better than daughters, or at least preferred by men. In public statements, Obama has made it clear that he could envision one of his daughters following in his footsteps and having a political career. Given his understanding of gender, there is not much that a son could do that a daughter might not do as well.

In many ways, images of Sasha and Malia have continued the political work of literature and iconography of the black girl as the innocent, non-threatening representative of her race. Numerous scholars have highlighted the real and imagined dangers of sexuality, especially vulnerability to violence that haunt cultural images of black girls (Collins 2002, 112–17). But the Obama girls "carry us forward to a promise . . . which encompasses hope, not only for black America but for all of us" (Schwarz 2011, 144).

But let's consider Obama's shadow sons. If his daughters are the most visible promise of a better America, then where are black boys in that imagined future? How would a fourteen-year-old son in the White House fit into the visual text of the First (African American) Family? Into the acceptance of them as beautiful? Black? American? Neither Obama nor the scholars, journalists, political pundits, and other onlookers have had nearly as much to say about these missing boys as they have the missing fathers. But on a few well-publicized occasions, Obama has reached out to a symbolic son: several times captured in a photograph or video, the other posthumously in the midst of national debate. These moments do not seem to have captured public attention to the same extent as the crying baby video did. They are harder to watch and hear, demand more difficult reckonings then watching the Obamas compete to quiet a white female infant.

Just a few months before the crying baby video, White House photographer Pete Souza caught another image that was both official and spontaneous. It is tradition for departing staff members to bring their families for an introduction and photograph with the president. Five-year-old Jacob Philadelphia took advantage of the opportunity to ask a question that surprised his parents. He wanted to know "if my hair is just like yours." In reply, Obama bent his head down to the boy and invited him to "touch it and see for yourself . . . Touch it, dude!" In the image, the president appears to be bowing down to the child who reaches up gingerly to touch his head. Despite the snapshot-like composition of the photograph, Souza chose it to display in the administrative offices. "That one became an instant favorite of the staff. I think people are struck by the fact that the president of the United States was willing to bend down and let a little boy feel his head."[26] Souza's interpretation of this image's popularity speaks to the significance of Obama's ability to extend his fatherhood to other people's children, here putting aside the formality of his position to invite the intimacy of a touch on the head.[27] As a black man, such intimacies must be carefully negotiated, and both Obamas are practiced at doing just that. But in this context Obama is authenticating his blackness to a child who needs to know that "his" hair could grow on the head of the president. For Jacob and his parents, the experience was undoubtedly about affirming that the president was black, like him, and therefore that his accomplishments were possible for other black children. Three years later, the boy reported that he wanted to be president when he grew up—or fly. Becoming an astronaut was a close second option.[28]

The second example is far more devastating. In February 2012, a self-assigned neighborhood watchman shot and killed an unarmed seventeen-year-old black boy he believed was "up to no good." When reports started circulating a few weeks later that police had not brought charges against George Zimmerman, outrage began to mount. Trayvon Martin's death, in his own neighborhood, on his way home from buying candy and a soft drink, came on the heels of too many stories and personal experiences of official and unofficial harassment of young black men.[29]

Obama had not been very successful in his previous attempts to comment on examples of racial discrimination during his first term in office.[30] He had made no comments on New York City police's "stop and frisk" practices, which studies had shown predominantly targeted young black men. He had not addressed the heightened scrutiny of black communities that contributed to higher rates of traffic stops, arrests for petty crimes. As we have seen, his more recent speeches about missing fathers had glossed over or ignored the systemic "whys" often behind their absence. But when he made a statement on the Trayvon Martin case, he connected himself directly to the situation by claiming Martin as symbolic family. After expressing condolences to Martin's parents, Obama somberly stated, "If I had a son, he would look like Trayvon Martin."[31] Amidst official scrutiny into how local Florida police had handled the case, this read to some activists as far too weak a statement. The wave of hooded protesters taking to the literal and social media streets demanding justice for Martin wanted more from the first black father in chief. But Obama's simple statement had complicated, and potentially transformative implications.

Obama's absent sons are the canaries in the coal mine of American racialism. It is to the statistical fates of black boys and young men that scholars turn first to when countering the hopeful claims that Obama's election marked a national turn to a "post-racial." The high school dropouts, the murdered, the imprisoned, the African American boys and young men "missing" from society: these are the brutal facts that remind us how far from post-racial we are (Neal 2005, 1–3; Gaines 2010, 197–99; Sugrue 2010, 83–91; Joseph 2010, 213–22). In the controversy that developed around the Martin-Zimmerman case two very different images of the young boy emerged: in one he was a violent young thug, exactly the sort of delinquent or criminal that Zimmerman was justified in targeting as suspicious. In the other he was a victim of the racialization of criminality as black, of the systematic hyperscrutiny and policing of young black men: a middle-class kid with no serious trouble or record.[32]

Obama's interactions with black boys and his statement on Trayvon Martin's death have not translated into policy changes, nor were they likely ever intended to.[33] Still, by simply inviting Americans to imagine Trayvon as his son (Handsome, Beautiful, Black, American), Obama invited young black men into the imagined framework of his family—a family he defines as representing our whole nation. In short, he invited us to do the same for all young black boys who could be seen as dangerous and threatening simply by being who they were.[34] For some of us, of course, those children are our literal sons. For Obama's employment of political fatherhood and family, they belong to all of us, and we to them.

This, I would argue, is the more realistic hope then "post-racialism" for what might emerge in the aftermath of the Obama administration. New definitions of racial and ethnic categories have come and gone before. Immigration and intermixing have shaped and reshaped seemingly consistent categories like "white" and "black" for generations. Racism has proven its ability to outlast legalized segregation and structures of overt discrimination. Collapsing the "double consciousness" of Du Bois is not a matter of African Americans coming to see themselves as simultaneously black and American: that is not new either. Rather, it is this ability to see each other as family, as connected, especially the ability of whites to simultaneously acknowledge race and make those connections across it.

For now, however, this inclusive reframing of the nation-family has not happened. So far Obama has only brought missing black boys and fathers back in rhetorical and limited ways. Furthermore, as Obama would have learned from some of his Harvard law school training at the height of the development of critical race theory, legal systems cannot control racism. Nor can presidents.

Notes

1. Michelle Obama, speech given at the Democratic National Convention, August 25, 2008.

2. Barack Obama, statement on Trayvon Martin, March 23, 2012, http://whitehouse.blogs.cnn .com/2012/03/23/president-obama-statement-on-trayvon-martin-case/.

3. "Crying Baby No Match for Obama," CNN, June 22, 2011, http://www.youtube.com/ watch?v=l6k6kIrTAGk. The high-volume posts of the video include http://www.youtube .com/watch?v=uqhzWlqN3uc (over 975,000 by November 10, 2012); http://www.youtube .com/watch?v=-uNoNnoKjZA (over 700,000 by November 10, 2012).

4. The "Magical Negro" trope was first applied to Obama by black liberal columnist David Ehrenstein (Ehrenstein 2007). But it was immediately taken up by political opposition, most notably with Rush Limbaugh's repeated airing of a song parody "Barack the Magical Negro," which was included in a campaign CD by would-be Republican Party National Chair Chip Saltsman. In the weeks following its release, copies of this thirty-second clip circulated on blogs, online news, and social media. It was also featured on major network newscasts and became the zen moment at the end of Jon Stewart's *Daily Show*. "Moment of Zen: Barack Obama Calms a Crying Baby, June 21, 2011; abcnews.com, June 21, 2011; "President Obama Can Charm Even a Hysterically Crying Baby," http://www.huffingtonpost .com/2011/06/21/obama-baby-crying_n_881288.html

5. Although I will use these terms largely interchangeably in this essay, they are not synonymous. Obama's own parentage does not fit the primary definition of African Americans as those Americans descended from West African slaves who arrived in the colonial or early United States by the early nineteenth century. This discrepancy, along with his mixed ancestry, fueled debates early in his campaign over his "legitimacy" as either black or African American.

6. "Father-in-Chief," Harry Smith interview with Barack Obama, *The Early Show*, CBS, June 22, 2009.

7. Philip Nel's analysis of these books compared to those of previous, recent presidents concludes that books about Obama for children are measurably more positive and embracing:

all but one "embrace him as 'ours.'" Furthermore, "attempts to reify Obama as an ideal American collide with his more complex history, sometimes even effacing his race."

8. No one has yet taken on the massive study these books would require, although analyses of individual and groups of them abound. John Avlon of *The Daily Beast* has been tracking Obama-hating books and counts eighty-nine "obsessively anti-Obama books" published by fall 2012, from a previous count of 46 in 2010. "The Obama-Haters Bookclub: The Canon Swells," *Daily Beast*, October 26, 2012, http://www.thedailybeast.com/articles/2012/10/26/the-obama-haters-book-club-the-canon-swells.html.

9. Schwarz is the only example I have found of a scholar analyzing Obama family photographs. He does so against a remembered past of African American disenfranchisement and activism, especially children's activism, in the mid-twentieth century.

10. Barack Obama, inauguration speech, January 2, 2009.

11. Day was the first African American woman to get a graduate degree in anthropology at Harvard University. Because of Day's focus on mixed-race families, the visual representation of blackness was not always obvious. Although none of the families she depicted were passing as white, about a third of them had relatives who did, and many had physical features that were ambiguous. In their dress, posture, tableaus, and use of middle-class possessions in the background, however, there was no difference between darker and lighter African American families' self-portrayals.

12. This was almost certainly the first time a sitting president has ever made a public statement regarding how he filled out personal demographic information on a federal census. The fact that the White House issued such a statement reflects the continued debate over the relationship between Obama's ancestry and his identity.

13. Schwarz also notes the close gradations of skin tone among the Obamas, but not in the context of Obama's contested blackness.

14. It is not within the scope of this chapter to consider the range and scale of racist and other negative images of Barack Obama that have circulated before and during his first term. Here, I am interested in his ability to be accepted as both African American and American enough to win two elections despite his outsiderness, both real and imagined, and despite very strong economic and political criticism from both the left and the right.

15. Slevin is quoting from a campaign speech in Iowa.

16. Michelle Obama, speech given at the Democratic National Convention, August 25, 2008.

17. Ron Kirk (U.S. trade representative) quoted in Chapell 2009, 8.

18. Obama, Father's Day Speech, Apostolic Church of God on Chicago's South Side, June 22, 2008.

19. Obama, "A More Perfect Union," March 2008.

20. Obama, June 22, 2008.

21. *Jet*, June 22, 2009, Cover.

22. Harry R. Jackson, "Father in Chief—Or Just Another Politician," June 19, 2012, http://www.thetruthinblackandwhite.com/Weekly_Column/?Father_in_Chief_Or_Just_Another_Politician&year=2012. While it is beyond the scope of this chapter to analyze comments on the many online newstories, photoessays, and videos I examined, I will note that it was quite common to find responses that stated both an opposition to Obama's politics, but an admiration for either him as a father or with children in general.

23. Political pundits made many comparisons between Obama and Kennedy during the 2008 election campaign, their youth and young families being just one of them. Just as they had during the Kennedy administration, White House and media photographers delight in finding formal and informal opportunities to catch the First Couple in their role as parents. Caroline Kennedy was three and her brother John, Jr., an infant at their father's inauguration, making them a truly unique First Family. Amy Carter and Chelsea Clinton would make better potential comparisons, particularly considering Obama's second term. Such an analysis, however, would have to take into account changes in both media technologies and behaviors as well as shifting and racialized expectations for girls and young women. Very few non-fathers have served as U.S. President, and none since the Kennedy administration. Johnson, Ford, and G. W. Bush had older teenagers or young adults; Nixon, Reagon, and G. H. W. Bush had adult children who were no longer living with them.

24. Obama, *Good Morning America*, June 16, 2011, http://abcnews.go.com/Politics/president-obama-opens-fatherhood-anthony-weiner-scandal-american/story?id=13862014.

25. Ibid. This question came from a "Little League Father" of two boys.

26. Quotes from "Indelible Image of a Boy's Pat on the President's Head," *New York Times*, May 23, 2012. See also Stebner 2012.

27. Jonathan Capehart wrote about this image in the context of African American experiences of their hair and white curiosity and interest in it. *Washington Post*, May 42, 2012.

28. *New York Times*, May 24, 2012, http://www.nytimes.com/2012/05/24/us/politics/indelible-image-of-a-boys-pat-on-obamas-head-hangs-in-white-house.html.

29. For summaries of the Martin case see Blow 2012; Macky 2012.

30. The most famous of these was the "Beergate" episode prompted by the arrest of Harvard scholar Henry Louis Gates. (Ogletree, vii, Joseph, 8).

31. Barack Obama, Statement on Trayvon Martin, March 23, 2012.

32. Elspeth Reeve offers a comparison of the photographs of Trayvon (or initially reported to be of him) on liberal and conservative blogs in the weeks after the case went national. "What Did Trayvon Look Like? That Depends on Your Politics," *The Atlantic Wire*, March 30, 2012, http://www.theatlanticwire.com/politics/2012/03/what-did-trayvon-look-depends-your-politics/50570/.

33. As I was completing final edits on this essay, the Sandy Hook shootings have prompted a renewed attempt at federal reforms to gun control.

34. At the time of this writing, the Zimmerman case is pending trial and much conflicting information about what happened that night has emerged. Zimmerman claims Martin attacked him, and there is some physical evidence that the two fought. But there is no doubt that Zimmerman followed Martin for blocks before the physical confrontation, frightening the teenager, and ignoring police requests to stop tailing his "suspect."

BLACK AMERICAN WOMEN'S POLITICAL EXPERIENCES

Leadership Lessons for Women Globally

Dionne M. Rosser-Mims

A web search in Google Books of the term "women's empowerment" brings up over 100,000 titles, representing widespread interest in feminist issues from around the world. Since the terrorist attacks on the Twin Towers in New York City on September 11, 2001, wars of invasion and religion have accelerated research related to the issue of women's empowerment in the United States and across the globe. Girls and women are being raped, burned by acid, kidnapped, and killed by individuals who oppose women's access to political power and their demands for increased social, educational, and economic rights. In recent years, the daily news has given the impression that women's participation in politics from advocacy and activist roles with an emphasis on expanding women's rights to holding formal political leadership positions can be hazardous to women's health. The cumulative effect is that, if women are not adequately represented in the political leadership ranks, there is the danger that public policy decisions will lack the distinctive perspective women bring to important issues.

What does "political experience" mean to female citizens in the U.S. and other countries, and why an emphasis on Black American women? Worldwide, it can be said that serving in political office means holding a role that potentially provides a platform for effecting social and political change. Black women leaders, for example, have been an important component of the struggle of Black Americans in the U.S., helping to shape the future of their people and of their country through their involvement in all areas of society, especially through political activism. In this chapter, "politics" is defined as strategies used to obtain power to overcome social, political, and economic disparities (Rosser-Mims, 2012). Furthermore, we posit that all women in various cultural contexts might profit from understanding Black women's leadership experiences within the political context of the United States. For example, the history of American Black women has direct parallels with current events elsewhere in the world, as these cultural snapshots show:

1850: Harriet Tubman was a leader in the Underground Railroad movement.

1961: Future television reporter Charlayne Hunter (later, Hunter-Gault) walked through hostile crowds to register as the first African-American student at the University of Georgia.

1963: Four African-American girls attending Sunday School classes in Birmingham, Alabama, were killed by the firebombing of their church.

2012: Targeted by the Pakistani Taliban, Malala Yousafzai was shot in the head because she spoke and wrote about Muslim girls' right to an education.

2014: More than two hundred Nigerian girls were kidnapped from their school in Chibok.

Black American women's struggle for leadership and political power remain examples for contemporary women to follow to combat today's education and social ails facing women worldwide. Although Black American women have a rich history of leadership within their communities, representation in the broader political arena has been limited.

Access to a range of political leadership positions remains an elusive dream for the vast majority of women in the world. According to the 2014 World Economic Forum's (WEF) *Global Gender Gap Report*, little improvement has been made in addressing the underrepresentation of women in political leadership globally. The head of the WEF's Women Leaders and Gender Parity program, Saadia Zahidi, articulated the concern: "We're talking about very small and slow changes" (Rupp, 2012, para. 3). According to Rupp, the reality of the political landscape is that women represent less than 20% of the global political leadership. The 2014 Women's Leadership

Factsheet published by Rutgers University's Institute for Women in Leadership summarized:

> Of the 197 self-governing countries in the world, 22 (11.2 percent) have women heads of state or government in the form of a president or a prime minister. This means that 88.8 percent of the countries in the world are led by men. In comparison, 6.8 percent of monarchies have women royal leaders. (p. 1)

Given that the United States is one of the wealthiest, as well as most politically and socially advanced nations in the world, the country might be expected to rank high among other industrialized nations in women's representation in political leadership. Yet the demographics of political leadership in the U.S. is not atypical (Paxton & Hughes, 2014). According to the World Economic Forum's Global Gender Gap Index, the U.S. ranking in female world leadership was 22nd as of 2012 (Rupp, 2012). This index ranks each country's progress on closing gender gaps related to economic, political, education, and health-based benchmarks (Hausmann, Tyson, Bekhouche, & Zahidi, 2013). Rupp explains a slight decline in the ranking of the U.S. as being due in part to fewer women serving in cabinet-level positions. The rankings make clear that even developed countries are not immune to the existence of gender disparities in political leadership.

In the sections of this chapter to follow, an overview of factors that have influenced the history and current status of Black women in political leadership in the United States is provided. The chapter concludes with recommendations for supporting greater representation by Black women in U.S. elective offices, including lessons that may be transferrable to women elsewhere in the world.

A FOCUS ON BLACK WOMEN AND POLITICS

Although women's representation at all levels of the U.S. government has increased over time, women remain underrepresented proportionally in elected leadership at the local, state, and national levels. This disparity has consistently been greater for women of color, defined by O'Connor (2010) as being a political category of groups of women who share the attribute of being non-White (e.g., Black American, Latina, Asian American, and American Indian women). Blacks represent the second-largest U.S. minority racial group among these political groups of non-White women according to the U.S. Census Bureau's 2014 *State & County QuickFacts*. Accordingly, an understanding of Black women's leadership experiences in the U.S. political arena may provide insights for others around the world (Kerby, 2012; Rosser-Mims, 2012). Although Black American women have a rich history of leadership at the level of local communities, their representation in the political arena has been limited for a variety of reasons. Jackson (2012) identified the barriers as "economic dependency; limited access to education and information; discriminatory cultural and social attitudes, and negative stereotypes; the burden of domestic responsibility; and intimidation..." (para. 3).

Now, as in the past, Black women's lives are influenced by the interlocking system of racism, sexism, and classism (Collins, 2000; Harris-Perry, 2011). The detrimental influence of these interlocking factors is evident in Black women's leadership experiences and career decisions, particularly in a political context. For example, a Black woman with an interest in pursuing a career of service through elective office must recognize that by virtue of her race, gender, and potential social class, her journey to political leadership will be more complex and challenging in comparison to males and White women. One explanation for this disparity is the tendency for men to approach politics as a career because their political ambition is cultivated and encouraged at an early age (Frederick, 2013). Because girls typically do not receive this same support, gender bias influences women's aspirations toward certain careers, and arguably toward political leadership roles (Smooth, 2010). Additionally, because women typically hold the responsibility of determining how to manage multiple social roles (e.g., wife, mother, employee, community/civic leader), their progression into a career, including politics, can be delayed (Dolan, Deckman, & Swers, 2010). For Black women, the challenges represented in managing multiple roles can be greater given that they face conflicting identity issues that surface between their professional and personal life (Stokes-Brown & Dolan, 2010).

In addition to the challenges of sexism and classism, a barrier to political representation by women of color is the reality of racism, which influences both their private and public lives. Despite these challenges, progress has been made toward the goal of greater political representation by Black women at the local, state, and national level of U.S. politics. Black women now constitute the majority of women of color in public office, with such representation having risen dramatically since the 1965 passage of the Voting Rights Act. In the past three decades, Black women's presence as state legislators has nearly doubled; while they made up only 7% of women state legislators in 1981, today they hold 13.4% of these legislative offices (CAWP, 2014). Notwithstanding this progress, work remains to be done in order to increase women of color's representation at the U.S. congressional and senatorial level as well as statewide elective executive offices (e.g., governor, lieutenant governor). The next section addresses this topic from a historical and contemporary view, offering insight into why Black women and women of color remain underrepresented in elected political roles.

BLACK WOMEN'S POLITICAL LEADERSHIP PATTERNS

In the history of the United States, White women were voted into state legislatures as early as 1894. However, it took another 26 years for the first Black woman—Crystal Byrd Faucet, elected to the Pennsylvania House of Representatives—to hold a seat in a state legislature. Similarly, at the national level, the first White woman was elected to serve in the U.S. Congress in 1917; it was 52 years later (1969) before a Black woman was elected to the U.S. House of Representatives. And it was more than two decades later, in 1992, that Carol Moseley Braun became the first Black female to be elected to the U.S. Senate. She served from 1993–1999 and remains the only Black female to have served in the U.S. Senate to date.

Data reported by The Center for American Women in Politics highlight the limited representation of Black women serving in political office at all levels of government. In 2014, Black women constituted:

- 14.2% of the 99 women who serve in the 113th U.S. House of Representatives. Fifteen years after the departure of Carol Mosely Braun, there remains no Black women serving in the U.S. Senate.
- 1.4% of the 72 women who serve in state-wide elective executive offices.
- 13.4% (242) of the 1,789 women who serve as state legislators nationwide.

Very few Black women have held significant political positions in the gubernatorial and mayoral levels. No Black women have served as the governor of the 50 U.S. states; of the 100 largest cities, to date only seven Black women have served as mayor. Further research is needed to understand why Black women remain underrepresented in the state-wide elective positions. A starting point is to examine Black women's leadership development experiences, given that racism, classism, and sexism can adversely influence progress on the traditional routes to gaining political experience. Accordingly, Black women have often invented their own strategies for gaining leadership skills by assuming roles in local institutions such as the church, schools, and grassroots political action (Harris-Perry, 2011).

BLACK WOMEN'S POLITICAL LEADERSHIP DEVELOPMENT

From the era of slavery in the U.S. (1500s–1800s) to the present, Black women have encountered barriers denying them full political participation and access to the traditional sources of power and decision-making afforded to males (Fredrick, 2013; Harris-Perry, 2011; Kaba & Ward, 2009). This lack of access has had an impact on the types of formal and informal leadership development opportunities that have been available to Black women. Despite the limitations in terms of official representation, Black women have found ways to influence political and governmental affairs. Historically, these women developed their political leadership skills by serving as educators and organizers of women's groups and community organizations. They took on leadership roles at family, community, and institutional levels to ensure community survival. Frequently, they served as a strong force behind political and social movements to lift their communities out of racial, economic, and educational subjugation (Williams & Sherman, 2009). They organized and led rallies and voter registration drives. Certain social institutions and organizations (e.g., churches, clubs, and societies) have been instrumental in educating and training Black women for roles in politics and government, developing their civic leadership skills.

Several political organizations were established with the goal of expanding the number of Black women seeking and securing political office. For example, in 1972 the National Black Women's Political Leadership Caucus was founded to help educate Black women in the fundamentals of politics and to encourage them to seek public office. Four years later, in 1976, the National Association of Black Women Legislators was organized to disseminate legislative information and policy changes affecting the Black community. Several other political organizations have served in similar capacities, among them the National Association for Colored Women's Clubs, the Congressional Black Caucus, and the National Political Congress of Black Women.

Black women's contributions to educational advancements at the family and community levels have also served as opportunities for political leadership development/training. The greatest number of Black women elected officials has been in the educational sector, where they have served as members of local boards of education and superintendents of education systems (Kaba & Ward, 2009).

Through service in positional and non-positional leadership roles, Black women have taken—and continue to take—action that has contributed significantly community change (DeLany & Rogers, 2004; Harris-Perry, 2011; Stokes-Brown & Dolan, 2010). The knowledge gained from the lived experiences of these women shapes the way in which they overcome the social and economic barriers that impede their access to leadership positions in the political arena.

BARRIERS TO POLITICAL LEADERSHIP

As noted previously, the vast majority of women of color face economic and cultural obstacles on the path to political power. Jackson (2012) identified some of the barriers to political leadership as including "economic dependency; limited access to education and information; discriminatory cultural and social attitudes, and negative stereotypes; the burden of domestic responsibility; and intimidation" (para. 3). The Gender and Multi-Cultural Leadership Project, a national study in 2005 that was funded by the Ford Foundation, offers insight into why this pattern exists (Hardy-Fanta, Pie-te, Pinderhughes, & Sierra, 2006). The resulting report, which represented the first comprehensive analysis of representation by women of color in elective office by specific racial groups, summarized reasons for the underrepresentation of women of color:

> Gerrymandered districts, racially polarized voting, specifically the difficulty of minority candidates to win the crossover votes of whites, and the higher costs associated with running for statewide and federal office are among the factors that contribute to patterns of underrepresentation for minority groups. (p. 5)

Research within the career development field and other academic disciplines has identified environmental factors contributing to or impeding Black women's career development success (Alfred, 2001; Bell & Nkomo, 2001; Cohen, 2003). The findings of numerous studies have implications for the developmental process Black women go through—or should go through—in preparation for seeking and serving in political leadership roles. Factors identified as contributing to Black women's career development success include the importance of having multiple mentors, peer networks, strategic career planning, and individual perseverance (Palmer & Simon, 2010). Described in the following sections are additional barriers which have had a particularly detrimental impact on women of color. These include the glass and concrete ceiling phenomena (Palmer & Simon, 2010), political influence, socially constructed stereotypes (Harris-Perry, 2011), and the double disadvantage phenomenon (Sokoloff, 1992).

Glass and Concrete Ceilings

In recent years, local, state, and federal governments, as well as many private companies, have had to reevaluate the steps they have taken to improve the representation of women—and women of color—in upper-level managerial positions. Numerous studies have identified the "glass ceiling" effect of invisible artificial and attitudinal barriers as a primary reason that women remain underrepresented in the highest leadership positions across most sectors (Adams & Funk, 2012; Palmer & Simon, 2010). For women who also experience race discrimination, the barriers to achieving senior-level leadership roles may represent, in fact, a "concrete ceiling" that appears to be unbreakable (Davidson, 1997). Women of color historically have not been able to see through a concrete ceiling to catch a glimpse of a corner office. Other terms used to represent invisible and attitudinal barriers are Teflon (Beach-Duncan, 2004) and plexiglass (Simpson, 1996) ceilings, which metaphorically represent the distinctive challenges faced by women attempting to move into more senior leadership ranks of their professions.

Political Influence

Acquiring political influence is a major challenge for Black women and women of color in general. Research by Smooth (2001) investigated how both gender and race play a role in determining who is regarded as influential in state legislatures. According to subsequent research by Smooth (2008), Black women serving as state legislators hold less power and influence regardless of the length of their political leadership or the type of leadership position they held (Smooth, 2008). This finding challenges the conventional thinking that power accrues with political seniority. According to Smooth (2008), the disparity between expectations related to power and influence and the lived experiences of Black American female state legislators results from the "preferences around gender and race [that] have become institutionalized and manifest as norms covering legislative behavior" (p. 3).

U.S. Congresswoman Maxine Waters, who has represented California's 43rd congressional district since 1991, observed that Black women have been held to different standards because of their race and gender (Clayton & Stallings, 2000). Waters explained the challenges for Black female political leaders:

> Voters and fellow congresspersons alike ... expect [Black women legislators] to be representatives on economic issues, health issues, housing issues, the issue of incarceration of Black males and drugs ....But at the same time, because of the nature of this job and the nature of our work, it creates the need to be assertive. And sometimes [Black women legislators] are criticized for being too aggressive. Somehow, there is a desire for [Black women] to be tough, but not show it, or to be aggressive, but to mask it in ways that men are not asked to do. (Clayton & Stallings, 2000, p. 579)

The literature suggests that Black women, once elected, must maintain a proper balance between representing the needs of their constituents and the needs of the Black and the female communities, while working within a male-normed political system (Dolan et al., 2010; Smooth, 2010). Although the number of women candidates for political office is increasing, women are still more likely to be elected to public offices that are perceived to be consistent with their social and domestic roles, such as superintendent of public instruction or secretary of state rather than attorney general, governor, and even president of the United States (Dolan et al., 2010; Smooth, 2010). As Representative Maxine Waters noted, the barriers of gender and racial stereotypes hamper Black women's ability to negotiate from strength.

Stereotypes

Another factor affecting Black women's efforts to seek and maintain leadership roles in the political arena is negative stereotyping. The most commonly known is the Black matriarch stereotype that depicts Black women as independent and domineering, suggesting that Black women can do everything and do not need the help of others, including Black men (Collins, 2000; Davis, 1989; Harris-Lacewell, 2001). The matriarch figure has historically been linked to slavery, both in its creation and in its sexual stereotypes. Wallace (1979) described how the characterization of Black women as matriarch of the family persisted throughout the late 20th century:

> [The black woman] was believed to be emotionally callous and physically invulnerable—stronger than white women and the physical equal of any man of her race. She was stronger than white women in order to justify her performing a kind of labor most white women were now presumed to be incapable of. (p. 138)

This image of the Black woman was reinforced by the controversial 1965 *Moynihan Report*. The late Senator Daniel Patrick Moynihan, then a sociologist serving as Assistant Secretary of Labor in the Department of Labor's Office of Policy Planning and Research, supervised the report, titled "The Negro Family: The Case For National Action." The Report stated that Black families had been destroyed due to slavery and the reversed roles of Black men and women, and argued that Black men were abdicating their leadership role within the family as head of household or the sole breadwinner. One of the study's many controversial findings was that the growing rate of single-parent families would hinder Blacks' social progress because of poverty and weakening family structure.

Collins (2000) elaborated on the misperceptions that were generated in part by the *Moynihan Report*: "Black family structures are seen as being deviant because they challenge the patriarchal assumptions underpinning the construct of the ideal family" (p. 75). As a result, Black women were historically viewed as emasculating figures who threatened both society and Black male power (Bova, 2000; Harris-Lacewell, 2001; Wallace, 1999). This stereotype promulgates a one-dimensional image of Black women as "a mother, loyal subordinate, and pillar of strength for others in the organization," an image that often limits Black women's access to positions of power at both the institutional and societal levels (Bova, 2000, p. 10).

Double Disadvantage Phenomenon

In addition to the barriers described previously as related to cultural and prejudicial stereotyping, several researchers have cited the perception that Black women politicians must work twice as hard as their male and female counterparts (Hardy-Fanta et al., 2006; Scola, 2006; Sokoloff, 1992). Smooth (2010) argued that Black women must constantly prove themselves by maintaining a balance of breadth and depth in terms of policy issues. Black women also feel obligated simultaneously to advance policies for the Black community and to advocate for concerns that have historically been identified as women's issues, including poverty, education, and health. Black women face a double disadvantage at the polls as well, confronting biases related to race and gender (Mansbridge, 1999). This double disadvantage forces Black women to choose between conflicting priorities; some argue that Black women's first priority should be to combat racism by advancing the situation of Black males (Sokoloff, 1992). Others argue that the issues facing all women should be a higher priority, thus Black women should focus on continuing the fight for educational and employment equality (Williams & Sherman, 2009).

In addition to these competing priorities, barriers to political success can make mutually exclusive demands on Black women. In character, they are expected to be both meek and tough, but not tough to the extent that Black men or White people feel disconcerted. As politicians, they must support the grandest dreams of democracy but, once elected, they must play nicely with colleagues who do not want to work from a place of collaboration. In light of these challenges, the following section examines practices that can assist Black women in resolving such personal and political dilemmas. Many studies during the past decade have examined strategies that smooth the way for Black women leaders to enter the political arena.

FACILITATIVE CONDITIONS—PATHWAYS TO SUCCESS

Recent scholarly attention has been devoted to understanding the factors that have contributed to political activity among Black women and the strategies they can use to achieve and maintain political leadership roles (Kaba & Ward, 2009; Rosser-Mims, 2012; Stokes-Brown & Dolan, 2010). Many of these factors are directly related to women's experiences with racism, sexism, and classism (Collins, 2000; Frederick, 2013; Kaba & Ward, 2009;

Smooth, 2010). Research related to the background profile of persons more likely to seek and be elected to office has identified certain political cues such as high social status and income (Kerby, 2012; Monopoli, 2009). Education, professional occupation, and activity in voluntary and community groups have also been associated with political ambition because of contacts gained, potential visibility, and possibilities for leadership in such activities (Boyd, 2012; O'Conner, 2010).

Research three decades ago conducted by Darcy and Hadley (1988), as well as Perkins (1986), concluded that political activism by women might have been associated with a politically active mother or an encouraging father; others were encouraged by the women's movement to move away from traditionally defined roles (Perkins, 1986). Age has also been traditionally associated with political ambition, in that women have typically waited until later in life to seek elected office, due in part to family and career obligations. According to Perkins, Black women's political activity in non-positional leadership roles, such as community organizing or political activism, are more likely to be driven into politics due to life circumstances (e.g., racism, economic and educational inequality, and sexism). Women often become involved in community organizing because they are personally affected by a social issue. Recent examples in the United States include the shooting death of young Black men such as Trayvon Martin and Michael Brown. The mothers of both young men, under the most difficult circumstances, forged an alliance to lead a social movement designed to raise awareness and reduce the number of deaths of unarmed Black male teens.

In a 1996 study, Reid-Merritt interviewed over 40 successful Black female leaders employed in the public arena and in corporate America to identify commonalities among them. The resulting book, *Sister Power: How Phenomenal Black Women Are Rising to the Top*, remains a relevant source today, reinforcing the point that access to political leadership *is* within the reach of women today. According to Reid-Merritt's findings, the successful Black female leaders possessed these qualities: self-assured, aggressive and assertive, and race-conscious and serious about social justice and change. Additionally, the findings from this study revealed that Black female leaders held a high degree of self-efficacy and demonstrated a deep sense of resilience. Notably, these women did not demonstrate "perfectly similar life patterns" (p. 15); they did, however, share core characteristics that made them unique as a group of powerful women leaders. The women had strong support systems that were rooted in their families, churches, schools, and communities. They focused intensely on clearly identified goals, political sophistication, and a spiritual foundation; they also nurtured a strong sense of identity and self-worth as Blacks and as women. The final shared leadership characteristic identified by Reid-Merritt's research was that all of the women were socially conscious and dedicated to a social agenda that transcended personal gain. Reid-Merritt also observed that all of the women in her study had mentors, ranging from faith/spiritual counselors to family members to professional colleagues.

Black women securing and succeeding in political leadership roles must prepare to meet barriers of race and gender stereotypes. Collectively, with self-confidence and self-esteem as well as strong professional and personal support networks, Black women will be better equipped to maneuver successfully around these barriers and to serve effectively as leaders in various spheres of influence (Easter, 1996; Erhart, 1990). Additionally, volunteering on political campaigns to learn the fundamentals of running for office, serving in community leadership roles (boards, professional associations and networks), and acquiring mentors can enhance the likelihood of Black women seeking and attaining political office.

CONCLUSION

Women constitute approximately 50.8% of the U.S. population. Women of color, however, are a growing demographic, representing 36.3% of our nation's female population and approximately 18% of the entire U.S. population (U.S. Census Bureau, 2014). As American women of color continue to shape the political and economic climate, it is important to acknowledge that they are not a monolithic entity. These women have different cultural and social experiences, as well as experiences in the workforce and political leadership. Thus, they bring diverse perspectives to the national discourse on issues directly related to their access to political power.

As more women within the context of the U.S. seek political office, there is a greater need to understand the influence of gender and race on their ability to access political leadership roles. A review of the literature reflects that women's representation in elected office matters for several reasons. First, the designers of the U.S. system of government strove to create a representative democracy. In order for this government to be truly legitimate, all members of society (irrespective of race, gender, and class), should have the same potential opportunities for serving their community and nation. Second, members of a society are more likely to trust and support a political system when they believe that all citizens have equal opportunity to participate in the decision making that affects their lives. Third, women constitute over 50% of the population in the United States. Similarly, from an international perspective, women constitute over 48% of the world's population of 7.1 billion people (Hughes, 2013), and their voices need to be represented in the political processes that shape the future direction of communities and countries.

The distinctive contributions of women in leadership roles have been widely recognized (Chandler, 2011; Eagly & Johannesen-Schmidt, 2007; Genovese & Steckenrider, 2013), thus their representation in public offices is important. Social science research has documented that children are influenced by external forces at very early ages. When children grow up seeing both men and women seeking public office, they are more likely to view elective office as an option for both genders. As a result of cultural and societal norms associated with gender socialization, both women and men have different life experiences and different points of reference. Thomas and Wilcox (1998) have observed that such norms "can translate into a distinctive way of viewing existing legislative proposals and can lead to different agendas. It is important, then, that women occupy our legislatures and executive offices so that their concerns contribute to policy agendas" (p. 2).

A final and critically important argument is the importance of ensuring that underrepresented segments of society are given voices in our democratic forms of government. Women, globally, represent a pool of talent with abilities, points of view, and ideas that can benefit communities, nation, and the world to the extent that they hold political leadership offices and roles. If Black women and other underrepresented populations of women worldwide do not have full and equal voice in the political arena, the community of women at large may feel powerless and voiceless, thus impacting how democratic governments function (Hughes, 2013). For these reasons, it matters that *all* women have access to and assume political leadership positions. Learning about the political leadership experiences of Black women in the U.S. may help other women of color around the world to navigate their own political terrain, thus improving their representation in political leadership on a global scale.

REFERENCES

Adams, R. B., & Funk, P. (2012). Beyond the glass ceiling: Does gender matter? *Management Science, 58*(2), 219–235. doi:10.1287/mnsc.1110.1452

Alfred, M. V. (2001). Expanding theories of career development: Adding the voices of African American women in the White academy. *Adult Education Quarterly, 51*(2), 108–127.

Beach-Duncan, J. A. L. (2004). *Career development factors of Black women who work in the professions.* Unpublished doctoral dissertation, University of Georgia, Athens.

Bell, E. L., & Nkomo, S. M. (2001). *Our separate ways: Black and White women and the struggle for professional identity.* Boston, MA: Harvard Business School Press.

Bova, B. (2000). Mentoring revisited: The Black woman's experience. *Mentoring and Tutoring, 8*(1), 5–16.

Boyd, K. S. (Ed.) (2012). *Encyclopedia of race, ethnicity, and society.* Thousand Oaks, CA: SAGE.

Center for American Woman and Politics (2014). Women in elected office 2014 fact sheet. Retrieved from http://www.cawp.rutgers.edu/fast_facts/levels_of_office/documents/elective.pdf

Chandler, D. (2011). What women bring to the exercise of leadership. *Journal of Strategic Leadership, 3*(2), 1–12.

Clayton, D. M., & Stallings, A. M. (2000). Black women in Congress: Striking the balance. *Journal of Black Studies, 30*(4), 574–603.

Cohen, C. J. (2003). A portrait of continuing marginality: The study of women of color in American politics. In S. J. Carroll (Ed.), *Women and American politics: New questions, new directions* (pp. 190–213). New York, NY: University Press.

Collins, P. H. (2000). *Black feminist thought: Knowledge, consciousness, and the politics of empowerment.* New York, NY: Routledge.

Davidson, M. J. (1997). *The Black and ethnic minority manager: Cracking the concrete ceiling.* London, England: Paul Chapman.

Davis, A. (1989). *Women, culture, & politics.* New York, NY: Vintage Books.

Darcy, R., & Hadley, C. D. (1988). Black women in politics: The puzzle of success. *Social Science Quarterly, 77*(4), 627–645.

DeLany, J., & Rogers, E. (2004). Black women's leadership and learning: From politics to Afritics in the context of community. *Convergence, 36*(2), 91–106.

Dolan, A. B., Deckman, M. M., & Swers, M. L. (2010). *Women and politics: Paths to power and political influence.* New York, NY: Pearson/Prentice Hall.

Eagly, A. H., & Johannesen-Schmidt, M. (2007). Leadership style matters: The small, but important, style differences between male and female leaders. In D. Bilmoria & S. K. Piderit (Eds.), *Handbook on women in business and management* (pp. 279–303). Northampton, MA: Edward Elgar.

Easter, O. V. (1996). Septima Poinsette Clark: Unsung heroine of the Civil Rights Movement. In E. A. Peterson (Ed.), *Freedom road: Adult education of African Americans* (pp. 109–122). Malabar, FL: Krieger.

Erhart, D. (1990). *Factors to which African-American women in high status careers attribute their success.* Unpublished doctoral dissertation, Georgetown University, Washington, DC.

Frederick, A. (2013). Bringing narrative in: Race-gender, storytelling, political ambition, and women's paths to public office. *Journal of Women, Politics & Policy, 34*(2), 113–137.

Genovese, M. A., & Steckenrider, J. (2013). *Women as political leaders.* New York, NY: Routledge.

Hardy-Fanta, C., Pie-te, L., Pinderhughes, D. M., & Sierra, C. (2006). Gender, race, and descriptive representation in the United States: Findings from the gender and multicultural leadership project. *Journal of Women, Politics & Policy, 28*(3/4), 7–41. doi:10.1300/J501v28n03_02

Harris-Lacewell, M. (2001). No place to rest: African American political attitudes and the myth of Black women's strength. *Women and Politics, 23*(3), 1–33.

Harris-Perry, M. (2011). *Sister citizen: Shame, stereotypes, and Black women in America.* New Haven, CT: Yale University Press.

Hausmann, R., Tyson, L. D., Bekhouche, Y., & Zahidi, S. (2013). *The global gender gap index 2013*. Retrieved from ttp://www3.weforum.org/docs/WEF_Gender Gap_Report_2013.pdf

Hughes, M. M. (2013). Diversity in national legislatures around the world. *Sociology Compass, 7*(1), 23–33. Retrieved from http://www.pitt.edu/~hughesm/Hughes %202013_Compass.pdf

Institute for Women in Leadership (2014). *The women's leadership factsheet*. Retrieved from http://iwl.rutgers.edu/documents/njwomencount/womenHeadsofStates .pdf

Jackson, S. (2012, September 4). *African women won't wield political influence without cultural change* [Web log post]. Retrieved from http://www.theguardian .com/global-development/poverty-matters/2012/sep/04/african-women -political-influence-cultural-change

Kaba, A. J., & Ward, D. E. (2009). African Americans and U.S. politics: The gradual progress of black women in political representation. *The Review of Black Political Economy, 36*(1), 29–50.

Kerby, S. (2012). *The state of women of color in the United States*. Retrieved from http:// cdn.americanprogress.org/wpcontent/uploads/issues/2012/07/pdf/ women_of_color_brief.pdf

Mansbridge, J. (1999). Should Blacks represent Blacks and women represent women? A contingent "yes." *The Journal of Politics, 61*(3), 628–657.

Monopoli, P. A. (2009). Why so slow: A comparative view of women's political leadership. *Maryland Journal of International Law, 24*(1), 155–168.

O'Connor, K. (Ed.). (2010). *Gender and women's leadership: A reference handbook*. (Vols. 1–2). Thousand Oaks, CA: SAGE.

Palmer, B., & Simon, D. (2010). *Breaking the political glass ceiling: Women and congressional elections*. New York, NY: Routledge.

Paxton, P., & Hughes, M. M. (2014). *Women, politics, and power: A global perspective*. (2nd ed.). Thousand Oaks, CA: SAGE. doi: dx.doi.org/10.4135/9781452275482

Perkins, J. (1986). Political ambition among Black and White women: An intragender test of the socialization model. *Women & Politics, 6*(1), 27–40.

Reid-Merritt, P. (1996). *Sister power: How phenomenal black women are rising to the top*. New York, NY: John Wiley.

Rosser-Mims, D. (2012). *How and why Black women are elected to political office: A narrative analysis of nine cases in the State of Georgia*. New York, NY: Edwin Mellen Press.

Rupp, L. (2012). *Women hold 20% of world's political power*. Retrieved from http:// www.bloomberg.com/news/2012-10-24/women-hold-20-of-world-s-political- power-report-says.html

Scola, B. (2006). Women of color in state legislatures: Gender, race, ethnicity and legislative office holding. *Journal of Women, Politics & Policy, 28*(3–4), 43–70. doi:10.1300/J501v28n03_03

Simpson, G. (1996). The plexiglass ceiling: The careers of Black women lawyers. *The Career Development Quarterly, 45*, 173–188.

Smooth, W. (2001). Perceptions of influence in state legislatures: A focus on the experiences of African-American women legislators. *Dissertation Abstracts International, 62*(12), 325A. (UMI No. AAT 3035826)

Smooth, W. (2008). Gender, race, and the exercise of power and influence. In B. Reingold (Ed.), *Legislative women: Getting elected, getting ahead* (pp. 175–196). Boulder, Co: Lynne Rienner.

Smooth, W. (2010). Intersectionalities of race and gender and leadership. In K. P. O'Connor (Ed), *Gender and women's leadership: A reference handbook* (pp. 31–40). Thousand Oaks, CA: SAGE.

Sokoloff, N. J. (1992). *Black women: Beyond the myth of double advantage.* New York, NY: Routledge.

Stokes-Brown, A., & Dolan, K. (2010). Race, gender, and symbolic representation: African American female candidates as mobilizing agents. *Journal of Elections, Public Opinion & Parties, 20*(4), 473–494. doi:10.1080/17457289.2010.511806

Thomas, S., & Wilcox, C. (Eds.). (1998). *Women and elective office, past present, and future.* Oxford, England: Oxford University Press.

U.S. Census Bureau (2014). *State & County QuickFacts.* Retrieved from http://quick facts.census.gov/qfd/states/00000.html

Wallace, M. (1979). *The myth of the superwoman. Black macho and the myth of the superwoman.* New York, NY: Dial Press.

Wallace, M. (1999). *Black macho and the myth of the superwoman.* New York, NY: Dial Press.

Williams, J. M., & Sherman, S. L. (2009). Black women's leadership experiences: Examining the intersectionality of race and gender. *Advances in Developing Human Resources, 11*(5), 562–581.

World Economic Forum (2014). *The global gender gap report 2014.* Retrieved from http://www3.weforum.org/docs/GGGR14/GGGR_CompleteReport_2014.pdf

Post-reading Questions

1. Why and how are Michelle Obama's working-class roots so important to her identity?

2. What are the essential characteristics of a father that Barack Obama is said to embody?

3. Would Barack Obama's image as a father/father-figure have been different if he had raised two boys instead of two girls?

4. How can those in power be convinced that empowering women politically is good for men, not bad for them?

5. How can people in the United States help empower women outside of the United States?

CONCLUSION

Intersections: A Contemporary Student Primer on Race, Gender, and Class has examined a variety of diverse topics all connected by the intersectionality of race, gender, and class. Tamara Winfrey Harris and R. Fleetwood reveal that Blacks and women must continually navigate America's fashion and beauty cultures—cultures that have been kind to the self-image of relatively few men and women. Kevin Gaines, Elizabeth Abel, Marsha J. Tyson Darling, Heidi Ardizonne, and Dionne Rosser-Mims all tell, in one way or another, of the economic, social, and political marginalization that people of color, women, the working class, and others have had to push back against. John Iceland and Patricia Hill Collins have provided the language and perspective to recognize, name, and, ideally, deconstruct the structures that divide and oppress in the name of power.

Because divisions created by racism, sexism, classism, and other arbitrary constructions of power are deeply entrenched in American history and culture, it can seem as if they will never be eradicated from American public and private life. At the same time, history reveals that seismic shifts were often unthinkable—until they became reality. Abolition, suffrage, labor reform, integration, the Black presidency, the (almost) female presidency—all seemed impossible before they were possible. This perhaps, is the collection's final and greatest lesson.

Credits